"SOCCER TOM" MULROY

90 MINUTES WITH THE KING

FOREWORD BY
SHEP MESSING
US Soccer Legend-Lifelong
friend of PELÉ

HOW SOCCER SAVED MY LIFE

International
Soccer Publishers

90 MINUTES WITH THE KING

Editor: Bill Summers

Hardcover ISBN: 979-8-35093-206-5
Paperback ISBN: 979-8-35091-108-4
eBook ISBN: 979-8-35091-109-1

Printed in the United States of America

This book is dedicated to the people who have made my life a wonderful journey.

First and foremost, my dear mother. Agnes Mulroy was a single mom who raised two boys at the time when few women would dare take that on. Through her hard work and selfless devotion to my brother and me, I learned that no hill was too high. Mom was kindhearted, compassionate, resilient. All the good in me is from my mom.

My big brother, JT Mulroy. JT had a heart of gold. He would have been a world-class artist had he not strayed onto a dark road. I learned from him. I only wish he had found a different path.

My coaches. Throughout my youth, I played for coaches who not only taught me soccer but also guided me in life. They were my mentors; they had a paternal influence on me. Hans Sautner, my first youth coach, gave me the captain's band. My junior high coaches, Rich Meszaros and Fred Bloom, and my high school coach, Gary Schoonmaker, helped me navigate those tough years and survive in school. My club coach, Frank Rottenbucher, was truly a surrogate father to me. My college coach, George Vizvary, lived up to his promise that, "You come here as boys, and you leave as men." Greg Myers, my first professional coach, gave me the soccer opportunity of a lifetime.

My soccer north star, Edson Arantes do Nascimento, or Pelé, also known as "The King" and "The GOAT." Pelé inspired me, not only as the best player in the world, but as a caring, compassionate man, a true ambassador of our game.

CONTENTS

FOREWORD

Tom Mulroy called me one day and asked me if I could write this foreword for his book. I've said no politely to several others who asked me to do the same thing for them. Could I say no to Mulroy? Absolutely not. This is a lifelong family friend, a former adversary and former teammate of mine . . . and possibly one of the best human beings I'm honored to have known.

I met Tommy (the rest of the world knows him as Soccer Tom) through my younger brother Roy, who was also a professional goalkeeper. These two young punks were hard to keep track of. My mom, Anne Messing, a college professor, often caught Tommy sneaking into our family house through a window after a night out with his buddies. She loved Tommy. Roy loved Tommy. My whole family adopted Tommy. I only tolerated him at first. But I came to love him too. Roy and I opened one of the first indoor soccer facilities in the country in 1980. We had to convince our potential commercial real estate partner, Joe Einbinder, that it was a good idea. Roy whispered to me, "Call Tommy." Thirty minutes later, Tommy jumps out of his car and on our front lawn puts on a dazzling demonstration, juggling the ball like few in the world can. His world-class ability to do that has over the years taken Soccer Tom beyond the sport. He jumped back in the car and we got our indoor soccer facility funded.

I have had an unbelievable life through the sport of soccer. One day, years ago, my son Zach (he loves Tommy too) told me that I had either played with or against five of the greatest players in the history of the sport. Pelé, Franz Beckenbauer, Eusebio, Johan Cruyff, George Best, the list goes on and on . . . Gerd Mueller, Nene Cubillas, Carlos Alberto, Gordon Banks, and Bobby Moore. These are unquestionably the most iconic names of players who plied their trade here as professional athletes in the prelude to Major League Soccer. They left an indelible mark on soccer in this country in our North American Soccer League.

But when it comes to who has made a bigger impact in the growth, popularity, and education of young boys and girls over the years, who has led this soccer evolution and revolution, out of the names above, I would say Pelé . . . and Tommy Mulroy. (Calm down, Tommy, I said impact. I'm not comparing him to you as a player!)

I'm serious when I say that. In this book, Tommy tells a true-life story for everyone. If you dream big, if you never give up on your dreams, if you find something that you love and you never give up, unbelievable things can be achieved. Tommy has done that, first as a professional player but more importantly, impacting generations of children to fall in love with our beautiful game. Pelé and Tommy had the same gift of being able to naturally connect with and inspire children.

I smiled when I read Tommy's account of our game in Yankee Stadium, and his coach's instructions to follow Pelé to the bathroom. Pelé had seen me hug Mulroy before the game started. When we walked off the field into the locker room at halftime, Pelé came up to me and said, "Shep, your friend, I think is going to follow me into the bathroom; tell him to leave me alone!"

There are very few things in the world that transcend race, politics, religion, and socioeconomic boundaries. Soccer is one that does that. Tommy has dedicated his life to doing that, all with a smile on his face, love in his heart, and a commitment to teach the beautiful game.

Tom Mulroy belongs in the National Soccer Hall of Fame for his contribution to the sport in this country. Read this book and enjoy it. His story will inspire you.

—Shep Messing, former goalkeeper, New York Cosmos, U.S. National Team

PROLOGUE

The next morning, I woke up in my Manhattan hotel room and hurried down to get the New York papers. The same photo was on the front page of every sports section—Pelé, the ball at his feet, his arms placed to give him balance and protection. You could see the dust rising around the moving ball. There was a defender leaning on Pelé's back, his arms also out for balance, yet at opposite angles to Pelé's arms. The defender had his chin just above the King's shoulder, trying to get a peek at the shielded ball. You could see the sharp cut of muscle in Pelé's legs—a muscle only seen on a soccer player. The defender's eyes were fixated on the ball while Pelé was looking up for his next move. And then I realized that defender was me. My jaw dropped.

"A picture is worth a thousand words" did not do justice to this photo. That black-and-white shot of Pelé, fending off his shadow, the 19-year-old kid from New York. It was the showcase photo of the match, taken by the Associated Press, which meant that nearly every newspaper in the world had access to it. That morning many of the world's biggest papers ran that shot on the front page of their sports sections. From Brazil to Germany, Asia to Africa, the world could not get enough of Pelé, and that day I was along for the ride.

Soccer was gaining popularity in the U.S.—Pelé the catalyst. He was changing how Americans saw the game. His spectacular bicycle kick that August night made clear that there was much more to the game than running around a field kicking a ball. He showed that soccer is an athletic art form worthy of respect from the U.S. media, sponsors, investors, and most importantly, the American public.

Even today, that photo from our game opens doors and gives me instant credibility. When people see it, they say, "You played against Pelé!" I joke back, "No, Pelé played against me." Then I tell them the story of that wonderful day as if it was yesterday.

CHAPTER ONE

LIFE BEFORE SOCCER

It was 1956, and Pelé had signed his first professional contract. I was born that September 28th to Agnes and James Mulroy, high school sweethearts from a little Irish neighborhood in the Bronx. This was a time when people identified themselves by the name of their church or temple and its location, which for our family meant Our Lady of Mercy Parish by Webster Avenue and Fordham Road.

At first the courtship of Agnes and Jim looked like it came straight out of the movie *West Side Story*. A nice Irish Catholic girl meets a nice Irish guy; they get married and live happily ever after. Or not. Soon after the honeymoon, Agnes began to realize that Jim's nightly carousing with his posse was the routine of an angry alcoholic. He would come home late and scream and yell and tear up the house. Agnes did her best to tolerate this dark streak, even as she moved through her first pregnancy.

Soon after my older brother John was born, Jim began to physically abuse Agnes. This was the 1950s, and he probably thought that no woman with a kid to raise would walk out on her man. Who knows, she may have never left him had he laid his hands *only* on her. But when John was four years old and I was almost two, not only did Jim strike Mom, but he also raised his hand on my brother and me. The next morning our mother changed the locks and my father was officially kicked out. Not long after, we moved into my grandmother's apartment on Valentine Avenue in the Bronx. Jim would pay a visit every once in a while, but in time he faded away and created a new life without Mom or his two boys.

In hindsight, I am glad my mother took this courageous step for herself and her kids. Amazingly enough, whenever Jim's name came up after that, Mom never said a bad word about him. He never paid her a penny of child support. When my brother and I were young, we would ask Mom, "Why don't we get him and make him pay?" She always replied, "Alcoholism is a disease, and he is sick and cannot help himself."

Mom stuck to that refrain; she never went after him. Instead, she went to work. She worked two jobs and always kept us clothed and fed. Whatever we had needed, Mom made sure to provide. Eventually we moved out of the city to a little community called Spring Valley in upstate New York. My mother went into a partnership with her brother, Frank Fuchs, on a property with a three-bedroom house and a small bungalow. That bungalow is where I would grow up and find the most wonderful game in the universe.

CHAPTER TWO

MEETING "THE BEAUTIFUL GAME"

In late summer of 1968, our gang kept busy playing all the games kids played: hide-and-seek, tag, ringalevio, baseball, tackle football, basketball. You name it, we played it. Everything but soccer. At the time, we thought soccer was a weird foreign game with hard brown balls, a game the gym teachers made us play once a year. We hated it because when we got home, our shins were sore. It seemed like one big mash-up, not the kind of game we would bring back to our neighborhood.

Back in those days, if you wanted to play with a friend, you went to his house, rang the doorbell, and said, "Hello, can Jimmy come out and play?" Then you and Jimmy would walk up the block to another house, knock on the door, and so on. No cell phone, no texting, just face-to-face. You looked people in the eye, stuck out your hand, and introduced yourself. You knew every kid on the block, their parents and siblings, even their pets.

One of my best friends, Paul Bianco, lived across the street from me. His family owned the Spring Valley Bar and Restaurant on Main Street, Route 45, about three miles from our neighborhood. Back then Rockland County was growing fast as builders put up houses and apartments to accommodate people moving out of New York City. The people building those homes were immigrants, mostly from Germany, Italy, Austria, and Norway. They did not always speak the same language or share the same culture, but they had a few things in common. One, they had all come to pursue the "American Dream," and two, they brought with them their passion for the beautiful game, known around the world as football, but called soccer in the U.S.

These young men lived all over Rockland County. They worked hard during the week and played hard on the weekend. In fact, they created the Spring Valley Soccer Club. Their men's teams played in the German American League, also known as the most competitive league in the United States. Soccer clubs such as the Greek Americans, New York Hota, Brooklyn Italians, Columbian, German Hungarian, Blue Star, and BW Gottschee all represented their various ethnic communities, both on and off the field.

In 1968, the German American League created a rule designed to help grow the game. Under this rule, any club that did not have a youth team would have to pay an extra thousand dollars to register their adult team in the league. A thousand bucks was a lot of money in those days. Luckily for me, our soccer club was sponsored by the Spring Valley Bar and Restaurant, my buddy Paul's family business. The teams would train two or three nights a week and stop in the bar for a quick one before they went home. On weekends after home games, the entire team would go to the restaurant, shower downstairs, and come up to drink and socialize with their families, as well as with opponents and their families. This is how it was done in Europe, and the custom was brought here to the United

States. Many of these ethnic soccer clubs still exist in pockets around the country.

Paul and I would spend many weekends working at his restaurant. We weren't really working, as we were eleven years old, but we would help by putting pizza dough on the pans. Because we spent so much time there, we got to know the players on the team. Collectively, the players didn't have enough children to make up a youth team, so they recruited Paul and me to be part of the first-ever youth soccer team north of New York City, the Spring Valley boys' soccer team. I went to the first practice in high-top sneakers and jeans. I didn't know you needed shorts, or special shoes, or these things called shin guards.

Spring Valley SC Boys Team 1968
First Youth Soccer Team North of NYC

Back (L-R) Coach Hans Sautner, Franky Rottenbucher, Ralph Reitmiaer, Eddie Hostetter, Paul Ritter, Mike Destifano, Herman Isker, Danny Janes, John Parkins, Tommy Mulroy, Paul Bianco

Front (L-R) John Sautner, Karl Yonkers, Peter Reitmiaer, Jimmy Everhardt, Richie Blum, Dan Von Taden

CHAPTER THREE

MY FIRST PAIR
OF SHOES

It was a Saturday and my mom had taken me to the local sport-ing-goods store. A young man greeted us with a smile and asked, "How can I help you?"

"I would like a pair of soccer shoes," I replied.

He looked confused. "Soccer shoes?" he repeated.

I might as well have asked for a can of paint. The clerk called his manager for help. First, they brought me a pair of baseball cleats. We agreed that the spikes might puncture a soccer ball, not that either guy had ever seen a soccer ball. I wound up settling for a pair of American football cleats. The manager's big selling point was the metal reinforcement in the front that would help me to kick the ball hard without breaking my toes. This was the summer of 1968, and it dawned on me that no general sporting-goods store carried soccer equipment. No shoes, not even a ball.

There was only one place where you could buy soccer equip-ment: Soccer Sport Supply on 1st Avenue and 87th Street in

Manhattan. At the time, nearly all soccer players in the country got their equipment from that mom-and-pop shop. The owner, Max Doss, and his family even had their own shoe brand, "Doss." Back then the Doss brand may have been even more popular than adidas. Nike had not yet made its first soccer shoe.

Soccer Sport Supply also had the first, real U.S.-based soccer catalog business. Later, in the mid-70s, soccer specialty shops began popping up all over the country: Soccer Locker in Miami, Massapequa Soccer Shop on Long Island, Niki's Soccer in Los Angeles, Kapp's Wide World of Soccer in Mamaroneck, N.Y., and Chicago Soccer, to name a few. By the early '80s, soccer shops had sprung up in every soccer community in the U.S. One shop, EUROSPORT, showed some entrepreneurial flair. Owned by brothers Mike and Brendan Moylan, the business started a catalog that today soccer people know as Soccer.com. Back in the day, instead of trudging into the city, it would have been easier if I could have ordered shoes from my phone.

CHAPTER FOUR

CINEMA 45 PARKING LOT: OUR NEW SOCCER MECCA

I was 11 years old, without a care in the world. Our big decision each day was what to do after school: shoot hoops, play football, or walk up the street to Hillcrest to hang out at the candy store. Pauly and I were the oldest kids in our group, and we organized the activities. At the time, we had been to a few practices with the Spring Valley boys' soccer team. Our Coach Hans Sautner and our teammates loved the game, and it was rubbing off on us. We brought that passion back to our neighborhood, and soon soccer became our favorite game.

The rest of America looked down on soccer. They saw it as a game played by kids who didn't speak English, or by kids who got cut from the football team. To many, it was a game played by sissies. But we couldn't play enough, and in time we turned my once-green front lawn into a patch of dirt. My Aunt Nancy planted a tree in the middle of the lawn to discourage us, but we played around it.

I started taking my ball with me wherever I went, in case we had enough kids to get up a game.

One afternoon I was dribbling my ball on the street up to Hillcrest. As we passed through the parking lot of the local movie theater, Cinema 45, we began kicking the ball off the brick wall. It was a movie theater with no windows. It was a weekday afternoon, no cars in the lot, and the kick-around turned into a game. We played for so long that it was getting dark. Had we been on my front lawn, that meant the game would be over, but not at Cinema 45. The parking lot had lights. This was our new soccer mecca. This was our American version of pickup games played in the favelas of Rio, the streets of London, and everywhere around the world except in the U.S.

Cinema 45 became our training ground. We spent thousands of hours playing pickup games or honing our touch by playing balls off the wall. My coach used to say, in his strong Austrian accent, "Five hundred with your right foot, then a thousand with your left foot." Heck, I learned to head a tennis ball off that wall a few hundred times before it hit the ground. I remember one night when the clock on the bank across the street read 12:20 a.m. My uncle Frank pulled up in his '64 Chevy Suburban, rolled down the window, and said, "Are you kids crazy? Everyone's parents are calling my house. Get in the car, you're all going home." It was a weeknight and we had school the next day. By the way, the temperature on the clock across the street read 27 degrees. We had no idea it was that late, nor that it was cold. It was a close game, and we were having a blast.

One Saturday afternoon we had a nice game going, and this little Haitian kid was standing off to the side, watching. When the ball rolled out of play, he asked, "Hey, can I play?" All eyes rested on me. I kicked a ball to the kid and said, "Give me ten juggles." He took the ball and juggled 1, 2, 3, drop. Again, 1, 2, 3, 4, drop. Last try: 1, 2, 3, drop. "Sorry, kid," I said, "come back when you can play."

These games were serious business. We couldn't let in any kid off the street. It wasn't because he was Haitian; we just didn't want to dilute the game. Wouldn't you know, the next afternoon we had another game going, and there's that kid again. The ball goes out of bounds, and he said, "Hello, you think I can play today?" I knocked him the ball and said, "Can you do ten?" He got the ball up and did 10 on his first try. I said, "Welcome, you're on the shirts team. What's your name?"

"Ron Dufrene," he said. Fifty years later we are still best friends, and my daughter Sabrina calls him "Uncle Ron." Ron is one of many Cinema 45 players who went on to do well on and off the field. He was a star at Ulster County Community College and then Florida International University. Later, he played professionally at Stade de Reims in France under the famous Argentinian Carlos Bianchi, and played for the U.S. National Team.

At a time when soccer was a cult sport played only by ethnic communities, a growing number of American kids in our neighborhood had embraced the game. Here are other kids from our Cinema 45 gang who would go on to play professional or collegiate soccer, or for our national team:

Professional Players:

Gerald "Magic" Celestin, New York Arrows

Kevin Clinton, Tampa Bay Rowdies

John Diffley, Tampa Bay Mutiny, U.S. National Team

Ronil Dufrene, France, Ligue 2, Stade de Reims, U.S. National Team

Frank Fuchs, Detroit Express

Herve Guilliod, Buffalo Stallions

Sammy Joseph, New York Express

Eddy St. Cloud, Columbus Capitals

Collegiate Players:

Harry Alexander, Southern Connecticut

David Braun, SUNY Fredonia

Ron Cadet, SUNY Geneseo

Will Cadet, University of Connecticut

Gerry Clinton, College of Charleston

Shaun Clinton, University of South Florida

Rick Derella, Cornell University

William Derella, Syracuse University

TJ Derella, Fordham University

Dan Derella, St. Thomas Aquinas College

Phil Diffley, SUNY Cortland

Danny Fuchs, Akron University

Emerson Jean-Luis, University of South Florida

Keith Murray, University of Connecticut

Richard Murray, University of Connecticut

Paul Rocker, Appalachian State University

John Sautner, Adelphi University

CHAPTER FIVE

THE BEGINNING OF A DARK ROAD

In 1968 I was about to turn 12 years old and begin my first year of junior high. My older brother John was almost 14. He was an altar boy at Saint Joseph's Church right up the road in Spring Valley. My mom was devout. In fact, she never divorced the old man because to do so would break one of the Catholic Church's seven sacraments, and she thought she would not be able to receive Communion.

John and I were both going through puberty, an important time in life. Puberty can bring mood swings and hard times, and things can get confusing and even difficult. My mother understood this and wanted to make sure that her two boys had the proper male mentors. What better role model than the local priest? After all, Agnes was raising two boys by herself with no financial or moral support from the father. She was on her own.

Mom worked for several years as a teller in the bank in downtown Spring Valley. Because she was a woman, she never received a promotion and barely got a raise. Never mind that whenever a problem cropped up, the bank managers would seek out Agnes.

She had been there longer than anyone else and she always helped solve whatever issues arose. Later, Mom left the bank to work in Kopelman's children's clothing store. She moved again when she got offered $65 a week from Nat Kaplan's Men's and Boy's Wear. What made the offer even more attractive was that Mom got a discount on John's and my clothes. All her jobs were located on Main Street in Spring Valley, a little over two miles from the house. We didn't have a car, so six days a week she walked to work and back home.

I remember when a blizzard dumped so much snow that every road was closed. That did not stop my mom. She tromped through the snow and opened the store. It was the only place in Spring Valley, or probably Rockland County, that was open that day. Toward the end of the day, when the roads were cleared, the owner stopped by the store, and to his shock Agnes was there. She had spent the day stocking shelves and organizing displays. When the owner asked her why she came in, she said, "I can't afford a day off, so I just walked in like I do every day."

Not only did we have no car; we had no phone as well. If we needed to make a call, we would go next door to Uncle Frank's. The few times we ate in a restaurant came after Sunday School. Mom would take us to a luncheonette in town, and we would get a bacon and egg on a hard roll with a slice of cheese, a New York special. I still get one every time I land at LaGuardia Airport, at the Neptune Diner in Astoria, on my way upstate. Along with a New York coffee, of course.

To understand who I am and how I traveled my life's road, you need to know my mother, Agnes Mulroy. She's a giver, not a taker. Seeing her raise me, I learned that women are equal to men, if not superior. My mom showed me that a woman can do any job a man can do. She woke every day and did a job that only men did at that time. Then she came home and did what women did at that time. She believed that all people were created equal, whether male or female, Hispanic or Jewish, rich or poor. In my house you learned to treat every person with the same respect. Mom always held two jobs, sometimes three. She never did anything for herself; she never went on a date and never took a vacation. She lived to raise her boys. She always made me feel that I was the most important part of her life, right up to her passing in late 2022 while I was still finishing this book. That's who she was.

Despite my mom's dedication, my brother and I were heading down the wrong road. John started to hang out with the kids your parents always told you to stay away from. Like many little brothers, I followed in his path. We were smoking cigarettes, drinking beer, and even sniffing glue. By the time I reached Pomona Junior High School, John had built the wrong kind of reputation. He had established a rap sheet, including being a skilled freehand tattooist.

I will never forget my first day of junior high. I had new clothes, notebooks, and pencils. You got your own locker, you moved from class to class, and you felt you were taking a big step toward adulthood. There I was, sitting in homeroom, and in walked a young lady who handed the teacher a note. The teacher read it, looked up, and said, "Tom Mulroy, please follow this young lady to the principal's office."

When I got there, both the principal and the dean of discipline awaited me. They read me the riot act: there will be no smoking, no drugs, no fighting, no skipping classes. They even checked my arms and legs for tattoos. I felt like I had gone from the first day of junior high to the first day of reform school.

To better understand why I was in the crosshairs, let me share a story told to me by my brother. John and his buddy Carl were smoking a butt in the boys' room when they heard the door open. They threw their cigarettes in the toilet and headed for the door. It wasn't a teacher, but a couple of Black students. They accused John and Carl of scrawling racist graffiti on the bathroom wall. My brother responded with, "First of all, I'm not racist, and second of all, that graffiti was ugly, way below me." John took pride in his artistic touch; no way would he have drawn those offensive images.

Word got out that the Black kids were after John and his greaser pals. John could feel the heat, and he stopped going to school. After a few days a truant officer showed up at our house. John had a choice: report to school or possibly face time in a youth institution. The following Monday, John went to school. He and his friends always traveled in pairs and did their best to avoid conflict. At some point, though, everyone needs a bio break. When John and a friend visited the boys' room, word got around. Before they could get out, they were surrounded by eight or so Black kids, ready to kick ass. The leader was a big albino kid with almost pink eyes. As these guys closed in on my brother and his friend, John took out a gun and yelled, "Stop, motherfuckers!" They stopped, hands up, eyes wide. John repeated that he and his friend had no hate and had not drawn the images.

Just then the leader said, "Let's get 'em guys; they can't shoot us all." At that moment my brother cocked his pistol, pointed it at the leader's forehead, and said, "You're right, I can't get you all, but I'm fucking getting you first." The leader backed off. John and his friend got out. School was almost over, so they never went back to class that day. Although school officials tried, no one could prove that John had the gun. Things eventually cooled off and John finished eighth grade at Pomona Junior High.

At the time, John and I shared the bedroom in our one-bedroom, 500-square-foot bungalow. Mom slept on the couch in the living room/kitchen. One night I was in bed when I heard the window opening. John was crawling out.

"Where are you going?" I asked.

"Shut up; you'll wake up Mom," he said. "I'm going to meet my friends."

It sounded like an adventure, and I said, "I'm coming with you."

"No way," John replied. "Go to sleep."

I said, "Mommy, Mommy, Mommy," a little louder each time. John knew she was going to wake up, so he let me go with him. I learned that not only were we meeting his friends, but that these guys had been meeting regularly to steal cars and go for joyrides. Back then it was easy, since most people left their cars in the driveway and the keys in the ignition. Heck, they even left the front door to their houses unlocked. Everybody trusted everybody. In some ways, the world was a nicer place back then.

We never stole any cars; we merely took them for joyrides. We would ride around all night until dawn, and then we would pull into the Shell station on Route 59 across from Jack in the Box. We filled the gas tank to the exact amount it had when we borrowed it. Then we drove it back to the house, left it in the driveway, and headed home. One night we took two Volkswagen Bugs out of the same driveway, and we raced them all night. When I look back now, it was crazy. I was on a dark and reckless path.

I was young but I knew something was wrong. John was always angry. He hated authority—teachers, principals, and the police. Over the next few years, John sunk deeper into the abyss. He was using and selling drugs. He dropped out of school and was running a few young hookers out of a van that he lived in for a spell. Eventually, he got into trouble with the local police. There was a controversy over whether he had given up some names. Whatever happened, he wound up leaving New York with a shotgun over his shoulder and a bag stuffed with his few possessions. His next stop was Houston, Texas, and the Black Dragon Tattoo shop. The story of John's wild and tragic life continues in chapters to come.

CHAPTER SIX

CAPTAIN'S ARMBAND

I played in my first official soccer game on September 28th, 1968, my 12th birthday. It was an introduction to a new sport, and to new and distinct cultures. I had opened a door to a world that was way bigger than the one I lived in. Everybody had a heavy accent, whether German, Yugoslavian, Hungarian, or Norwegian. Whenever I carpooled to an away game, the ethnicity of the driver would determine the language I would hear that day and what kind of music played on the built-in cassette tape or the eight-track player. We played in every ethnic neighborhood in New York City, say, in Astoria, to play the Greek Americans, or in Brooklyn to face the Italians. You name it, if there was an ethnic neighborhood, they had a soccer team playing in the German American League. I was learning to open my mind and think beyond my little world. This was an atmosphere where a young man could hone his people skills and prepare to be successful in all walks of life.

We trained twice a week, and at that time the youth teams played on Saturday and the men's teams played on Sunday. Our coach, Mr. Sautner, would invite me to watch him play with the over-30 team. They would play a match and the first team would play right after, which was like a double-header for me every Sunday. Soccer was becoming a huge part of my life. Off the field, I was still spending time with John and his friends. But for once I was on the path toward a healthy addiction, the same addiction that people have for soccer around the globe.

About halfway through the season, I got a new perspective on what soccer means to the people in my new community. Our captain, Danny Janes, had lost his mother. It was the first funeral I ever attended and an experience I'll never forget. The team was asked to come to the funeral in our uniforms. We lined up on both sides of the coffin as the priest gave the eulogy. It was emotional and moving. Now, people not steeped in soccer might wonder why someone would ask kids to wear their soccer uniforms at a family funeral. But that's what our club had become. We were more than friends and teammates; we were extended family. I didn't realize it then but I know it now: standing in our uniforms by Danny's mother's coffin was our way of showing our love and loyalty for our teammate and his family.

Back then, no matter your age, you played 11 versus 11. You played on the same size field as the adults. You played with the same size goal, and, in most cases, with the same size-5 ball. Think about the effort asked of an eight-year-old to get from one goal to another 120 yards away. It was also a challenge for young goalkeepers, who couldn't come close to reaching the crossbar eight feet off the ground. Back then, the standard soccer formation was the WM system, comprised of one goalkeeper, two backs, three midfielders, and five forwards. This is how the numbers on the uniforms went: Goalkeeper #1, Right Back #2, Left Back #3, Right Midfielder #4, Center Midfielder #5, Left

Midfielder #6, Right Winger #7, Inside Right #8, Center Forward #9, Inside Left #10, and Left Winger #11.

After each game, our shorts and socks were ours to take home. Our coach, Mr. Sautner, would collect our jerseys to take home to wash. At the next game when Coach handed you a shirt, you knew by the number if you were starting or not, and you knew your position and your responsibility for that game.

That year I played in my first indoor tournament, the Rudy Lamonica Oceanside Tournament. At the time, it was the first and only youth indoor soccer tournament held in the country. I remember seeing Rudy's picture in the high school trophy case as we entered the gym. He was a legendary youth player before bone cancer took his life at age 17. His parents would go to the tournament and help hand out trophies every year. I won my first trophy there. Launched more than 50 years ago, the tournament still takes place every year.

Later that season, I got picked to play on the German American League Boys' All-Star Team. I played my first international game with that team at the Metropolitan Oval against a team visiting from Germany. I carry one vivid memory from that game. I was defending in front of our goal when I dove to head out a cross. Just after I put my head on the ball, a German forward swung his boot into my face. He was a split second late on his attempted volley, but he landed a direct hit on my front teeth. I was in serious pain, but this was 1969, before any concussion protocol. In fact, the medic or ref would simply ask you if you knew your name. Whether you did or not, as long as you could answer the question, you kept playing.

German American League Boys All-Stars 1969
Young Tommy Mulroy front row far right kneeling

Toward the end of the season, I got a thrill that I remember to this day. At the end of practice, Coach Sautner began to give one of his talks. Coach had a harsh German accent, and he stuttered a bit when he spoke English. He talked about working hard, improving over the season, and being a leader. He pulled out a captain's band and described what that role meant. Then he looked at me and said, "Tommy, come here."

As I walked toward Coach, a feeling of euphoria swept over me. Coach said I had earned this band through my effort and leadership. It was a moment that changed my life, a moment that gave me a huge shot of self-confidence. As a 12-year-old kid still trying to choose between right and wrong, this was a game-changer, even a life-changer.

It's a moment that I share with others whenever I can. I share it when I'm giving coaching seminars for coaches. I want them to realize that they are not just coaching a "soccer kid," but a little human. Those kids could use a pat on the back and a little positive support from someone they looked up to. When I am on the field working with kids, I aim to make every kid feel special. Sometimes it might be a little smile of approval, a smile that can turn something that seems trivial into something important, even memorable.

When I got home after practice that afternoon, I was still high as a kite. That night I couldn't fall asleep. That was not unusual; I often had trouble drifting off after we won a big game. But this night was different. I felt like I was glowing. Looking back, this was truly my first soccer "high" across physical, mental, and emotional realms. You hear big-time athletes, musicians, and other successful people say how they can't describe the feeling. I'm pretty sure that's what I was feeling.

Later in life I would realize that this was a tipping point, a time when I stood at an intersection, one road full of death traps, the other leading to a life in soccer. Being on a soccer field felt so good, so motivating. I began training every free minute I had. It didn't matter if the kids in the neighborhood wanted to play. I would happily dribble my ball up to Cinema 45 and pound it off the wall for hours on end. If I was working on my instep, I'd kick it off the wall 500 times with my right and then 1,000 times with my left, exactly how coach told me to do it. Somehow, kicking my ball always made me feel good. If I was having a bad day—maybe I had failed a spelling test—I could get my ball and juggle, kick it off a wall, or go for a run with it. The stress melted away. Soccer was beginning to become my personal identity.

One day early in the season, my aunt could not drive me to practice and I couldn't drum up a ride, so I took my gym bag and started walking. We trained at Clarkstown Junior High, almost four miles from my house. About halfway there, I realized I was going to be late and maybe even miss the whole practice. So, I stuck out my thumb. I figured it was safe, because my brother and his friends did it all the time. It wasn't long before I got my first ride as a hitchhiker. For the next few years, hitchhiking became one of my primary forms of transportation to and from soccer fields all over Rockland County and beyond.

The more I played, the more I wanted that high like no other. I would train and play between 40 and 60 hours a week. When my mom wanted me to become an altar boy with my brother at Saint Joseph's, you can imagine how I reacted. I would have to miss all my games, since they took place on Saturdays. It was a battle early in the school year when the church was recruiting 13-year-old boys for the role. But my mom knew what soccer meant to me. She eventually relented, and I never missed a game.

I set my goals high. I wanted to be the best player in the world, the first American Pelé. At times I felt like I should have been born in Argentina, Germany, or some other country where soccer ruled. I was in the wrong place, I thought, but that didn't stop me from training every day. I was not competing to be the best player on my team, my state, or my country. In my mind I was competing against some kid in the favelas of Rio de Janeiro, or in the streets of Berlin, some kid who might be practicing harder and improving faster than I was. I wanted to be the best player I could be. According to the role models in my life, that meant no smoking, no drinking, and no wild and crazy behavior. It meant dead-on focus and hard effort. It meant teamwork. It meant leadership, and it meant choosing a path at this crossroads that would take me in the right direction.

My First Ball

My Jr. High School Coach Rich Meszaros and I during one of my many visits back to Rockland to do youth clinics when I was a professional.

CHAPTER SEVEN

MY SCHOOL HAS A TEAM

In the fall of 1969, I was a big-shot eighth-grader but I hated school. All day I would stare out the window thinking about soccer. Of course, the cafeteria was fun, and I loved gym class. Gym was the only class where I never worried about a teacher asking me a question in front of the class. The gym—and the athletic fields—those were the places where I was confident.

When we were choosing teams, I usually got picked early, no matter what sport. Often, the gym teachers would name me a captain and ask me to choose a team. Looking back, I think that was because of all the sports and street games I played with my gang back in Hillcrest. That experience gave me an advantage, no matter what sport the gym teachers were teaching, be it football, basketball, wrestling, or volleyball.

The sun was out on a perfect September afternoon, gym class about to begin. I stepped out of the locker room and up the hill toward the athletic fields, eager to see what sport we would play. To my delight. and nearly everyone else's despair, Coach Meszaros and Coach Bloom had set up a soccer field. Small goals did not yet exist, so big orange construction cones had been set out as goal posts. Even the soccer balls were primitive—brown, plastic, and rock-like. The coaches threw out a ball, and what ensued was how I imagine soccer was played by the Greeks, Egyptians, and Chinese back in 2500 B.C. A huge cluster around the ball with everybody kicking each other in the shins.

Most kids hated it, and I can see why. Nobody had a clue, as nobody had ever seen a soccer game, either live or on TV. The one rule kids knew was that only the goalkeeper could use his hands, which meant that every athletic kid wanted to play in goal. Maybe that explains why the U.S. has always been a little ahead in developing goalkeepers as opposed to field players. Ten minutes after kickoff, the coaches pulled me to the side. I remember Coach Bloom saying, "Hey, Mulroy, you got some serious twinkle toes." Then Meszaros jumped in with, "Where did you learn to play like that?"

I told him I played on the Spring Valley boys' team that competes in the German American League. Both the coaches were surprised, as they had never heard of a youth soccer league. And why should they have? We were the first youth soccer club north of the New York City line. At the time there were only two youth teams, our A team and our C team, a total of about 30 kids ranging in age from seven to 13. They were mostly first-generation European ethnics who lived all over Rockland County, and both teams met twice a week for practice.

Coach Meszaros had played some soccer in college and loved the game. He flicked up one of those rock-hard balls, juggled it a bit, and then kicked the ball to me and asked me to juggle. Now, Coach had kept it up 10 or 15 times, which might have impressed the other kids on the field. But I'm sure I had a big-ass smile, because that summer I had hit 100 for the first time. I got the ball up and started juggling. I was still at it when Coach said, "Why didn't you play on the school team last year?"

I asked, "There's a school team?"

He said there was and that tryouts started this week every day after school. The final cut would be that Friday.

I told Coach I'd be there that afternoon. He said he needed a permission slip signed by a parent. If I brought it back in the morning, I could start tomorrow. At this point, I had graduated from the metal-tipped football cleats to a pair of Max Doss kangaroo leather soccer shoes. I had my own pair of shin guards and a pair of shorts made for soccer. That night, I couldn't wait for my mom to get home to sign the form and learn that I had another place to play.

But was I spreading myself too thin? At the time I had training with my club team on Tuesdays and Thursdays, which began later in the evening. That meant I'd have to get from Pomona Junior High School to Clarkstown Junior High School, eight miles away. Hitchhiking at that time of day was not reliable. The next day, however, I was relieved to learn that an activity bus would drop me in Hillcrest, which was closer, and I could hitchhike from there and make it to my club team practices. So now I could have seven formal training sessions every week, club games on Saturdays, and I could watch adult games on Sundays. Beyond that, I would spend every free moment either organizing games in Hillcrest at Cinema 45 or training on my own.

I was pumped for my first day of tryouts with my new school team. I ran out of the locker room and up the hill. To my surprise, there were only 25 kids, barely enough to have a scrimmage. What I didn't know was that American football coaches were holding tryouts on the field next to us. After they made their cuts, we had three times as many kids trying out. This was further evidence that I had picked a sport that was still considered a cult. We had to fill our rosters with leftovers from other sports. We were last in line for everything.

Neither cheerleaders nor the school band ever came to soccer games. Thankfully, we had Coach Bloom and Coach Meszaros, who would fight to get us whatever they could. When the final cut came that Friday, I made the seventh- and eighth-grade team. In addition, I found out that the coaches were checking to see if I could also play with the ninth-grade team.

Once the team was set, Coach Meszaros would hold practice early in the morning before school started. That meant it was practically dark when I left the house, and Coach didn't think it was a good idea for me to be hitchhiking. So, he looped me into a carpool with three of my teammates—Eddie Weiner, Irving Myones, and Brad Mattis—and we all became good friends. The only catch was that I had to walk a few blocks to the corner of Eckerson Road and Trinity Avenue so they could pick me up on the way. No sweat, not when I'm catching a ride to soccer practice.

A few words about my neighborhood. I lived on Pascack Road, right off East Hickory at the bottom of "The Hill," or, as most people called it back then, "N****r Hill." We didn't have railroad tracks, but if we did, we would have been on the wrong side. Eckerson Road represented the divide between the neighborhoods. Poor to lower-middle class on our side, and middle class, all-white, and predominantly Jewish families on the other side.

I'll never forget one morning when it was Eddie's family's turn to drive. I'm standing on the corner of Eckerson and Trinity when up pulls a big Cadillac. I jumped in the back with Brad and Irving, with Eddie up front with his mom. She was in a robe, her hair up in those big pink curlers women used back then. She was complaining to Eddie about having to drive us so early. Then she looked at me in the rearview mirror and asked, "What about him, how come his mother never drives?"

I was a little stunned, and before I had time to respond, Eddie blurted, "His parents are dead, and he doesn't have a car."

I could feel my heart pounding. I didn't know what to say. Eddie looked back at me and winked, while Irving and Brad just stared out the side windows. Not a word was said for the rest of the ride. My three buddies thought it was funny. I didn't, and maybe that's why I remember it to this day.

The four of us got along, no matter that we came from different economic and religious backgrounds. I would get invited to their social events and parties. There were some bang-up parties thrown when parents were out of town. I also got invited to lots of bat mitzvahs and bar mitzvahs, but I usually couldn't go because I had games on the weekends. It was just as well because my mom didn't have much money for gifts, and my closet held no fancy clothes for formal events. To no surprise, those guys grew up to be lawyers and business execs, and I stayed on my soccer path.

Soon, I got word that I would be able to play up on the ninth-grade team. That team would open the season playing against perennial powerhouse, Nyack. I couldn't wait. Now I was going to play games on the weekdays and on the weekends. Who needs a day off?

The day before our first game, our coach ended practice early. We showered and met in the gym for a team meeting. The coaches gave a motivational talk and then said, "Gentlemen when we call your name come up and get your uniform." Now, when you're a kid and somebody hands you a new uniform, it is better than Christmas. When my name got called, I went up to the table. Coach Meszaros handed me my uniform, and then he dropped a bomb. He told me that Mr. Schuster, our athletic director, said that I would have to stop playing for my club team until the school season was over. By the time I got back to the bleachers, my heart was thudding on my chest. They continued handing out uniforms and then dismissed us. I walked over to Coach Meszaros and handed him my uniform. I said, "I'm sorry, but I won't be able to play with the school team. I learned to play with the Spring Valley boys' team, and they have always been there for me. I appreciate you offering me a position on the team, but if I must pick then I must take my club team."

I saw Coach Meszaros look over to Coach Bloom. I think I caught them off guard. Coach Meszaros said he'd talk with Mr. Schuster. Perhaps because I was only in eighth grade, that rule may not apply. Later that afternoon, I waited outside the gym office while my coaches met for 10 minutes with Mr. Schuster. At that point, Coaches Meszaros and Bloom walked out with big smiles and my uniform in their hands. They told me Mr. Schuster thought it would be okay. They gave me my uniform and told me to go home. I ran toward the activity bus, hoping I hadn't miss it, or I'd have a long hitchhike to my club practice. In hindsight, I think that coaches Meszaros and Bloom fought hard for me, stressing that I needed the club team environment to keep me out of trouble and off my brother's path.

The next day we got out of class a few minutes early, changed in the locker room, and boarded the team bus for our game against Nyack. We won, 2–0, and I scored the first goal off a free kick. I remember getting on the bus after the game. Coach Meszaros stood up and asked the guys to give the little eighth-grader a warm welcome to the team. As cheers rang out, there was that feeling again, that "soccer high." I was still "high" when I got home and that night it took me too long to fall asleep.

The next morning came another high. In homeroom, during announcements over the intercom, the front office mentioned that the ninth-grade soccer team beat Nyack and that eighth-grader Tom Mulroy had scored the first goal. You will recall that the last time I had heard from the front office, the principal and the dean of discipline had read me the riot act and checked me for tattoos. That episode made this day even sweeter. All day, in classes and in the halls, my friends and teammates congratulated me. Even kids I hardly knew were giving me high-fives. Talk about positive reinforcement.

By the time eighth grade ended, just about every kid in the school knew I was the "soccer kid." In ninth grade, I became the captain of the team and was growing into a leader. There was even talk about me moving up to play at the high school, but it turned out there was a rule against that. I figured they didn't want me hitchhiking from Pomona to Ramapo.

While soccer was going well, my academics were another matter. I had a learning disability, maybe dyslexia, maybe attention deficit disorder. Back then, no one really knew. They would round up the "slow" kids and stick us in a room so we would not impede the "normal" kids. They called us the BA kids which stood for below average. I went to all the special reading classes, received an evaluation for this or that, and then got sent back to the slow class. In fact, in ninth grade I took German as an elective so I could understand what the German families were saying at training, games, and other functions. There were only six kids in the class, so I thought this would be a good learning opportunity. But about three weeks in, the teacher told me I was slowing down the class and I got kicked out. I do remember learning the German word for "library," which is *bibliothek*. Later in life, I trained and played in Austria and Germany and I picked up German quickly. Maybe I wasn't stupid; I just had my own way of learning.

Where I grew up, junior high was comprised of seventh, eighth, and ninth grades, but academically, ninth grade was considered your freshman year of high school. Most students entering ninth grade would meet with their guidance counselor, who would try to steer each student along an academic path. When I got into my guidance counselor's office, he had my file in front of him. My grades were lousy. I figured he already had me ticketed for failure. The counselor said, "Well, Mister Mulroy, when you grow up, what job or occupation would you like to do?"

That must have been a loaded question because it didn't take me long to answer. I leaned back with a smile and said, "I'm going to be a professional soccer player." I figured he knew I was on the soccer team. I'm the soccer kid, and my file is in front of him. Besides, he must have heard the morning announcements, when I got plugged every time there was a soccer update. Well, he knew I was the soccer kid, and he couldn't give a rat's ass. He began to rip me a new one. "Who do you think you are?" he bellowed. "Every kid that walks in that door tells me that they want to be a professional athlete or a rock star. Stop dreaming! Come down to reality!"

His outburst hit me hard. I didn't even enjoy practice that day, and that never happened. When I got home that night, Mom was cooking dinner and she could tell I was upset. She asked, "What's the matter, are you okay?" I told her about my exchange with the guidance counselor. For some reason, I figured all adults thought alike and that she would echo his sentiments. Instead, she was miffed. She told me she didn't care who he was or what kind of degree he had, no one can tell you that you can't dream. She added, "As long as you put your heart and soul into it, you should never stop dreaming. Where would we be without dreams?"

My mom's words had reminded me that no matter what others say, I needed to believe in myself. Right there I went from being sad to being motivated to prove that guidance counselor wrong. Less than six years later, I would call and leave a message at the Pomona Junior High School guidance office. In it, I had invited that guidance counselor to come watch me play at Yankee Stadium, on August 10th, 1976.

Pomona Junior High School 7th and 8th Grade Team

Front Row L-R: James Koch, Pat Allen, Mike Vitolo.

Second Row L-R: Brad Mattes, Irving Myones, Ed Weiner, Hagay Gerber, Coach Fred Bloom, Tony Marciano, Klaus Goldmann, Doug Austin, Vinnie Selecchia.

Third Row L-R: Andy Kaye, Dan Scott, Andy Jacoby, Harvey Kaplowitz, John Yeager, Jim Minkin, Doug Kane, Jeff Lipnicky, Steve Schuster

Fourth Row L-R: Steven Muchnikoff, Bruce Pynes, Scott Cooper, Al Smith, Fred Kobb, Elliott Greenberg, Bruce Symanski, Marty Goodman, Larry McGinty, Tom Mulroy, Stuart Schimmel.

Pomona Junior High School 9th Grade Freshman Team

Standing Row L-R: Coach Meszaros, Alan Smith, J. O'Sullivan, D. Osborne, S. Mayer, Gary Berzon, Jeff Bloom, Fred Kobb, Tom Mulroy

Middle Row L-R: I. Newman, Harvey Kaplowitz, Tony Marciano, Irv Myones, Ed Applebaum, Ed Weiner, Michael Klingher, M Goodman, Jeff Lipnicky

Kneeling Row L-R: R. Wolfe, Todd Lesser, B. Krell , Eric Bergstol, Todd Essig, Scott Cooper, S. Muchnikoff, Jimmy Minkin

Missing: P. Allan, V. Moscatello, M. Bergman, D. Lambros, E. Lambros, J. Williams

CHAPTER EIGHT

WILL I HAVE A TEAM?

As my final year with the Spring Valley boys' team came to an end in the spring of 1970, I was in a pickle. There was no juvenile U-16 team in our club or anywhere else in Rockland County. I had begun to gain a reputation in the New York City area, having been named to the German American Junior League All-Star boys' team for the past two years, and having played in international games each summer. So, where was I going to play?

At the time, Ben Bohem was the mastermind behind the most successful youth development soccer program in the country. Bohem was the director of Blau Weiss Gottschee Youth Soccer Club, which had turned out some of the best players raised on U.S. soil. Among them were Arnie Mauser, a top goalkeeper in the NASL, and Joey Fink, a proven scorer in the U.S. pro ranks. Bohem, who walked with a cane, was known for identifying young talent. Legend had it that if he lifted his cane and pointed to a kid and said, "Now that one, he is going to be a player," it was a sure bet that that kid had a bright career ahead.

Bohem knew that Spring Valley did not have a juvenile team at that time. He reached out to my coach, Mr. Sautner, and my mother, and tried to recruit me to the BW Gottschee. I remember Bohem telling my mother that he thought I was a fine young man and that there would always be a place for me with BW Gottschee. I appreciated his interest. But how would I get to practice at the Metropolitan Oval in Maspeth, Queens, when it was both illegal and dangerous to hitchhike within New York City limits? Besides, there was talk that Spring Valley was planning to start a juvenile team. If that happened, that would make my life so much easier.

Here was the big question: If Spring Valley started a juvenile team, who would be the coach? Mr. Sautner had a full plate; he was coaching both his sons, who played on different youth teams, John on the A team and his younger brother Peter on the C team. A quick aside: My younger cousin, Frankie Fuchs, started off the season playing on the C team. However, after he scored an own goal in one of his first games, the assistant coach wanted to drop him. That would have ended Frankie's soccer career, but Mr. Sautner had other ideas. He moved Frankie up to his A team. He had two good reasons to do so. One, he thought that every kid should have a place to play, a chance to grow. And two, he knew Frankie's parents drove me to and from training. Sure enough, Frankie grew into an exceptional player, winning two Junior College National Championships and then playing professional soccer. Later he earned his A Coaching License and still is contributing to the sport today.

Back then, there were only volunteer coaches. It's not like today, where if you need a coach for your youth team, you get out the checkbook. Pay to play had not begun yet. The coaches didn't get paid; the administrators didn't get paid. The only people who did get paid were the referees. Heck, I think the entire U.S. Soccer Federation (now U.S. Soccer) had only three or four full-time employees, who worked out of a rented office in the Empire State Building. Yes, soccer in America was still a mom-and-pop shop. In fact, our sport was like an ethnic cult, run by immigrants who spoke English as a second language and in most cases with heavy accents. There were no coaching licenses, as the federation had yet to develop a coaching curriculum. The USSF national A, B, and C licenses were later introduced in 1970, with the D, E, and F state licenses following in the 80's. There was no formal coaching education at that time. Even if you did get a license, no one knew what it was. The one quality a coach needed was true passion for the game. Too often now, money comes first, the game and its people a distant second.

In the last week of our boys' season, after practice Mr. Sautner told us he had good news. We were going to field a juvenile team for next season and we were lucky that they had found a coach for the job. He told us it was someone that we all knew, Mr. Rottenbucher. His son Frankie was the tallest kid on the team and almost two years younger than me. Mr. Rottenbucher was a big, strapping guy. When you shook his hand, it was like scratching your hand on sandpaper. When I played for the boys' team, he had been at every practice and every game. At halftime of games, he would approach me and whisper something in my ear. When I went back in the game and tried whatever it was, it always worked. Frankie's mom, Teresa, always brought the oranges and drinks, including my favorite, hot tea with lots of lemon, for when we played on those freezing days in the middle of winter.

Little did I know that the guy taking over our team would have a hugely positive influence on me for years to come. In fact, not only would Mr. Rottenbucher become my mentor on and off the field, but he would also eventually serve as a surrogate father for countless young men, underserved, lower-middle-class white kids, and poor Haitian kids alike. He was known to all simply as "Coach." Coach asked nothing in return. He loved what he was doing and the people he was doing it for. In today's world, it may be hard to understand how someone would invest their time, energy, and money into a bunch of kids on a soccer team. Never mind that most kids on our team didn't have the money to pay for a uniform or a registration fee. Coach paid out of his own pocket. He thought no kid should miss out because he lacked means. After all, Coach came to this country with three shillings in his pocket. He came to pursue the American Dream, and he was going to share that dream with every kid who crossed his path. Coach was one of the special ones, part of a small breed that sacrificed much in their own lives to help kids that needed a hand up. We all loved him like a father.

It was early summer 1970 and the Spring Valley Soccer Club had just changed its name to the Clarkstown Sports Club. This enabled the club to secure more training and field permits in Clarkstown, a more central location for the players who traveled from all over the county to play in the only club north of New York City. We didn't have enough kids from the boys' team that were old enough to move up to the juvenile team, so the club started to recruit. They took out ads in the local paper and tried to get the ethnic newspapers to write stories. They also reached out to our main paper, *The Journal News*, but this was 1970 and soccer was still looked upon as the foreigners' game, a second-class sport for kids who could not make the football or basketball teams. Many Americans called it a "pussy" sport, a game for sissies. They would whine, "You can't touch the ball with your hands, what's that?" Now and then you would hear someone say that, "Soccer will be a big sport in ten years." I heard that over and over right up until 1994 when the FIFA World Cup took America by storm.

It turned out that the best way to recruit players was word-of-mouth. By this point, most players on the club team were also playing school soccer. We all knew some kids from our school teams, kids that might want to take the next step into the ethnic cult where soccer turns into "fútbol" and becomes a priority in your life. To my surprise, players from around the county showed up to the first training session of the newly formed Clarkstown Sport Club juvenile soccer team. One who stood out was Rick Derella, a little guy with huge, muscular legs. He was a skillful, gritty scorer who knew his way around the field. The prior season he had played for the German Hungarians boys' team, winners of the New York State Cup. Rick lived in West Nyack, which to me was, and still is, a rich kid's neighborhood. His family was fed up with driving into Queens for training and games, and they were relieved that a team had been formed in Rockland. Rick and I became thick as thieves; we trained together, we socialized together. I introduced him to girls from my school; he reciprocated in kind. Later we became college roommates. We were not just friends but family. Our mothers, Joan and Agnes, became fast friends. Our siblings and cousins all love each other. Here we are more than 50 years later, and we are still family.

As the juvenile team was firming up, other changes were taking place at the club. Our men's team had earned promotion into the Uber League (first division) of the German American Football Association, which was then the most competitive soccer league in the United States, amateur or professional. That promotion came after the team beat Bridgeport in a playoff. During that game, the president of the Bridgeport club suffered a massive heart attack and died in the stands. For me, that sad event was a stark example of how much soccer meant to its followers.

I was enjoying the summer, my favorite time of year. Without school, I could play soccer 12 hours a day. I would often run while dribbling a soccer ball from Hillcrest to Pomona Junior High. A few minutes after I arrived, my Aunt Nancy would show up with a car full of soccer balls, cones, water, and lunch. I would practice by myself all day, and she would come by to get me around dinner time. Then every evening I would head off to a place where I thought I might be able to get a game.

One evening at Spring Valley Junior High, I met up with one of my teammates from the club team, Mike DeStefano. He was the captain of the Spring Valley Junior High team, Pomona's biggest rival. Mike introduced me to a guy who was a few years our senior. His name was Ronald Clemente, and he came from Haiti, wherever that was, somewhere in France, I thought. Mike said this kid was good, so right away we picked Ronald for our team. After one of our games, Ronald asked me where I lived. When I told him Hillcrest, he asked why I didn't play at Memorial Park. I said, "Memorial Park? I had played Little League baseball there years earlier. Who plays soccer at Memorial Park?" He said a lot of Haitians play there. I thought to myself, *Haitians? There's more of you guys? Awesome!* So, I had another place where I could play and practice. That next Saturday I met Ronald at Memorial Park, where kids my age, older teenagers, and adults had started a pickup game.

At first, I was a little uneasy. I didn't know how good they were, they didn't know how good I was. I noticed that everyone was speaking a foreign language. That wasn't unusual, but what was odd was that they were all speaking the same foreign language. Usually, it was two or three guys from Yugoslavia who spoke Serbo-Croation, a few Germans who would communicate in German, and so on. Here everyone spoke in the same tongue, which I thought was French but later learned was Creole. I also noticed that I was the only white guy on the field. Not only on the field, but in the park. That didn't bother me; I had hung out on the hill before I ever saw a soccer ball. I grew up in a household where you didn't see color, only people. I walked out to the baseball outfield where they had two big iron garbage cans set up as goalposts on each side of the field, the teams in shirts and skins. Ronald stopped the game and introduced me to a bunch of guys who would later become lifelong friends.

In situations like this in my early soccer days, expectations were low for any American kid, or "El gringo." That kid would not be much of a player, especially on the ball. Well, it took me only a few minutes to surprise my opponents. I dribbled past two players and slipped one past the goalkeeper standing between the two garbage cans.

That's all it took. After that it didn't matter that I didn't speak Creole, or that I was white. My teammates knew they could share the ball with me. Soccer is a common international language, the words spoken with the ball. How you dribble, how you pass, how you shoot. It's all part of how a soccer ball brings people together from all around the world. I soon became a regular at Memorial Park. It was hard to find people who loved soccer the way I did, but these guys fit the bill. I spent lots of time that summer building close bonds with my new Haitian friends. In fact, I can still taste the Haitian rice, beans, and chicken dish that Herve's mom used to make for us.

Soon, I was recruiting the more serious Haitian players to play with us at the Clarkstown Sports Club. It started with Ronald "Frenchy" Clemente, and soon to follow were Herve and Gerard Guilliod, Wilbert and Ron Cadet, Ralph Dennis, and then Eddy St.

Cloud. This was the beginning of an ongoing flow of skilled players to our club. Coach Rottenbucher was overjoyed. For me, it was the onset of a lifelong connection to my Haitian brothers and the wonderful culture of the Haitian people.

As the summer wound down, the juvenile team was coming together, with only a few roster spots to fill. Coach had asked us to keep an eye out for good players. Coach was a savant; he had an intuitive feel for the game, a knack for knowing who should play where and what tactical role each kid should play. Sometimes in the middle of a game, he would change the lineup because he saw an uneven match-up that might cost us a goal, or a weakness on the other team that he wanted to exploit. Coach was known around the league as the guy with the big work boots. A contractor, he usually came straight from work to our games, and after the games he often went back to work.

In today's world, coaches would love to lead a team like ours, where most parents were hard-working people who didn't have the freedom to attend their kids' games. Here's how one coach put it: "We wish we could coach only orphans, no parents to bother us." Well, no parents bothered Coach. He was a one-man band, paying fees, running practices, handing out player passes, and managing our games. In fact, we didn't have to carpool to away games. Coach pulled up in his van and we jumped in the back, sometimes 15 or 16 of us packed in. Seat belt? Hell, no. When we came to a toll booth, Coach told us to hide under his painting drop cloth so the guy in the booth couldn't see all the kids huddled in back.

One time we were signed up to play in the Goya Cup, an indoor tournament in Staten Island. One of the parents who was supposed to drive the younger kids didn't show up. So, Coach offered to throw all those kids in the back of his van. There must have been 20 kids in that van, myself included. It was winter, and Coach cranked the heater. Before long, between the hot air, the full sun hitting the van, and the fact that the windows didn't open in the back, we were roasting. One of the younger kids got carsick, then came the chain reaction. Kids were throwing up all around me. Coach had to pull off the road. A few kids were grunting, while the older players laughed it off. I would have laughed, but I was trying not to breathe.

Clarkstown SC First Juvenile Team

Back (L-R) Frank Rottenbucher Coach, Tom Mulroy, Ron Cadet, Ken Fisher, Herve Guilliod, John Feger, Danny Janes, Paul Rocker

Front (L-R) Ralph Dennis, John Parkins, Gerrard Guilliod, Herman Isker, Rick Derella

CHAPTER NINE

WORLD CUP, 1970

The summer of 1970 also marked my introduction to the FIFA World Cup Tournament, "MEXICO 70." Everyone in my new soccer community, whether European or Haitian, was talking about it. It wasn't like today, when you can watch a World Cup game on your phone or tablet, or on TV in any other language, anywhere. Back then the event was not televised in English anywhere in the U.S.; the only coverage was week-old highlights shown on ABC's *Wide World of Sports*. One network, SIN TV, broadcast the games in Spanish. At the time, only nine million Hispanics lived in the United States, compared to more than 62 million today. SIN TV didn't have a national footprint, but New York was one of their markets and Uncle Frank got the channel on his black-and-white TV.

On the Sunday of the final match, I returned home from church and adjusted the bunny ears on Uncle Frank's TV so we could watch Brazil play Italy. The picture was so fuzzy we could barely see the ball, and we understood none of the Spanish commentary. There was, however, one name we kept hearing. Every time that player touched the ball, the commentator, Tony Tirado, whom

I would later meet when I turned pro, would constantly repeat Pelé, Pelé, and more Pelé. I saw my first World Cup goal, a header from Pelé. It was not an ideal way to watch the tournament, but it was enough to ignite a love affair. This was my first taste of what would become my most cherished soccer experience every four years. More notably, this was my first connection to Pelé, the man who would become my North Star. Since then, I have experienced nine World Cup finals in person.

CHAPTER TEN

CAMP HILL

The summer was coming to a close, and one night Coach Meszaros had left a message with my Aunt Nancy for my mom to call him. We still didn't have a phone in our house so we went next door. It turned out that there was going to be a first-of-its-kind soccer camp in Rockland County, at Camp Hill. The camp was for older high school kids, but when my coaches Bloom and Meszaros heard about it, they approached the soccer camp owner, Les Solney, a Hungarian gentleman who was the soccer coach at Hunter College. Not only did they ask Coach Solely if he would let a younger kid attend; they also asked if I could go for free because they knew my mom couldn't afford it. Like so many soccer people back then, Coach was happy to help a kid who loved soccer and might not have the means to attend camp. Coach Solely gave me a full scholarship to camp and we wound up being friends. In later years, he would often pick me up and drive me into the city so I could take part in offseason training with his college team.

CHAPTER ELEVEN

WATCH OUT, CRAZY DRIVER

School was back in session and the ninth-grade soccer season at Pomona was under way. By now my classmates and even my teachers knew me as "the soccer guy." Wherever I went I had a ball with me, and my schedule revolved around soccer. There was a rule where you had to be in school by the lunch bell at 11 a.m., or you couldn't participate in an athletic event that day. On game days, I would sleep in for an extra hour or two, then hitchhike to school to make sure that I signed in and was eligible to play.

One day in late fall, I was hitchhiking to school along Pomona Road, which was lined with apple orchards on both sides. A state trooper whizzed by, lights on, siren blaring. Less than a minute later another police car roared up and came to a screeching halt. An officer jumped out and told me they were pursuing a stolen car and the driver was out of control. He told me to be alert and get out of the way if I saw anything coming. I thought nothing of it.

A few minutes later, I scored a ride and got to school on time to play in the game that day. When I got home that night after my game, I learned that the stolen car was being driven by my brother John, his friends along for the ride. My poor mom. I had come home with good news about my game. I knew she wanted to celebrate with me, but my brother had been arrested for stealing a car and taking a joyride. It was a lot for a single mom to handle.

Our juvenile team had lots of new faces including a few of our new Haitian brothers. Funny to think that I would be playing with these guys on weekends, and against them when our school's teams met. The fall flew by, and our Pomona team had a great season. There was, however, one disappointing development. Coach Meszaros and Coach Bloom had invited the head varsity coach from Ramapo High School, where I would attend next year, to come see us play. That coach was Gary Shoonmaker, or "Schooney." We hit it off, and the school tried to get permission for me to play up on the varsity. I was super excited, but there was a rule that prohibited me from doing so.

By the time the fall school season ended, we knew every good soccer player in Rockland County and we were adding talent to our juvenile team. Once the winter indoor season ended, we had enough kids for two teams that spring. Our first team was becoming well-known in the German American League, and we were playing games on Long Island and in New Jersey. We were building a reputation across the entire Metropolitan New York area. When the season ended in late spring, that meant school was almost out. Then I had the summer days that I could fill with soccer from morning to night.

CHAPTER TWELVE

PELÉ VERSUS BOBBY MOORE

Santos of Brazil versus West Ham United of England. Pelé versus Bobby Moore. Dowling Stadium on Randall's Island, New York City. As a gift for my 14th birthday, Mom was taking me to my first international soccer game. The tickets were only $9. That was the easy part. Getting from Spring Valley to Randall's Island on a Tuesday night via public transportation—a single mom, a 14-year-old kid, and his 11-year-old cousin Frankie Fuchs—that was the challenge. But we all had been raving about Pelé since the World Cup held in Mexico that summer. No matter the strain, no matter how late we would get home, no matter how early my mom had to get up for work, Mom would make sure that I got to see my idol play in person.

Not only did I see Pelé play, but I also saw him score two spectacular goals against one of England's top teams. I was surprised that 22,143 people attended the game, and I bet that neither the promoter nor the Randall's Island stadium crew had any idea there would be that many avid international soccer fans. Looking back now, as someone who has promoted many large international games, I can tell you it was a cultural disconnect. The people running the stadium had no idea that just a few weeks earlier, the entire world was watching Pelé win the most important sporting event on the planet, the 1970 FIFA World Cup. To top it off, the captain of the English national team, Bobby Moore, was in uniform for West Ham. Every bus and train heading toward Randall's Island was oversold. Nobody who worked at the stadium had any clue that so many fans would attend the game.

The chaos started before the game. Dowling Stadium was shaped like a horseshoe, and the general admission tickets for the game were behind the goal. The sideline tickets were much better seats and cost more. Just a few minutes before the kickoff, thousands of fans had packed into the general admission seats behind the goal. However, there were plenty of empty seats on both sidelines. Suddenly, two guys jumped out of the general admission seats and ran across part of the field to the sideline seats. They hopped over the wall and settled into unused, reserved seats, swapping high-fives to celebrate their upgrade. Then I saw a few more fans jump over the wall and sprint for the reserved seating section. Within a few minutes, the trickle grew into a stampede, as nearly everybody in the general admission seats chased the same upgrade. There were no ushers and no security, except for two or three off-duty New York City policemen.

There I was with my cousin Frankie and my mom, who might have been the only woman in the stadium. She wasn't about to jump over a wall in her skirt and make her way to reserved seating. The atmosphere was electric. The fans were treated to an action-packed 2–2 draw.

Dowling Stadium had a rich history of hosting major sporting events, none more notable than Jesse Owens competing in the Men's Olympic Trials on July 11, 1936. Negro league games (1936–1940) and numerous music concerts followed, and in 1974 and 1975, the stadium was the home pitch for Pelé and the New York Cosmos of the North American Soccer League.

CHAPTER THIRTEEN

MY FIRST INTERNATIONAL TRIP

In late spring of 1971, tryouts were under way for the German American League All-Star teams. I had an advantage, having played for the boys' all-star team the year before. If I made the juvenile all-star team, I would be one of the youngest players. As usual, tryouts were held at various venues in New York City. That meant the field would likely have more shards of broken glass than blades of grass. These were places like College Point, Throgs Neck Stadium, and of course, the iconic Metropolitan Oval. By now I had experience trying out for teams, but this was different. The players were bigger, stronger, and faster, and the game was played at a quicker tempo. Every player was going in for tackles like it was his last game. This was a win-at-all-costs atmosphere.

Most of these kids weren't driven to the tryout by their parents; they took subways and buses. They were street kids, mostly from the city, and there were only a handful who, like me, had to make their way from the suburbs. Once they had selected the team, they announced that we would be competing in an international tournament in Toronto, Canada. Today the Robbie Cup remains one of the most competitive youth soccer tournaments in North America.

Those were the days when pay-to-play didn't exist. No one even knew what pay-to-play was (paying to join a team or a league, or to gain access to a facility). In fact, the entire trip was paid for by funds raised by the German American Junior League. All we had to cover was our personal expenses, like candy in a gift shop or souvenirs to take home. The German American Junior League had put together three all-star teams: the boys U13, the juveniles U16, and the juniors U19. With the three teams traveling together, that meant we would take two vans and one tour-style bus.

New York City to Toronto sounded like a long way to drive. It took 9 or 10 hours, and honestly the time flew. I was sharing a bus with the best soccer kids in the New York City area, and together we represented what New York City looked like: Germans, Greeks, South Americans, Italians, you name it. I think I was the only Anglo-American; there may have been one other. As I boarded the bus at the Neptune Diner in Queens, I learned that this was the most common departure point for soccer teams leaving the city to play away games. Every soccer kid in New York City knew the Neptune Diner.

Looking back, I still have fond memories of my first international soccer experience in Toronto. What is more, a handful of kids who were on that bus became some of my closest friends in life. One guy was Ron Atanasio. His nickname was "Brillo" because his afro sprung about a foot off of his head on all sides. An Italian kid, he had a left foot like a cannon and speed no one could match. He was a Long Island superstar who lived in Oceanside and played for New York City youth soccer legend Joe Goldberg.

The other lifelong friend that I met on the ride to Toronto played on the U-13 team. I roomed with him when we were staying at a YMCA in downtown Toronto. We were supposed to have two kids in a room but we had at least six. Although we were three separate teams, we did everything together. One night we were walking from the YMCA to a restaurant where we had reservations for the whole group. We were in three lines. At the front of the line was the younger team, the U13 boys. Then it was us, the U16 juveniles, and behind us were the U19 boys.

This was the seedy side of downtown. We passed adult stores and all manner of shady characters. At one point, I saw one of our U13 players step out of line and stop in front of two women, both dressed provocatively. At first, I thought the boy had strayed by accident. But when the women tried to step around him, he blocked their path. They tried again, and he slid in their way a second time. By now our entire line had stopped. Then this young player took something out of his pocket, held it up to the women, and said, "I offer you the key to my hotel room."

We were shocked. A coach grabbed him by the collar and threw him back in line. The coaches started to apologize, but both ladies had burst out laughing. Our entire group began cracking up. There he was, Nicky Megaloudis, the U13 Casanova, offering his hotel key to two women of the night in Toronto.

Ronnie, Nicky, and I became like brothers and have remained lifelong friends. We played with and against each other over our amateur and professional careers. Ronnie would become a first-round draft choice for the New York Cosmos, and Nick started his professional career with the Houston Dynamos and played for the U.S. National Team.

CHAPTER FOURTEEN

DID I DIE AND GO TO SOCCER HEAVEN?

As I got older, more soccer opportunities emerged. Coach Schooney had planned a team trip to a camp at Colgate University in Hamilton, New York. It would be all soccer, all the time. Wake up, eat breakfast, go out for skill sessions. Come in, wash up, eat lunch. Go out for an afternoon tactical session, come in, wash up, eat dinner. Go back out for an evening session, usually games. Return to the dorms, shower, eat pizza, and watch a soccer movie. Did I die and go to soccer heaven?

Back then, the college dorms were different from what they are now. Our team was in one big room with bunk beds. The coaches were in another part of the building, but close enough to make sure the kids behaved. I was the youngest kid in camp, and I was having the time of my life. Most of the kids were juniors and seniors, and I was one of a few incoming sophomores. The camp director was George Herrick, an American guy from Binghamton, New York, where he had built a name as coach at Vestal High School. George was also a businessman who partnered with his wife Linda to run the camp.

The week flew by, and now it was Friday. We were told to pack our stuff and be ready to go when we came back from the afternoon session. That morning we would play games, and in the afternoon the staff would play against the campers. A juggling contest would follow the games, with trophies presented to winners in each group: sophomores, juniors, and seniors. It was a memorable day for me, as a I scored on a free kick against the staff and won the sophomore juggling contest with nearly 400 juggles. A junior had the most juggles in the camp, just over 500, which was big stuff in those days. He was a Turkish kid named Sinan Baskent, the little brother of one of the camp counselors.

At the closing ceremonies, they called me up and gave me my first-ever individual trophy. But something ate at me. I wanted to have the most juggles of all the campers. I did not care if I was younger, second was not good enough. I swore to myself I would come back next year, beat everyone's records and be the top juggler in the entire camp, even as a junior. I was growing into my competitive fire.

CHAPTER FIFTEEN

WELCOME TO HIGH SCHOOL

Where I grew up, high school really started in 10th grade because ninth-graders spent freshman year at the junior high school. So, sophomore year you moved to the high school campus and started at the bottom of the social totem pole. That first day is both exciting and scary. For me, it was exciting because I couldn't wait to play varsity soccer. It was scary because I was such a poor student.

Ramapo was a typical New York high school, populated by various factions. There was a Black faction, a smaller Jewish faction, the jocks, the nerds, and the greasers, who supplied the drugs and tattoos. Of course, the one group most kids wanted to be part of was the cool crowd. That group included the hottest girls along with some well-dressed boys with cars and confidence from their family money.

Luckily for me, the soccer season kicked off when school started. I had just finished a summer camp with the varsity guys, and I had become friends with a handful of juniors and seniors. So, I had the jock box checked. My brother, John, was king of the greasers, even though he had already dropped out of school. I was friends with many of these guys, so another box checked. The Jewish faction? Well, my mom worked at Kopelman's Kitty Shop and then Nat Kaplan's Men's Clothing Store on Main Street in Spring Valley, where she was respected by the largely Jewish clientele. In fact, outside of my soccer posse, the kids that I ran with the most happened to be Jewish. One of my best friends was Barry Rothbaum, at whose house I had lox and bagels on many Saturday mornings. Another box checked.

In the Black faction, there were many reasons why I could check that box. I lived at the bottom of the hill, and unlike most white kids at that time, I was allowed to hang with anybody I chose. It didn't matter what color, it didn't matter what religion, and it didn't matter if they were rich or poor. That was the message from my mother Agnes: people are people; there are good ones and bad ones. In elementary school I used to hang out on the hill with my classmates Ronald Hauser, TT, and Boogie. The four of us were tight. We thought little about color or neighborhood; we simply had fun. We loved going to North Main Street School in the summer to play dodgeball and hoops. Most days I was the only white kid in the gym.

I remember one time I was so caught up in a game of basketball that I didn't realize the street lights had come on, my signal to get home. If I didn't get home, my mom would come looking for me. She would be worried, and, after a long day at work, she would be pissed. Suddenly, two kids ran onto the court and yelled to me, "Hey you, a white lady is looking for you, and you better hurry up because she got a belt." I threw down the ball and started running toward my house. I caught up with Mom as she walked up Slinn Avenue, and she did have a belt in her hand. She never really used it, but she threatened my brother and me with it, and we were scared to death of what that belt could do.

Many mornings, I would get up early and walk to the bus stop at the top of the hill at the corner of Slinn and Ewing Avenues. There were all kinds of activities going on near that intersection—tag, keep-away, even tackle football. Over a hundred kids, mostly Black, caught buses on that corner. One incident stands out. Two girls, maybe 12 or 13 years old, began to shout at each other. Everybody gathered around. One girl slapped the other across the face. A slap, not a tap, a hit that would have knocked me off my feet. Then the other girl grabbed her adversary by her hair and swung her around. Kids began to chant, *fight, fight, fight.*

I had never seen anything like this, not even on TV or in a movie. This was the ultimate catfight. They were scratching with their nails, kicking, biting, and tearing out hair. No one tried to break it up. The circle around the combatants was six or eight kids deep, all howling each time a blow was landed or a hunk of hair was tugged out. The girls tumbled to the ground, one on top, then the other on top. When the buses pulled up, not one kid got on. The drivers wouldn't dare try to break this up. One girl had a bloody nose and the other girl's face was cut. Then one girl ripped the other girl's shirt and her boob popped out. The crowd went wild, and then the fight stopped. It was as if there was an unwritten rule: the first one to show a breast loses. Still cursing and yelling, the two girls walked off in different directions. I think they each went home. I had thought girls were sissies and couldn't fight. Now I knew better.

Anyway, I had hung out with enough members of the Black community to check that box. I was as comfortable sitting at their lunch table as I was anywhere in the cafeteria. I considered myself lucky; as a sophomore, I had a foothold in every social clique. By the time I was a senior, nearly everybody in the school knew who I was. Even if they didn't know my name, they knew me as the soccer kid. Heck, I would often jog to school dribbling my soccer ball while the school buses passed me along the way.

It took me a couple of weeks to learn my way around the school. It had two floors, with 1,500 kids or around 500 per grade. Soccer was going well, as I made the starting eleven as a sophomore. However, my academics were another story. Since I could remember, even back in first grade, I struggled to pay attention in class. Somehow the letters were always backward. In some cases, I didn't spell the same word the same way twice, even in the same paragraph. Studying was a drag; I couldn't wait for class to end. Most of the time I would stare out the window thinking about my next soccer practice or game. Then the bell would ring and I would blow a sigh.

I guess the special reading classes and after-school programs that I had attended in junior high were not enough. Every assignment, every test, was a battle for me. School administrators had a way of dealing with me and other kids who struggled in the classroom. They put us in what they called the Below Average classes, referred to then as the "BA" classes. Educators didn't like to say "below average" out loud for fear that it would create a stigma. A few kids were assigned to BA classes in every subject: math, English, science, and social studies. For me, I was all BA except for physical education, which was my favorite class anyway.

Back then the kids in the BA classes were considered the dumb kids, the kids who were impeding the others. Looking back, it was a case of good kids having some learning disabilities, most commonly dyslexia and attention deficit disorder. Public schools did not know how to handle us. I think there were lots of bright kids in those BA classes, kids who didn't learn well in that structured environment but were intelligent and capable in their own ways.

One of the boys in my class was Wayne Courts. Wayne and I became friends early on as part of the BA brotherhood. Turns out he started mowing some lawns in our junior year. By our senior year, this below-average student was flipping some real estate, one property after another. Just a few years ago, Wayne wanted to hire me as a consultant on a possible sports complex that would include soccer. When I told him that I could not get to a meeting in New York on such short notice, he offered to fly me up in his private plane. Not bad for a dumb kid who was slowing down the rest of the kids.

From a social standpoint, BA classes did have a stigma. One day I heard some kids in the cafeteria saying they heard that Ramapo had some "retarded" classes. I was not sure that they were talking about the BA classes, but suspected as much. It was not cool going into those classrooms, and I did everything I could do to avoid being seen in them. Here is an example. I would be sitting in class, there would be a knock at the door, and this hot girl who worked in the main office would deliver a note to my BA teacher. Whenever that would happen, I would drop my pencil and bury my head under the desk until I heard the person leave the room.

What took real skill was slithering in and out of the BA classroom each day. Here's how I did it. Before class, I would stand in front of the locker nearest my next classroom door. I would spin the dial on the locker, pretending to be opening it. Once the hallway emptied, just after the second late bell rang, I would dash in and take my seat. Getting out without being seen was all about timing. I was packed up and ready to dash before the dismissal bell would ring. For me, when that bell went off, it was like the starting gun at a track meet. I would sprint out the door and get as far away from that classroom as I could, and then I would slow down to escape notice. As students left the other classrooms, no one knew which room I had exited.

Looking back now, it seems kind of silly. I knew I wasn't stupid, but I also knew I wasn't very good at the academic stuff, especially reading and writing. During my senior year, something wonderful happened. I got introduced to a program called Distributive Education Clubs of America (DECA). This was the most valuable classroom experience I ever had. The program was run by two wonderful teachers, Ms. Liscio and Mr. Gulker, kindhearted souls who were passionate about the kids in their charge. The program was like a business school, and somehow everything we did in those classes made sense to me. They taught us how to be entrepreneurial, not just how to make a product, but how to package it, price it, and market it. From day one, I was locked in.

Later in life, after my playing career, the principles I learned from the DECA program helped me build a successful company, Soccer Marketing and Promotions. I was able to apply what I learned in that class and rely on my people skills, work ethic, and grit to find a way forward.

Before long, our high school soccer season was under way. In every game, I was the smallest guy. I stood 5 feet 2 inches and weighed 105 pounds. I played center midfield, and took the goal kicks, corner kicks, indirect kicks, and free kicks. On nearly every restart, I was called to the ball. After the season, I was named to the second-team all-county squad.

My biggest disappointment that season was missing a penalty kick, in a road game that we won anyway. After the team bus arrived back at Ramapo High, I still felt terrible about it. Instead of getting a ride home with one of my teammates, I let everyone leave. When I was alone, I took my ball and went on the field and started taking penalty kicks. It was pitch black, and from 12 yards away I could barely see the whites of the goalposts and crossbar.

A few hours later, my Uncle Frank pulled into the parking lot, screaming my name out the window. My mom was worried when I didn't come home, and she started calling the coach and all the players' parents. In hindsight, I am sorry that I scared my mom, but I never did miss another penalty.

We ended the season ranked among the top three teams in the county. Soon after our last game, I was one of the six or seven players who were asked to gather in the athletic director's office. Coach Schooney wanted to share his thoughts about our prospects of playing soccer in college. He said, "Gentlemen, you can either be a small apple on a big tree or you can be a big apple on a small tree. Which one would you prefer to be?" He then asked each guy to state which option he preferred. He came to me last, probably because I was the only sophomore in the room. I said, "Well, Coach, you never mentioned my option." Coach shot me a puzzled look and said, "What do you mean? What's your option?"

"I want to be a big apple on a big tree," I said.

The seniors laughed, but I was serious. I didn't want to be a small apple on a big tree, and I didn't want to be a big apple on a small tree. I wanted to be the biggest apple on the biggest tree, and that's how I always set my goals.

As soccer season ended at Ramapo, the big winter sports were basketball and, to my surprise, wrestling. Wrestling was huge. Our varsity soccer coach, Schooney, was the assistant wrestling coach and a few soccer players, including my close pal, Tony Marciano, were wrestlers. At home matches, our gym was packed to the roof. The head coach was Tom Canty, an awesome teacher and mentor who spread passion for his sport to everyone he met.

That wrestling program had a big impact on me. At most high schools, basketball and football players are the big dudes on campus. In my high school, wrestlers were absolute bad-asses. Our team featured some of the best wrestlers in the state, and the country. Top college programs like Nebraska recruited at Ramapo. These grapplers were more than a team; they were a family. They did everything together, and they treated every kid on the roster with equal respect.

Think about this: in every weight class two guys had to compete against each other to earn the right to wrestle in the next match. Aside from when they went head-to-head on the mat, these guys helped each other every chance they got. They supported each other in the weight room, they worked on moves together, and they even helped each other make weight. One wrestler who also played football weighed 210 pounds during football season, and three weeks later, he was wrestling at 154 pounds. At some matches the weigh-in beforehand was among the most exciting parts of the day. Guys did whatever it took to make weight. They would starve themselves, dehydrate themselves. It was that culture that blew me away. I knew I had found athletes who loved their sport as much as I loved soccer. Even though I wasn't a wrestler, these guys appreciated the dedication I showed to my sport. I became the team's biggest fan, and I would hitchhike all over Rockland County to watch them wrestle.

CHAPTER SIXTEEN

COACH HAD EVERYONE'S BACK

It was spring of 1971, and never had my schedule been more frenetic. Every day after school, I would train with my varsity team, and three nights a week after practice I would hitchhike seven miles from Ramapo to Clarkstown Junior High School to train with my Clarkstown juvenile team. It was our second year competing in the GAJSL, and Coach Rottenbucher had taken us from a mediocre side to one of the most competitive teams in New York State.

We made it to the semifinals of the State Cup where we played to a 2–2 draw against the Greek Americans, one of New York's top clubs. Sadly, we lost on penalty kicks. I remember Coach calling me over after the game and congratulating me for "great leadership and a wonderful season." He said, "Come sit with me; this is a moment in life that we will never forget. Let's make it last." Coach hated to lose, but he knew that sometimes you could still win even when you lose on the scoreboard. Coach knew it was about the journey.

We were no longer a team made up only of the sons of European members of our adult soccer club; now we had kids from all over

Rockland County. Back then, interracial teams were unusual. The Greek-American kids we played against were all Greeks. They spoke Greek as a first language, and English, if they spoke it, was their second language. It was the same with the Brooklyn Italians. Their kids were all Italian and they spoke Italian. The German Hungarians, well, they were German Hungarians. The Colombian team was pure Colombian, and they all spoke Spanish. That's how it was. People stayed in their neighborhoods and hung out with people like them.

But Coach saw America differently. He didn't care about where you came from, or who your parents were, or your nationality, or your color, or your religion. He had emigrated from Austria to the United States to meet new people, learn a new language, and experience new customs. Coach saw America as a place for everybody, a place where different people met and shared their cultures. Coach said America was the greatest country because we mixed. Back in Europe, he said, everybody did everything the same way, and there was only one way to do things. He marveled at how in the U.S., people come from all over the world. Just when you thought you knew the only way to do something, you would meet some gringo from someplace you never heard of and he had a new and better way to do it.

Coach's approach was not popular with all his constituents. At one point in the season, he encountered pushback at a board meeting of the Clarkstown Sports Club. A few members from the old country, one of them a member of Coach's family, told Coach that he had too many Black kids on the team. As a result, their own kids were not getting enough playing time. These members also wanted Coach to know that his Black kids were not welcome at the upcoming Christmas party.

Coach didn't take that well. He was a big guy, built like a grizzly bear. Word was that Coach flipped over a table and had to be held back by several members. No one got hurt, but it was ugly. Coach had made it clear: any boy who was a good enough player and a nice enough kid could play on his team, no matter his color. If his Black players couldn't attend the Christmas party, nobody was going, including Coach and his family. To Coach, the team was his extended family. He cared about each kid, from the stud to the last player off the bench. He was our mentor. For many of us on the team who didn't have fathers, he was our father.

Tommy and his Surrogate Farther, Mentor and Coach Frank Rottenbucher

CHAPTER SEVENTEEN

MY EXPERIENCE WITH THE "OTHER" FOOTBALL

My first experience with American football came in eighth grade when I was playing soccer on the freshman team at Pomona Junior High. It was a late fall afternoon, and on the schedule were both a soccer game and a freshman football game. I arrived late to the locker room because I had attended a special reading class that met a few days a week. The coaches were okay with that—academics first. They knew I would arrive late, but before kick-off. When I got to the locker room, my teammates had already left to warm up on the field. The freshman football team was still in the locker room.

I went to my locker and started to change. I could hear players screaming and banging lockers. It was new to me, but I figured this was how football teams prepared for battle. Then I heard the coach yell something like, "We're gonna kick their ass on our field today!"

Players started stomping their cleats and banging more lockers. It was a little intimidating. As I put on my uniform, I looked across the room and saw that one of the coaches had grabbed a player by the facemask. He started banging the kid's helmet off the locker, never mind that the kid's head was in the helmet. The coach yelled, "Do you know what they're saying out there? They're calling your mother a N****r!"

 Bang, bang, bang, he bounced the kid's helmet off the locker. "Did you hear me? What are you going to do about it?"

It was a loud, angry voice. My sense of intimidation had turned to fear. I shut my locker, grabbed the rest of my uniform, and ran out barefooted until I made it up the hill to my team's bench. I was shaking, maybe from the cold, maybe from fear. I put on my shin guards and was pulling up my socks when Coach Meszaros came over. He told me I was not late, that I could have dressed in the locker room. I never told Coach what happened that day. I figured that was how football coaches fired up their players. Who was I to question it?

A few years later, as a junior in high school, I had a more intimate experience with American football. It started when Chuck Scarpulla, our athletic director and head football coach, came to watch our soccer team play a game. He noticed that I was launching my goal kicks 50 to 60 yards down the field. The next day, Coach Scarpulla approached me in gym class and said, "Hey, Mulroy, you got some leg, think you can kick a football?"

I said, "Sure, Coach, no problem." He asked me to come to his practice that afternoon. I told him I had soccer practice. He assured me that Coach Schooney would let me miss soccer to work out with the football team. I thanked Coach Scarpulla but told him I wasn't going to miss soccer practice. He looked at me like I was from another planet. Then he said, "Okay, how about when you finish practice you come over and find me?" I told him I'd do that. This wasn't a big deal to me. I almost felt like I was doing them a favor.

At the beginning of soccer practice, Coach Schooney told me if I wanted to leave early to try kicking for the football team, no problem. I told him no, that we always scrimmage at the end of training, and that's my favorite part. Well, Coach Schooney ended our scrimmage while we still had some daylight. I think he cut practice short to make sure I got to the football field. After all, Coach Schooney worked for Coach Scarpulla.

By the time I got to the football field, Coach Scarpulla, his assistants, and a few players were waiting on me. Coach asked me how much I knew about kicking field goals. I replied that the ball must go over the bar and between the posts. He said that's right and that it's a lot harder when big and fast opponents are rushing you. He added that the good news is those rushers are not allowed to touch the kicker.

Coach said, "Let's start with some extra points. First, we'll kick some off the tee, then you'll kick it out of a player's hold." We moved onto the field, maybe ten yards from the posts. My first thought was that this was like taking a penalty kick without a keeper in goal.

Coach said, "What do you think? Can you put it through the bars from here?" Was he busting my chops?

I said, "You want me to kick with my left foot or my right foot?"

Coach broke into a grin and everybody was laughing. I made the first one with my left foot, then made another with my right foot. Coach knew I had plenty of pop. Then Coach wanted me to kick while a few players ran at me with their hands up. In my soccer brain, I figured I would chip the ball, similar to chipping a ball over a defender in soccer. But then I thought about how different those kicks were. In soccer, the ball rests on the ground, not a tee, and the ball is usually moving. Your target is also moving, so you have to be that much more precise. And defenders come at you not just from the front but from every conceivable angle, and they certainly could make contact.

I shut my brain off and we moved to the 20-yard line, then the 30, the 35, and the 40. Rather than kick straight on, I rotated between the hash marks on both sides. I was consistent until we got to 50 yards, which was about my limit. I still made most from that distance, but a few fell short, never wide. Not bad for the first time I kicked a football. Right then and there, Coach welcomed me to the Ramapo varsity football team. He told me to come to his office in the morning to get my uniform and equipment. I have to say, it was a pretty cool feeling.

I was riding high for another reason those days. My mom was worried about all the hitchhiking I was doing, so she put a down payment on her credit card for a 1968 GTO convertible. I had my first car; what a thrill, and what a relief. Of course, I would have to get a job to pay for it, and that proved to be another story. Anyway, after football practice, I got in my car and headed home. There was no social media and we didn't have a phone, but come tomorrow, everyone at Ramapo High School would know that I would be kicking for the football team. That night at home, I got my head back into soccer. It was Thursday, only a few days from our season-opening game against our biggest rival, Spring Valley. This was the big one, the one for bragging rights. That's what I thought about as I crawled into bed.

The next morning, I went to the office by the gym expecting to get a jersey, a pair of pants, and a helmet. I soon learned that there was a lot more to a football uniform. We're talking about a helmet, chin snap, visor, shoulder pads of different models, a game jersey, practice jersey, gloves, game pants, practice pants, rib protector, elbow pads, knee pads, and thigh pads. What really caught my eye was the mouthguard, this little brick of white plastic that hung from your helmet. During plays, you were supposed to stick it in your mouth. I didn't think I'd be able to kick with all that stuff attached to my body. The more stuff I put on, the more uncomfortable I became. And then I wondered, *If no one is allowed to touch me, why do I need all this protection?* One thing was for sure: I wasn't going to wear football cleats, I would wear my soccer shoes, the ones in which I had spent thousands of hours kicking a ball.

First, they fitted me for a helmet. I picked a lighter one with no real face mask, just one thin bar in front of my mouth. The shoulder pads took forever. I tried a bunch before settling on a pair that had flimsy plastic flaps. The jersey was cool because it had the number 10. Wait a second, how did I, the last guy to get a jersey, manage to get number 10? Were these guys nuts? That's Pelé's number, and no one picked it?

When it was over, I had a jersey, shoulder pads, a helmet, and that little plastic doohickey that even came in its own plastic bag. I was geared up and ready to go. As I was leaving, Coach Scarpulla said, "It's Friday, and the game is tomorrow. Aren't you going to put your jersey on? You know the players all wear their jerseys on the Friday before our Saturday games. That lets everybody know they're on the team and that there's a game they should come out to support."

I liked that idea. I wondered why the soccer team didn't do that the day before our games. I put on my jersey and headed to my locker to put away the rest of the equipment, and then I was off to my first class.

By lunchtime, I had received more than 100 comments and high-fives. People would wave and say random stuff like, "Kick Spring Valley's ass." It felt cool. Later that day, right before my last class, the halls were emptying. I was at a locker near my BA classroom door, acting like it was my locker. When the bell rang, I was about to jump into class when I felt a hand on the back of my shoulder. I turned to face this big kid, maybe 6-foot-3-inch tall, and built.

He said, "Hey, Mulroy, I see you're wearing the varsity football uniform."

I said, "Yeah, I'm going to be the kicker."

He replied, "Do you know what an honor it is to wear that jersey? Do you know that kids train for years, dreaming about being on the varsity football team? Well, many of those players either stay down on the JV team or get cut. Then you show up out of nowhere, with one thirty-minute training session, and you're walking around the halls wearing a varsity jersey."

At this point, there was nobody left in the hall but us. I had sensed agitation in his voice. He was not wearing a varsity jersey, while I was. Was I about to get my ass kicked?

I said, "Sure, I only had one training session. But I can kick, and that's a specialty. I'm sure I've spent more time working on my kicking ability than any athlete at this school has spent honing his game. Besides, I didn't take the position from anyone, certainly not from anyone who works as hard as I do."

He nodded, and it seemed that I had defused the situation. We shook hands and I slipped into class a few minutes late.

That afternoon, after soccer practice ended, I ran to the locker room, changed into my football gear, and jogged to the field. When I arrived, they had begun to work on special teams plays to prep for tomorrow's game. It was more formal than the day before. The defensive special teams unit was playing against the offensive special teams unit. They would hike the ball and place it for me to kick. Now, instead of one or two guys running at me, it was a full line. I kept telling myself they are not allowed to touch me. After I knocked through a few extra points to warm up, we kicked field goals from various distances and angles.

After practice ended, Coach Scarpulla called everyone together. I looked around. There must have been at least sixty players and half-dozen coaches, a much bigger crowd than you see at a soccer practice. Coach said something like, "Good job this week, men. Tonight's pregame meeting will be at seven o'clock sharp; see you there." The coaches left, and the captains spoke a few inspiring words. Everybody clapped and screamed and then headed into the locker room. On my way to my car, I was thinking, *A team meeting on Friday night? Do they do this to make sure nobody goes out the night before a game?*

That night I returned to the high school for the pregame meeting. It was held in a science classroom I had never been in. When I walked in, a few players in the back were fooling around with Bunsen burners. The rows of desks were tiered, probably so the teacher could see what students were doing with the burners. Soon the room was packed. First, Coach Scarpulla talked about the Ramapo-Spring Valley rivalry. Then he turned it over to the defensive coach. When he started talking, it sounded like a foreign language to me. He described plays the opposition would run and what we would do to counter. Just when I thought I would doze off, the defensive coach introduced the offensive coach and we got hit with another round of tactical blather. I thought I was Linus, the character in the Peanuts comic strip, listening to his teacher, Miss Othmar, go Wah, Wah, Wah.

Finally, they addressed the special teams. Coach Scarpulla said, "OK, on field goals, Knapp you hike to McIntee, McIntee you place the ball, and Mulroy you put it through the uprights." Once I heard my name, I perked up a bit. Then Coach added, "Mulroy, if McIntee drops the ball, don't try to pick it up and run with it; we don't need any heroes. Just throw your body on it and cover it up." *Hang on, did Coach say something about throwing my body on the ball?* My mind flashed back to, "They can't touch the kicker." I stood up, looked at Coach Scarpulla, and said, "If McIntee drops the ball, he better throw his body on it because I will be standing on the sideline next to you."

That didn't go over well. Coach Scarpulla nipped the tension with, "There is nothing to worry about, McIntee won't drop the ball." In hindsight, I am glad Coach doused the flame before the room turned on me. At 10 p.m., the meeting ended. Everyone was heading to Hillcrest to get a slice of pizza before they went home. When I arrived at the pizzeria, not only were the guys stopping for a quick slice, but they were stocking up on beer and other party items as well. So much for holding a team meeting the night before a game so the players could get a good night's sleep.

Before I knew it, my car was full of players and I was following a caravan of more than a dozen cars. Somebody had heard there was a party in Spring Valley and we were going to crash it. This was new to me. Not that I was a goody-two-shoes, but if I had a soccer game the next day no way I'd stay out late. I wasn't a big drinker, and I certainly didn't drink and drive. But if the team was going to a party, I thought why not? It wasn't like I had to run seven or eight miles the next day, like I do in a soccer game. All I had to do was step up to a ball and kick it.

Soon after we arrived at the party, it was obvious that we weren't welcome. The entire Spring Valley football team was already there. Everyone was drinking and it looked like things were going to get ugly quick. There was pushing and shoving and someone called the police. Sirens were blaring, lights were flashing, and I jumped in my GTO and drove back to Hillcrest. Most of my teammates met back there and we called it a night.

As I drove home, I was thinking about the contrast between soccer and football cultures. Sure, our soccer team wanted to win as badly as our football team did. But we didn't want to go to our opponents' turf and rumble. In fact, soccer players had our own way to bond, no matter what school you were from. You fought hard, you hit hard, you were all-in during the game. But when it was over, we shook hands with our rivals and we were friends. For me, American football was a new and strange way to compete.

Game day. The whole team would meet at Denny's on Route 59 to eat breakfast together. The game was midday, so it was important to down a hearty breakfast. This made sense, as that's what we would have done before a soccer game. When I arrived at Denny's, the team had taken over the entire restaurant: tables, booths, and counters. As the waitress arrived, I was still trying to decide if I wanted home fries or French fries with my two eggs and bacon. She started to take orders. One guy said, "Six over easy, three stacks of pancakes, two orders of home fries, two orders of French fries, two orders of bacon, and ham on the side, please." I thought he was ordering for the whole table. When I realized he had ordered for himself, I looked over my shoulder at the other tables. When the food arrived, forks became front-end loaders. For these guys, eating was sport.

After breakfast we headed to our locker room to get dressed and meet the team bus. Getting ready for a soccer game took only a few minutes. You put on your shorts and fiddled with your shin guards until they felt tight. Dressing for an American football game was another matter. First, there were three or four tables where players got taped. The only tape you would see on a soccer player might be around the ankle. Here, guys were getting taped on their wrists, shoulders, and knees. Oh, and just about every guy got both ankles taped. A coach asked me if I wanted to tape my ankles. I did not want to restrict my ability to feel the ball, so I declined.

There were other things I had never seen in a locker room. Guys had paired off, standing face to face. One guy would pound his fists on the other guy's shoulder pads, and then the other guy returned the favor. I was afraid to ask if they were doing this to get fired up or to make sure their shoulder pads were on correctly. Some guys were screaming like warriors. A couple of guys were punching lockers or banging their heads on lockers. It was quite a ritual.

It didn't take me long to get ready. All I had was my trusty soccer shoes, game pants, shoulder pads, a jersey with the number 10, and, of course, my helmet with the mouthpiece now hanging from the bar. I had no intention of putting that thing in my mouth. It was uncomfortable. I couldn't understand how anybody did it. I thought they were all crazy.

As our bus took off for Spring Valley High School, the guy next to me said, "Hey Mulroy, what's with your mouthpiece? Why didn't you boil it?"

"Boil it? What are you talking about?" I replied.

He said, "You were supposed to take your mouthguard home and boil it in hot water, then put it in your mouth, so it molds and fits comfortably."

I said, "Nobody told me anything about boiling it."

Then another guy said, "Don't worry, Mulroy, you're a kicker, so no one is allowed to touch you." That's what I needed to hear as the bus pulled up to Spring Valley High School.

We arrived two hours before the game and yet the parking lot was almost full. Fans from both schools streamed toward the bleachers. We entered the visitors' locker room, where Coach Scarpulla reviewed some tactics and then delivered a compelling motivational speech. Even I was ready to kick some ass. Then we gathered outside the locker room door at the top of a small hill, where we could hear the marching band playing in the stadium below. The captains took over, "This is the day we make history!" Something to that effect.

Our captains led us in a light jog down the path and into the stadium. One side wore the orange and black of Spring Valley, and the other side was togged up in Ramapo's green and gold. As we entered, the announcer said, "Here comes Ramapo High School!" The place went crazy, half cheers, half jeers. Butterflies flapped in my stomach and goosebumps raced down my arms. But I wasn't nervous; I was ready.

As I warmed up, I felt adrenaline flow through me. We started with a few kicks from the extra-point spot. Then we moved back to the 20, then the 30, and finally the 45. I told myself that every fan was watching my kicks sail through the uprights. I didn't miss one kick, and I felt invincible. As the coaches called us to the sidelines for the national anthem, any doubt I had about playing American football had been erased. There I was, facing the American flag, hand over my heart, listening to our national anthem and feeling high on life. I was ready to win this game by myself.

The game began, and soon we had a third-down on the Spring Valley 25-yard line. A special teams coach told me to warm up. I scanned the sideline for a place to get loose. I felt like I was at a block party, surrounded by 75 teammates and coaches. I jogged along the sideline, right knee up, then left knee up, side shuffles. I started jumping off one leg, as if I was heading a soccer ball. That's when the coach ran up and said, "Mulroy, what the hell are you doing?"

I looked at him and said, "You told me to warm up." He pointed up the sideline and said, "Use that."

I had no clue what he was pointing to. He grabbed a bag of footballs and walked me to a lacrosse goal. I still didn't know what he wanted me to do. He called over a player and had him hold balls as I kicked into the lacrosse net a few feet in front of me. I kicked half-dozen times. Now it was fourth down on the field and I was ready to go. But instead of trying a field goal, we went for the first down. Spring Valley made the stop, so I quit warming up. Three times in the first half we moved inside their 20-yard line, but not once did I get called out. At halftime, we trailed, 7–0. Had they given me a chance, we would have led, 9-7.

In the locker room Coach started with, "It's not over, the second half is ours." Then each assistant coach chimed in with his form of Wah, Wah. I never understood anything they said. After the talk ended, the players gathered at the top of the hill. As we were waiting for a few stragglers, one of our players, Jay Feinberg, started to scream, "Let's kick Spring Valley's ass!" A short, stocky guy, Jay, was holding his helmet by the facemask and swinging it over his head. He started to dart back and forth, apparently trying to fire up the team. The look on my face must have been priceless. I had not seen an athlete behave like this. In fact, if my club soccer team saw our opponents doing jumping jacks and counting in chorus, or chanting some hokey cheer, we knew we would kick their ass. American football was a big culture shock to me.

While Jay was still bouncing around, my teammate Kenny Furnish came up to me. He pulled out his mouthpiece, and said, "Look at Jay dance. He looks like a monkey in heat." Then it got really weird. Jay looked in our direction and screamed, "No fucking smiling!" Now he was running in our direction. "Why are you fucking smiling?" he wailed. I looked over my shoulder to see who he was running toward. By the time I looked back, he had launched himself like a human torpedo, planting both knees just below my shoulder pads onto my chest. I flew backward with him on top of me. I landed on my back, and then the back of my helmet hit the ground. Jay was now sitting on me with his knees on my chest. He was banging his helmet into my helmet while screaming, "No fucking smiling! No fucking smiling! We are losing!"

I didn't know what hit me. I had no time to brace myself, and I was dazed. Finally, other players ran over and pulled Jay off. Jay jumped up, held his helmet over his head, and screamed, "Beat Spring Valley." Then he ran down toward the field, most of the players following him, shouting in unison, "Beat Spring Valley." As I was getting to my feet the coaches were coming out of the locker room. Kenny and a few other players were still with me. Kenny said, "If you had your mouthguard in, he wouldn't have seen you smiling." Then he added, "But he did look like a monkey." I bit back a laugh and jogged down the hill.

The second half was merely an extension on the first half. The only kicking I did was into the lacrosse net. The game ended—Spring

Valley 7, Ramapo 0. To this day I still believe that had they given me a chance, we could have won the game. As we piled onto the bus to head back to Ramapo, Kenny sat next to me. I could hear players whimpering, even crying. I was not so invested, but I could still empathize with these guys. Just then one of the players in the back let out a loud sob. Kenny leaned in and whispered, "That's big Willy, bawling like a baby. That's the same guy that runs around school like a tough guy."

Kenny snapped off a couple more zingers, but this was not the moment. The last thing I wanted to do was smile on that bus, never mind laugh. I finally had a use for my mouthpiece. I put it in and bit on it hard. I rested my head on the back of the seat in front of me, my eyes closed. Kenny was whispering junk in my ear the whole ride. I tried my best to block him out.

Finally, the bus pulled into the school lot. Coach told us how proud he was, and that he'd see us at practice on Monday. He left the bus, and then I saw something I had never seen. The players emptied out of the bus, but not by walking up the aisle and stepping out the front door. No, these players left like there was a bomb scare. The emergency back door flew open and players started jumping out. The emergency side windows were pushed or kicked open, players crawling out. A few others joined me in leaving through the front door. I didn't go to the locker room. I went straight to my GTO and drove home.

On Monday morning, I was waiting at the gym office door as Coach Scarpulla arrived. I told him I had thought hard about this, and then I said, "Thank you for the opportunity, but American football isn't for me." I handed him the team shorts, the number 10 jersey, the helmet, the shoulder pads, and, of course, the mouthguard. We respectfully parted ways.

This might just be my own "pipe dream", but here's how I would like to see American football and international football change roles in the United States. I propose that all public high schools reallocate the resources that are traditionally provided for American football high school teams to their soccer teams. Here is what I would like to see considered:

Soccer teams play games at prime times on Friday nights and weekend afternoons at the stadium. American football teams play two weekday games immediately after school, with no lights and no stadium, exactly like soccer now.

The school band, cheerleaders, and other school groups participate as part of the soccer team's game day at the stadium, i.e., pregame and halftime performances.

School pep rallies and other social events usually scheduled for and around the American football teams now become part of the soccer team's environment.

Local media devotes the same time and space to soccer as they do to American football, i.e., front-page coverage as opposed to a small mention on Page 3.

Sure, in the '70s, soccer was a foreign game, and few people cared or understood. Today, more than 18 million kids play. There's passion for the sport. It's time for soccer to take its place at the front of the line.

CHAPTER EIGHTEEN

A HUNGER FOR ACHIEVEMENT

A year later I was packing my bags to head off to my second Colgate soccer camp. This time I knew exactly what to expect, and I couldn't wait. To add to the fun, I was going not only with my high school teammates, but with a bunch of my teammates from the Clarkstown Sports Club. I might have been the camp's best salesman.

As I had done the year before, after each session, I stayed on the field for a bit and worked on whatever we had just learned. On the last night, we had eaten dinner and were watching a soccer movie when the director, Coach Harrick, picked up the mic. He announced that on the last day, in addition to the juggling contest, there would be dribbling, passing, shooting, and penalty kick contests. Trophies would go to the winners of each category. I was pumped. I loved competition, and I wanted another go at Sinan Baskent, who had won last year's juggling contest and was back again this year.

That last day of camp was always the most fun, starting with the morning matches between campers and the game pitting the staff against the kids. The skills contests and closing ceremonies would follow in the afternoon. When we arrived at the fields after lunch, they walked us through the skills contests. Each contest had a point system, and, in some cases, you would be timed as well. The person with the most points in each age group would win the trophy. In addition, they would compare the results of each event across all age groups to determine the overall winner of each contest. Hearing that got my juices going.

After the contests, we gathered at the assembly for the closing ceremonies. Coach Herrick began with the sophomore winners, where a different camper won each category, including some of our Clarkstown kids. Then he started with the junior category winners. "Let me begin with the juggling contest," he said. "Our overall camp juggling winner, with over two thousand juggles, is Tommy Mulroy from Ramapo High School." He mentioned how I'd come in second the prior year but came back determined and now had the all-time camp record. I stepped up and got the trophy. As I started back to my seat, Coach said, "Tommy, don't go anywhere." He turned to the crowd. "You see, Tommy not only won every junior skill contest; he had the top overall camp score in every skill category."

I needed help carrying the trophies back to my seat. The ceremony continued with the senior category winners, and Sinan won the juggling contest. Once they gave out the last senior trophy, I thought it was over. But then Coach Herrick said, "Now, for our final honor, the Camper of the Week award. This award goes to a player who the coaching staff believes is not only a good player, but a hard worker and true leader of the game." Then Coach called Sinan Baskent back to the podium and presented him with the award. You would think having won five trophies and taking the juggling contest would have satisfied my hunger for achievement. But no. Sinan was a nice kid and a good player. But why wasn't I chosen? Did I not work hard enough or was I not good enough?

I now had an intense desire to go back to camp next year and win that award. I wasn't sad or disappointed; I was motivated. I had started to set individual and personal goals. After all, in my mind, I was up against every kid in the world who was kicking a ball, from Brazil to Germany to South Africa to Japan. I wanted to be the best, and I was driven to do everything I could to achieve my goals.

CHAPTER NINETEEN

MONEY BRINGS HARDER TACKLES

A new summer, a new opportunity. For the first time, there would be a New York State All-Star team. The team featured the best players from the German American League All-Star team, along with a few players from leagues across the state. We would compete against teams from New Jersey, Massachusetts, and Connecticut. We would also host teams from Europe and play exhibition games before Cosmos games at their stadium.

This summer would also mark the first time I played in an adult league, the Caribbean League, along with my high school buddies, Herve Guilliod and Medrick Innocent. We were by far the youngest guys on the team and probably in the league. The Haitian community from Nyack had entered this team in the league, which played games in Brooklyn every Sunday during the summer. Our team was named Blouson rouge, after a famous pro team in the Haitian First Division. There were many long rides to Brooklyn in a Volkswagen van packed with Haitians speaking only Creole. That gave me a new-found empathy for my club teammates who didn't speak English.

Our first game was played in a high school football stadium in Brooklyn. The bleachers were packed with Haitians, Jamaicans, and other natives of the Caribbean, some 5,000 strong. They were ready to enjoy football, celebrate their heritage, and cook up island fare such as Haitian pork griot, polenta corn dogs, and Jamaican meat pies. Even rice and beans made it into this venue in the Italian stronghold of Brooklyn.

All the ethnic newspapers and radio stations would send reporters to cover the league matches. This was a new rung for me, a 16-year-old American kid. It was my first game in front of an international audience. There was money on the line. Most players received some form of compensation, and people were betting on the game. Soon after the opening whistle, I learned that money brings harder tackles. The game was played at a fast pace, end to end, chances created in one box and then the other. For young players like Herve, Medrick, and me, it was a new soccer high.

That summer, I would get my first experience as a coach. The Clarkstown Sports Club was looking for someone to lead the new U10 boys' team. On that team were many kids I knew: Coach Frank Rottenbucher's youngest son, Stewie; Rick Derella's brother, William; my cousin, Danny Fuchs; and Ron Dufrene and a few other Haitian kids. Frank Rottenbucher was my club coach at the time, and he told me I should take the job. He would be my back-stop, helping pay the kids' fees and driving them to practices and games when needed. Taking that job turned out to be one of the best experiences of my life. I learned to see the game differently. I saw that you had to be a perpetual student to keep getting better, as a player and a coach. Many of the kids from our group went on to play in college and even in the pros. Here I am 50 years later, writing this book in between the coaching sessions I lead nearly every day for girls and boys of all ages.

CHAPTER TWENTY

THE IMPACT OF PROFESSIONAL PLAYERS

Summer had arrived, and I had started my daily training routine of eight hours of practice followed by a game each evening. One night, my mom floored me with a big surprise. We had family that lived on Long Island in Garden City, a border town to Hofstra University, where the New York Cosmos played their home games. Mom learned that the Cosmos had scheduled a camp at Hofstra. My Aunt Sally had offered to put me up at their place in Garden City, and to shuttle me to and from camp every day.

I was thrilled at this chance to spend a week practicing with the pros. The director of the camp was Gordon Bradley, the player-coach for the Cosmos. He would participate in the camp every day and was later inducted into the US Soccer Hall of Fame. The coach of my team that week was John Kerr Sr., a Cosmo who was a first-team all-NASL player. He was a wonderful coach with a cracking wit and a sharp Scottish accent. I was used to international accents, but this was my first Scottish one, and I had to concentrate hard to keep up with John's rapid-fire delivery. He gave me my first autograph from a professional player. Years later, we crossed paths many times after he became the representative for the NASL Players' Association.

That camp was the first time that I felt the impact a professional athlete can have on a young kid. Throughout my life, I have often heard this question asked: "Is it a professional athlete's responsibility to be a role model?" To the people who say no, let me ask this. What do you think about a pro player who behaves badly, on or off the field? Isn't that player having a negative influence on young people? Professional athletes have a powerful platform; I believe they have a duty to set a worthy example for their young followers.

Let me share two life experiences that show how a professional player can influence a young person. The first came at the Cosmos camp. I had been selected as the camp's Most Valuable Player, and I was invited to receive the trophy at halftime of the Cosmos' final match the night after camp ended, August 12, 1972. The Cosmos beat the Rochester Lancers that night and John Kerr, my camp coach, had scored a goal. There I was, 15 years old, cheering from the sideline for a handful of pros I had spent time with at camp. My mom was in the stands, having been driven to the game by my Uncle Frank.

Receiving the trophy in front of thousands of people was one of the most exciting moments of my life. I still have the picture of me standing next to Gordon Bradley. That said, what happened after the game has stuck with me forever. I was standing outside the locker room door as the players made their way inside. John Kerr grabbed me and brought me into the room. The door was shut and then Coach Bradley said a few words, and everyone started celebrating. I was in awe. There I was in the Cosmos locker room, and they were there too! I noticed that the players were wearing bikini-style underwear. Now this may seem like a trivial detail, but from that day to this one 50 years later, I still wear bikini-style underwear.

My second example of how a pro can influence a kid can be traced to the late '60s. At that time there was no soccer on TV, but now and then I would see a clip of Pelé scoring a goal, jumping, and punching the air. Pelé became my first soccer idol. I remember seeing his autograph on the cover of a book I found at the school library. Pelé drew the top of the letter P in a circle. I thought, *Wow, what a cool signature!* Later in class I doodled away, signing my name with a big circle on top of the T, instead of a horizontal line. At age 13, that became my signature, and it has remained so to this day. That's how deeply influenced I was by the King.

NY Cosmos Soccer Camp MVP Award

L-R: Coach Gordon Bradley, Tom Mulroy, GM John Young

CHAPTER TWENTY-ONE

A DANGEROUS DUO

On the first day of my junior year of high school, I was helping kids get acclimated, just as others had helped me the year before. Many of my Haitian friends were new to the school, and few understood English. Their class schedules had been printed in English. On that first day, they had only a few minutes between classes to figure out which classroom they belonged in next. I knew most of these guys from our high school team tryouts, so I did what I could to help. Soon we had a pattern; before each class started, I would meet a few guys in the cafeteria and walk each one to his next class. Word spread in the Haitian community, and before long, I was escorting a dozen or so Haitian boys and girls to their classes. After every class we would meet in the cafeteria and repeat the drill. After two weeks, everybody had memorized their schedules.

For a change, I had one class that I looked forward to, Driver's Education. My teacher was Gary Schoonmaker, coach of our varsity soccer team. I had the class in first period, and every morning on our driving route, Coach, the other students, and I would stop at the diner to pick up coffee and breakfast for the ride. Coach was also the director of the school's audiovisual department. That meant he knew all the teachers and had insights into all the students. If any of Coach's players skipped a class, he made sure it wouldn't happen again.

Luck was on my side that fall, as my close pal Herve Guilliod and his family moved to the hill, just a few blocks away from my house. That meant they lived in the Ramapo School District, and Herve, his little brother, and I would be high school teammates. In one family's move, we added to our roster a highly skilled scoring machine and a top goalkeeper. Herve and I became a dangerous duo. We both earned first-team all-county honors that year and our team finished near the top of the league table. Above that, we won the State Section 9 Championship.

That fall was also the first year Clarkstown entered a U19 boys' team in the Junior Division of the German American League. Coach Rottenbucher enrolled us in the First Division, even though we fielded the youngest team. Early in the season, we rode in Coach's van to a game in Passaic, New Jersey. We got to the field, and after the players spilled out of the van, the Passaic coach approached Coach Rottenbucher and asked where his team was.

Coach said, "This is my team, right here."

The Passaic coach smiled. He said, "Are you kidding, coming here with those youngsters?"

Coach replied, "Don't worry about my team; just worry about your team, and we'll talk after the game."

Our opponents were big and physical, but not technical or tactical. Herve could fit in the pocket of the guy marking him, and Rick Derella was the smallest guy on the field. Well, Herve bagged three and Rick scored once and set up two others. We put on a clinic and won, 5–0. As we were walking back to our van, I saw Coach Rottenbucher walk up to the Passaic coach. With a big smile, he said, "So, what did you think of my boys? Not bad for a bunch of youngsters, eh?"

Ramapo High School Section 9 Champions

CHAPTER TWENTY-TWO

UNFINISHED BUSINESS

It was the summer of 1973, and I had won a scholarship to the Hubert Vogelsinger soccer camp by virtue of my juggling record of over 3,000 taps. However, the dates of that camp conflicted with what would be my third straight trip to the Colgate University summer camp. I had unfinished business in Hamilton, New York. I headed there with my sights set on winning the Camper of the Week award.

For the first time in my three years at this camp, a torrential rainstorm forced us indoors to the gym. Coach Herrick asked me if I would give a juggling demonstration to the other campers. I had no experience speaking to a crowd, and I could feel the nerves. But once I lifted the ball and started to juggle, my fear eased. Coach helped by talking me through it. "Tommy, show us how to lift the ball. Now show us your shoelaces with spin, without spin, thighs. Okay, let's do some with the head." I thought we were done, and then Coach said, "Okay, Tom, show us some tricks."

I had just learned to flick the ball up with my foot and catch it on my forehead. I had seen the famous coach Dettmar Cramer do this in a video, and I had practiced until I got it down. Now, in the grand finale of my routine, I juggled for a bit, kicked the ball high, and did a forward roll. I let the ball bounce once on the wooden floor, and then I headed it into the basketball hoop. The kids went crazy, and asked me to do it again. I wasn't stupid; I knew the odds of me nailing it twice in a row were about one in 100. We ended the show there. Little did I know that session would be the forerunner to similar demonstrations I would give to groups of kids around the country.

On Thursday night, Coach Herrick told the campers that the skills contests and juggling contest would be held the next day. He added that the camp had a new policy whereby each camper could enter only one contest. After I had run the table past year, that sounded like the Tom Mulroy rule. My teammates kept asking which contest I was going to enter, a question I stewed over that night in bed.

On Friday, players went to their stations and began to compete. I walked from station to station, encouraging my teammates and friends to do their best. The last contest was the juggling competition. I had opted out of that contest, and every other one. This year, I cared about only one trophy. Later that morning, Coach Herrick began to announce the contest results. As I watched the winners step up to collect their trophies, I felt anxious. Finally, Coach Herrick picked up the Camper of the Week trophy. This was the moment; I had set a goal, would I achieve it? Coach described the attributes he looked for and then he announced the winner, "Tommy Mulroy, Ramapo High School!"

Now and then, I fondly reflect on these soccer moments of my youth. I know they helped me grow.

CHAPTER TWENTY-THREE

WRONG PLACE, WRONG TIME

For me, winter was indoor soccer season. It was too cold to play outside, so our Clarkstown Sports Club rented the gym at the junior high. It gave us a way to train all year long and prep to play in indoor tournaments. For mainstream America, however, winter was basketball season. Friday was the big night for high school hoops. Basketball games were the place to meet and socialize. Everybody at school was talking about this Friday's game, to be played at Spring Valley High School, our arch rival. As usual, everybody met at Hillcrest in the shopping center parking lot. I hitched a ride with one of my best friends, Paul Bianco, and a few guys on the football team. We got to the gym, which had been set up so Ramapo fans would sit on one side, and Spring Valley supporters on the other side.

As soon as the final whistle blew, fans began to leave the stands. Both groups were heading for the doors in the front of the building, behind one of the baskets. In hindsight, this part of the night was not so well thought out. A few thousand pumped-up high school kids from rival schools were merging toward the same doors.

We were mushed together like pickles in a jar. As I neared the doors, I looked around and realized that I had gotten separated from my crew. Out of the blue, a big African-American kid grabbed my coat collar with both hands. He screamed in my face, "Any of you motherfucking Ramapo guys looking for trouble?"

I replied, "Who's fucking looking for trouble?" I grabbed both his wrists and squeezed tightly with my hands. I thought, *I've got his hands, he can't hit me.* I was right, he couldn't hit me. However, his buddy next to him could. That kid threw a punch that landed on my nose. It came from nowhere and it was hard. I was staggered but managed to keep my footing. Then this ugly, blonde-headed punk hit me in the face and screamed, "Fight, fight!" I fell and started to roll. Now we were at the top of the steps that led out the front doors. Before I could get back to my feet, two kids started kicking me. At this point, I was fearing for my life. I was crawling, scrambling, whatever I could do, to get out those doors.

Finally, I got to my feet and ran for the door. Out I went, only to encounter a crowd in front of the school. At this point I thought everybody was after me. I was scanning the area, trying to figure out how I could get away. I was moving fast toward a car parked in front of me. I jumped onto the hood and then rolled off the other side into the driveway. Another car crept toward me but stopped short. I got up and ran across the driveway and onto the huge lawn in front of the school. I looked over my shoulder, and now I was really scared. A pack of kids was chasing me, a few screaming, "Fight, fight, there's a fight."

I was running so fast that a Puma Clyde sneaker flew off one of my feet. I continued my one-shoe getaway and soon I neared Route 59, the road that ran in front of the school. Route 59 is an east-west state highway in southern Rockland County. As I approached, cars were whizzing by in all lanes in both directions. My first thought was to cross the street and hide in what appeared to be a dark and deserted parking lot. They shouldn't be able to find me there. My second thought was, there wasn't much light over there. It was the Orange and Rockland Utilities headquarters, and if I got cornered there, I might get killed.

At this point my face was cut, my nose was bleeding, and I wore only one shoe. I decided I couldn't chance that dark secluded area. I had to stay in the light. I looked to my left, and there was a big Cadillac barreling down Rte. 59, heading east. The road was straight, so I stepped into the lane, waving my hands above my head. I thought they could see me, and figured they had plenty of time to stop. The driver hit his brakes. As the car neared, the driver and I locked eyes. A woman was in the passenger seat, another couple in the back seat. As the car rolled to a stop, I could see the woman in the front seat staring at me. There I was, blood on my face, wearing one shoe, standing in the middle of a busy highway. The driver started to open his window. The woman next to him glanced to her right and saw a mob running toward us, screaming. She grabbed the driver's shoulder and pointed at the mob. I was about to lean into the window to ask for help, but the driver hit the gas.

I was desperate. As he started to pull away, with both hands I grabbed the big side-view mirror. I put my forearm on the side of the car and kicked my feet up onto the hood. I was now clinging to the side of the Cadillac like I was a parade ornament. Westbound traffic was flying by us.

I felt secure as we started to speed up, felt like I could hang on until we hit Route 45 a mile up the road. About fifteen seconds later, I think the driver realized I was not letting go. He hit the brakes. My feet flew off the hood, but I held onto that side-view mirror like my life depended on it. The car came to an abrupt halt. The driver opened the door and stepped out. I let go of the mirror, dashed around him, and dove into the front seat. I was bleeding all over the woman in the passenger seat.

Seconds later we were surrounded by two police cars, four police officers, and a gang of angry Spring Valley fans. Traffic had stopped. There I was, sprawled out in a stranger's front seat, with my head bleeding and buried on some lady's lap. The next thing I knew, my boy Paul Bianco, the rest of my crew, and two Spring Valley police officers were helping me out of the car. Pauly handed me my shoe. He said, "Don't worry, bro, we were right behind you."

I had known there was a crowd running behind me. What I didn't realize was many in the crowd were my schoolmates from Ramapo, trying to make sure I was safe. The police officers had me checked out by a team of first responders and then put me in their car and drove me to the station to take my statement. When I got home that night, very late, my brother John and a carload of his friends were waiting for me. They wanted me to give them the name of the kid who had thrown the first punch. They wanted to take care of him without the police. The last thing I wanted was more trouble for my brother, so, even though I knew who the kid was, I gave John nothing. He was hard enough for my mom to handle without this growing into a retaliation.

A few days later, for the first time since the incident, I saw my club buddies and Coach Rottenbucher at indoor practice. My eye was still black and blue, the cuts on my face still evident. Everybody wanted to know what happened, so I had to relive the story. That night, as I was leaving the gym, Coach Rottenbucher pulled me aside. Coach was my mentor, really a surrogate father. In his thick European accent, he asked, "My boy, what did you learn from this fight?"

I answered, "Well, Coach, it wasn't much of a fight; it was pretty one-sided."

Coach said, "In life, you must learn from your experiences, especially your bad ones. So, think about what happened. What could you have done differently that might have changed the outcome?"

I was thinking, but had no answer. Coach said, "It was a fight the second that kid grabbed your jacket. Unfortunately for you, this fight started without you. You see, when a man lays his hands on you with an aggressive attitude, there is no talking your way out of it. As you now have learned the hard way, when there is a fight, whether you started it or not, getting the first punch in is a huge advantage. It sends a message. The message is that you're no victim. I'm not telling you to run around hitting people. Each situation is different. You just need to think about how you could learn something from this experience. What will you do the next time you're in this situation? This is something we each have to decide for ourselves."

I spent hours thinking about what Coach said. I replayed the situation in my mind time and again. Coach was right, there was no way I was going to be able to talk my way out of that trouble. I also may not have won that fight. But had I landed the first punch, the outcome could have been different. After a few days reliving the experience in my mind, I concluded that I would no longer allow anyone to physically threaten me. Life lesson learned.

CHAPTER TWENTY-FOUR

LIFE LESSON LEARNED; LIFE LESSON APPLIED

Six weeks later, I still had faint scars on my face. We were on the back half of winter, and some high school seniors had rented a building on Route 306 near Pomona, where they would host a party. The legal age to buy alcohol in New York State was 18, and high school kids often threw keg parties. This one was a blowout, the who's who of both Ramapo and Spring Valley high schools, every big-time athlete, every cheerleader, and the hottest girls in both schools on hand. I had a game the next day with my Clarkstown club team, so I would not drink. Not that I drank much anyway, but when I had a game the day after a party, I never crossed that line.

Another line I never crossed was smoking pot or doing drugs of any kind. It wasn't working for my brother and I wanted to stay off that path. At the time, most of my pals outside of soccer were smoking dope and dropping Quaaludes, a big drug back then. One time, when I refused to inhale a joint, my friends held me down and blew pot smoke in my face. I wasn't quite a goody-two-shoes, but nothing would get in the way of my soccer.

Back to the party. The keg taps were flowing and the music was blaring. I was standing with Mitch Heine, a wrestler, outside the front door, and we were talking with two hot girls from Spring Valley. Mitch was tall and wiry; I think he wrestled in the 102-pound class. By the way, being small on our wrestling team was not seen as a handicap. The team captain, Joe Goldberg, wrestled in the 112-pound class, and he could bench-press 220 pounds. So, up walked two guys who looked older than high-school age. They approached the girls and one guy snapped, "Come on, let's go." The girl standing next to me told the guy to get lost. When the guy grabbed the girl's arm, Mitch said something like, "Did you not hear the young lady? They're not going anywhere with you guys."

It was brave of Mitch to step in, but I saw two problems. For one, Mitch was slurring his words, even rocking a bit. And two, these dudes were a lot bigger than us. The guy with the big mouth leaned toward Mitch and said, "Who the fuck are you?" Mitch shot back something like, "These girls are with us and you dickheads better get in your fucking car and get out of here before you get your asses kicked." Now, I guess if you were on the wrestling team you could talk smack and know your brothers would jump in and take care of you. Me, I was a peaceable soccer guy.

I stepped in and offered something like, "Let's all calm down." Before I could finish that sentence, big-mouth turned to me and grabbed my shirt. He started to say something but I don't recall his words, because I snapped. You will recall that the last time somebody grabbed my shirt, I got my ass kicked all over the front steps at Spring Valley High School. I had told myself I could never let it happen again. So, this time, when the fight started, it did not start without me.

First, I cold-cocked him with a right fist to the face. I landed a left jab and followed with another hard right. As he was falling backward, I jumped on him and grabbed him by the hair as we hit the ground. My adrenaline taking over, I banged his head on the sidewalk. I was mad, I was scared, and I wasn't going to stop. A few guys pulled me off him, while a few of my football and wrestling pals held back his friend, who wanted a piece of me. Many of these guys had seen me get whipped at Spring Valley High School. This time, I was not the victim. Coach Rottenbucher was right, getting the first punch in made a difference. My Ramapo boys put the guys back into their car and they were on their way. My life lesson learned had become my life lesson applied.

Back to the relative calm of soccer. Early that spring, we were warming up to play the German Hungarians when the referee blew the whistle and summoned the captains to the circle. I jogged out and shook hands with the other captain. After the coin flip, I was about to head back to my team when the ref pulled me aside. He said, "Hey, you better keep those N****r monkeys under control because I ain't taking no shit from them." I could feel my heart banging around in my chest. At first, I felt shock, then a pang of fear. By the time I had jogged back to Coach and the team, I was steamed. Coach could tell by my expression that something was off. He asked what happened. I told him and my teammates what the ref said, which in hindsight was unwise. Half our team was Haitian and it was a direct hit on them. Herve, normally calm, was seething and wanted to go out and kick the referee's ass. Then Herve started running to his car, where rumor was he kept a gun. We had to restrain him. Once we restored some peace, Coach said, "Stay here and stay cool. I'm going to go have a word with the referee."

The referee denied calling our players N*****s but was proud to admit he called them monkeys. When Coach returned, he said, "Here is what I think our choices are. First, no matter what we decide, we must report this racist referee to the league and try to get him suspended indefinitely. Our first option is we do not play the game. We can send the German Hungarians back to Queens without a game and we can all go home. Our second option is we can play with total control of our emotions. No yakking at the ref, no dirty fouls, because we know he's looking to get us. Just straight-up beautiful soccer."

Coach wasn't done. "Boys, I can't imagine how it must feel for someone to talk about you or treat you this way. You have every right not to step on the field with that animal. However, we can also take the field and show that son of a bitch that he can't get to you and that he is wrong. We are first-class people and we play with honor and discipline. We cannot let that idiot ruin our day. We can, if you choose, go out there and play our game."

That's what we chose to do. We were so hyped that we creamed the German Hungarians, 4–0. I was proud of Herve and our Haitian brothers. They never even looked at that referee. Instead, they showed him that they were bigger than he was. Coach reported that ref and we never saw him again on our fields. Years later, I heard that the league may have chosen him to ref that game, because we were the only team in the league that was not of pure ethnic origin. Looking back a half century later, I can't imagine how difficult life must have been for my Haitian brothers. They not only had to learn a second language; they had to confront systemic racism on and off the field.

Clarkstown SC Juniors 1974

Back (L-R) Danny Janes, Ken Fisher, Paul Rocker, John Feger, Coach Frank Rottenbucher, Tom Mulroy, Ron "Frenchy" Clement, Frank Rottenbucher Jr.

Front (L-R) Floyd Land, Ray Lipnicky, Tim Lynch, Karl Gueldner, Rick Derella, Rich Murray, Wilbert Cadet, Medrick Innocent

CHAPTER TWENTY-FIVE

GOD IS NOT AGAINST US

As we geared up for our senior season at Ramapo, the soccer land-scape in Rockland County had shifted. Nyack used to rule the county. Then five years ago, along came the Spring Valley Soccer Club, the first youth club north of the Tappan Zee Bridge. Our club, now the Clarkstown Sports Club, recruited and developed players from all over the county, players who could play year-around with the club. Every high school coach knew it; the more players he had playing club soccer at Clarkstown Sports Club, the better his team would be. Now Ramapo, Clarkstown South, and Pearl River were in the hunt to dethrone Nyack.

Life was good; I didn't have a care in the world. I had school games during the week and club games on the weekend. I had lots of friends at school, along with my teammates from my club team. I hung tight with my club boys, and we did our best to introduce each other to girls at our respective schools. I had landed my first job, working as a stock boy at the delicatessen on the corner of Eckerson Road and Route 45. I wanted to earn some cash to pay off my 1968

GTO, which got me to school and back and took me to training or games all over metropolitan New York. No more sticking out a thumb.

Well, that job didn't last very long. Neither did the car.

Our Ramapo High School team had just won at Clarkstown South, 2–1, putting us in first place with Clarkstown now in second. Both the Ramapo and Clarkstown South rosters were filled with Clarkstown Sport Club players. Our teams had knocked Nyack out of first place for the first time in six years.

Off the field, I was dealing with a personal challenge with one of my Ramapo teammates. His name was Alan Smith, and he was one of our Hillcrest gang. He had moved into town about a year before and become a regular at Cinema 45, our soccer mecca. Smitty, as we called him, was a year older than me but in the same grade. He had spent the summer in rural Montana, planting trees on a family farm. When he came back a few days before school, he was like a different person. Smitty still loved soccer but had made a few dramatic life changes, ranging from his diet to his religion. The kid we knew as Alan Smith now wanted to be called Patrick or Pat. We didn't care what he wanted to be called, as he was still our pal and the starting goalkeeper for Ramapo. Heck, we didn't care what he ate or what religion he practiced. Well, we didn't think we cared, until we learned that Smitty's new religion forbade him from playing sports from sunset on Fridays to sunset on Saturdays.

So here we were, about to play Clarkstown South in our biggest game of the year, and our goalkeeper was telling me that God would punish him if he played. Smitty lived across the street from me on Pascack Road and I was probably his only close friend. Except when he came out to play soccer in the hood, Smitty kept to himself. That

Monday he announced that he wouldn't be able to play on Friday night due to his new religious beliefs. I could tell he was burning to play, so I started to chip away at him. First, I tried to understand why God would punish a kid for playing soccer. Over the next few days, I had more conversations about religion and philosophy than I care to remember. I remember pleading my final case to him, when I said something like, "Do you think God wanted us to work so hard together and sacrifice so much, and then he was going to tell you that you can't play alongside your teammates in the big game?" To this day I don't know if it was something I said, or if it was a conversation Smitty had with his God, but he agreed to play.

I remember sequences from the game as if we played it last week. Late in the first quarter, John Parkin, one of my club teammates but an opponent on this day, dribbled down the left side and crossed the ball. He struck it well but not on his intended line. The ball sailed over Smitty's head and punched the far side netting just under the bar. A fluke, a costly one for us.

While our opponents and their fans went crazy, my eyes were on Smitty. He stood frozen, staring up at the sky as if he was having a moment of reckoning with God. I ran over and grabbed the ball out of the net. Then I got in his face. I told him that it was not God that put that ball in the net, it was John Parkin, and it was one of the luckiest shots of his life. I said that was not a shot, but a misplayed cross. I closed with, "I promise you we are going to win this game. I promise you God is not against us."

I ran the ball up to midfield, handed it to Herve, and off we went. The match flowed, chances created at both ends, but none cashed in through three quarters. We were still down 1–0 in the final quarter when we were awarded a free kick from 30 yards out. I stepped up and cracked one past goalkeeper Tad Delorm, my club teammate. With only a few minutes to play, I wriggled free with the ball just outside the box. I cocked my left foot and let fly, lashing a dart inside the far post for the winner. On my jog back to the center circle, I thought about those hours I had spent kicking balls with my left foot off the wall at Cinema 45. As the game ended and we were running around the pitch celebrating, I looked back and saw Smitty gazing up into the sky with a big smile. That game marked the end of the Nyack High School soccer dynasty and the beginning of a new soccer paradigm in Rockland County, one led by the Clarkstown Sports Club. This turned out to be a special day on my soccer journey, one that I'll never forget.

CHAPTER TWENTY-SIX

NO SOCCER?
NO SCHOOL

It was business as usual the following morning, when our Clarkstown Sports Club U19 junior team was scheduled to play host to one of New York City's most powerful clubs, the Greek Americans. We were glad to be on home turf, rather than playing the Greeks in their Eintracht Oval Stadium, especially after playing an epic match the day before. As we warmed up, all we could talk about was the game Ramapo had just played against Clarkstown South. Sadly though, Medrick Innocent, our star from the Nyack team, was injured and wouldn't play.

The game was about to kick off when one of my teammates came over and said, "Look who's on the sideline, it's Coach Nelson from Nyack." At the time, I didn't think much of it. Lots of coaches, parents, and soccer fans would show up at our games on a Sunday, especially when we faced a team like the Greek Americans. Well, Coach Nelson's visit to this game would turn out to be one of the biggest nightmares of my soccer career.

The next day, just before I headed out to practice, I got called to the principal's office. When I arrived, Coach Schoonmaker was there, along with my teammate and best friend, Herve. I knew we hadn't done anything wrong. Maybe we were about to get an award for beating Clarkstown South and moving into first place for the first time in the school's soccer history? I couldn't have been more wrong. The Public School Athletic League executive committee had called the principal's office to inform them that we had broken rule #13 of the PSAL: "Outside Competition." The committee claimed that we had a total of 14 players from various teams throughout the county. I thought to myself *only 14? They must have counted only the varsity guys.* Club soccer had developed much faster than anyone could have imagined. Someone had opened the can of worms, and they were going to have a hell of a time putting those worms back in the can.

As we stepped outside the principal's office, Coach Schooney told Herve and me it was business as usual until we heard back from the PSAL executive committee. Let me tell you the next few days were extremely stressful. We didn't know what lay ahead for our school team careers. This did not look good for guys who were looking at college scholarships; it could all be ruined because someone blew the whistle on a bunch of innocent kids. It didn't take long to find out who reported our Clarkstown brothers to the PSAL executive committee. Recall that Coach Nelson from Nyack had come to our last club game? He had walked up to his injured player Medrick on the sidelines. When Medrick saw coach Nelson coming, he gave his soccer shoes to his friend sitting next to him. When Coach asked Medrick if he would be playing, Medrick said no, that he was there to watch his friends.

We concluded that the only reason coach Nelson reported us was because he knew that Medrick would not be playing. Therefore, any forthcoming punishment and forfeits wouldn't apply to his Nyack team. A few days later, the PSAL executive committee suspended all the players and came up with some bogus system of which team forfeited which game and what the PSAL official league standings were after including the forfeited games. All these legal decisions were made while the kids being affected were given no chance to respond. The next day, Coach Schoonmaker notified Herve and me that we were suspended and would not be able to play in any of the remaining games. Not only that, but we had forfeited all the games that Herve and I had played, or every match that season.

I was devastated. I couldn't believe they were taking soccer away from me. How could they do this? The only reason I got up in the morning and went to school, made every class on time, and did whatever work I could get done was to advance my soccer career. I went to my mom and said, "If they're not going to let me play soccer, I'm going to quit high school." My mom didn't like that idea but she knew how much soccer meant to me. It wasn't like school was the end-all in our household. The most important thing was that you were a good human, you worked hard, and were honest. That said, if I were to graduate, I would be the first one in my family to earn a high school diploma.

Next, I went to my surrogate father, Coach Rottenbucher, to tell him my plan. Coach said, "Okay, if you quit school, that's half your plan. But how the hell do you feed yourself, how do you make a living? How far do you think you can go stocking beer bottles in the deli refrigerator? You need to learn a trade, you need to know how to make a living." Things got quiet for a bit. Then he looked at me with a big smile and said, "I guess you're going to have to come and work for me. Can you paint?"

For the next two weeks, every night the soccer team held some kind of protest, some kind of meeting at a lawyer's office, some interviews with the newspaper. I didn't go to school. I had quit. I woke up one morning and met Coach at his jobsite. He was a one-man construction crew. He could build a house by himself with his bare hands. I was a hard worker, but wasn't much good with my hands. I didn't have the knack or the passion to be a carpenter, a bricklayer, or even a painter for that matter. After a few days of humbling work with Coach, every night I was praying I'd figure out some way to make a living out of soccer. At that time my only real option was to find my way to the pros. Beyond that, no one got paid to do anything, other than the referees and a few college coaches. I had dropped out of high school, so coaching college wasn't going to happen. It wasn't like today with pay-to-play, when there's a paid coach on every sideline.

I will never forget the first day I worked for Coach. During our lunch break, he looked at me and said, "Some people are painters, and when someone needs a painter, that painter has work. Some people pour cement, and when someone needs cement, they have work. Some people are roofers, and when someone needs a roof, they have work. The more trades you learn, the more work you will have. That's why I have work every day. You do a good job, you work hard, you stay honest, and you will always have work. Whether you're in construction, marketing, or maybe even soccer someday." Coach was no philosopher and he didn't run around telling people what to do. So, when he did talk, I listened. On that day I didn't know how important his words were. But anyone who knows me knows that

that little conversation would later shape my entrepreneurial path after my playing career ended.

In the middle of the chaos around our soccer team, a group of players and their parents filed a lawsuit that resulted in a temporary injunction against the PSAL. Judge Joseph Hartwick granted the injunction in the Rockland Supreme Court. The judge also questioned the PSAL procedure in ordering the suspension. As he put it, "Apparently no opportunity was accorded to the pupils to have their parents present, so as to accord a modicum of due process." Eventually, the suspension was dropped, and we were able to resume playing. The PSAL executive committee would keep records of on-the-field standings and forfeit standings, but the only thing that mattered was that we were able to rejoin our teams and play.

The next day I was back in class, staring out the window, dreaming about my next game. Although I think Coach had enjoyed my company on the job, I'm sure he was happy I was back in school and back on track. We played out the rest of the season and when it ended, the only standings I cared about was the one that said, "ON THE FIELD RESULTS." In those standings, Ramapo won the league with Nyack in fourth place. Even in the standings that included forfeits, Nyack did not finish as champion. It was over for them. For me, this episode sharpened my focus on setting goals. At the end of my sophomore year, I promised myself I would lead Ramapo High School to the Rockland County PSAL League Championship and take one step closer to my dream of becoming a professional soccer player.

Now 50 years later, with a lot of life under my belt, I truly believe that blowing the whistle on these young men was not good for the players or the game. It was a selfish gambit made by a win-hungry coach trying to hold on to a legacy that was slipping away.

CHAPTER TWENTY-SEVEN

COACH VIZVARY AND THE WINTER GAMES

Winter was approaching, indoor soccer just around the corner. By now there were plenty of indoor tournaments to keep us busy during the cold months. It was also time to start deciding what my next steps would be to become a pro. I thought that in an ideal world, I would try out for a pro team and skip college. Unfortunately, back then it was not so simple. There were not many professional teams in the U.S., with only nine teams in the North American Soccer League and 12 teams in the American Soccer League in 1973. Back then, scouts from around the world were not looking at the U.S. for up-and-coming talent like they do today.

I had made a reputation as a standout player in high school, and quite a few colleges had approached Coach Schoonmaker about me. Well, not only was I a marginal student, but I hadn't even taken the SAT exam. My options seemed limited, until one night in late January 1974. I was hanging out at my uncle's house next door when the phone rang. My Aunt Nancy answered and handed me the phone. She said it was a man, some college coach, and he wanted to talk to me. This phone call, from a complete stranger, from a school I had never heard of, would change the course of my life. The gentleman spoke with a strong European accent, one that I had never heard before, and by then I thought I had heard them all. He sounded a little like Count Dracula. He said, "I am George Vizvary, the coach at Ulster County Community College. I have been following your career with the German American League All-Stars and the New York State team."

Right there, this guy had my attention. He was the first college coach who wasn't reaching out because of my high school career. Instead, he knew the real pool of soccer kids, my ethnic friends from my club team, guys who dedicated their lives to the sport. The more we spoke, the more I realized this guy was legit. Not only did he know where to find talent; he had played professional soccer himself.

Coach Vizvary started telling me whom he was recruiting, rattling off some of the best players in the New York City area. That included my good friend Nick Megaloudis and various other all-star teammates and league rivals. Vizvary added that he had connections to the pros, where his friend Al Miller was the coach of the Philadelphia Atoms, NASL champion. He said that he had other contacts that could help players move from community college straight into the pros. This was music to my ears. The more we talked, the more I knew we were on the same page. When he asked me about Herve, I knew he had a sharp eye for talent, because Herve was a badass, one of the best scorers anywhere. I was thinking that I would love to continue playing with Herve as a teammate in college. Vizvary asked me for his number, which I gladly provided. It wasn't long before Vizvary would set up a school visit, and he would come and pick up Herve and me for my first and only college visit.

It was sometime in early spring when Coach Vizvary arrived at my house on Pascack Road. Herve and I were eager to meet the man that we had only spoken to on the phone. Into my driveway pulled a late '60s Volkswagen Karmann Ghia, midnight blue with a white convertible top. It was a two-door, two-seater sports car. As this car came to a stop, out stepped this man, standing 6'3" and weighing about 250 pounds. He was bald, except for a few long hairs that were strategically raked across his head. Later, that mop would be known by his players as the Vizvary three-stripe adidas hairstyle. He was a giant; it was hard to believe that he fit in that little car. He was dressed business casual, a rare occasion when he wasn't clad in an adidas sweatsuit. As he stepped out of the car with a big smile, he put his hand out and said, "Hello, gentlemen, I am George Vizvary."

A few minutes later, Herve and I got in his car to head up to Ulster County Community College. The car was even smaller on the inside than it looked from outside. Herve sat in the front seat and I sat in the storage area behind the two front seats. When Vizvary opened the roof, it fit right behind the two seats. The ride up to Ulster took about an hour and a half with no traffic. As we entered the college and drove through the apple orchards in front of the school, Coach told us about his role as the director of the engineering department. He stressed how important it was for us to pick the right classes and be sure to graduate. That way, we could move on to a four-year school with a top soccer team or try to find a way to the professional ranks.

We started the tour in the student union building where Coach treated us to lunch. Then we walked around campus and saw all the educational buildings: English, science, blah blah blah. Finally, we walked across the parking lot to the athletic area. We started in the gymnasium, then went to the soccer locker room, and then down a little hill onto the beautifully manicured, full-size FIFA soccer field. Herve and I were impressed because we were used to playing on fields of rock and dirt. The last stop was coach's office. Hanging on the wall were the awards his Ulster players had received: All Mid-Hudson Conference players, All-Region 15 players, and even a few NJCAA All-Americans. I remember pointing to the All-American plaques and saying to Coach Vizvary, "That's me right there; I am going to be a first-team All-American." Vizvary looked at me and said in his thick Hungarian accent, "Those are big shoes to fill, my boy, only time will tell."

Soon we got back in Coach's car, and luckily it was my turn to sit up front. On the way home, Coach told us stories about his Hungarian soccer background and how he played with Ferenc Puskás of the 1954 Hungarian National Team, one of soccer's first international superstars. Vizvary also told us that the Ulster team would play in some indoor tournaments later that spring. Then he invited Herve and me to come watch his Ulster team play in the field house at Sullivan County Community College, where a big indoor tournament was held every year. By the time we got home, there was something about this guy that mesmerized me. For one, he told me that none of his players could beat him in foot tennis and that I would be no different. He made it clear he was the foot tennis king. Soon, I had decided that I was going to Ulster County Community College next fall, 1974. Herve was not as convinced, because he looked at a few more schools before accepting a scholarship at Fredonia State University in upstate New York. He would play for another legendary U.S. soccer coach, Jay Hoffman, and earn first-team All-American honors in 1977.

One Friday night in late February, I was about to head out to my Clarkstown SC game when my cousin knocked on my door and said my boss, the deli manager Lou, was on the phone. I ran next door to take the call at my uncle's house. It was raining ice, and by the time I got across the yard I was wet and freezing. The manager said that the stock boy who was scheduled to work that night lived in Pomona and his family did not want to drive him to work in the storm. Could I cover, since I only lived a few blocks away? I said, "I'm sorry, but I can't make it." After all, I was about to head out to my game. Lou didn't believe that I was going to a soccer game in an ice blizzard. I politely told him I was meeting the team van at the New York State Thruway entrance, where we would get on the Garden State Parkway and head to Route 29 in Union, NJ. We would play against Elizabeth SC, a big rival, on their home field, the historic Farcher's Grove. He still didn't believe me and told me I could come to work or get fired.

Well, nothing was going to get in the way of my soccer. We hung up and I headed to our team meeting spot on Route 59 at Dunkin' Donuts where Coach was waiting, and we made our way to Farcher's Grove. We played an exciting game, ice, or snow falling for most of it. Canceling games back then wasn't really an option. It wasn't like you could ruin a field made of dirt and frozen rock. If the snow got too deep, they painted the lines in blue so you knew where the penalty area was and where to take corner kicks.

After the game, we stopped in the clubhouse for some hot tea and German bratwurst before we got back in the van to head home. The next morning, I woke up and headed into the deli for my shift. The manager, Lou, called me over and handed me an envelope with the few hours' worth of money he owed me. He said it was bad enough that I couldn't help out the prior night, but when I had lied about playing in a soccer game, that was just too much. He felt he couldn't trust me, and we had to part ways. Looking back, I guess

I can't blame him. After all, Friday was a big night for high school kids to go out and party. And back in those days, what were the odds that I was telling the truth about going to play a soccer game in the middle of a snowstorm?

I didn't like working anyway because it ate into my practice hours. I remember dreaming back then that maybe I could find a way to make soccer my lifelong profession. Was this a kid's pipe dream, or could this be Soccer Tom's reality?

The next week, my best friend and soon-to-be college roommate Rick Derella, and I skipped school and headed to the Philadelphia Spectrum. We went to watch the first-ever international indoor soccer game played in the U.S., between the touring Red Army of Moscow club and the Philadelphia Atoms of the North American Soccer League. We didn't know it then, but this game would mark the "birth of indoor soccer." Al Miller was coach of the Atoms and he put together an all-star team from around the league: Paul Child (from the defunct Atlanta franchise); Alex Papadakis, an All-American at Hartwick College (also from Atlanta and today an owner of the USL); Dick Hall (Dallas); and Jorge Siega (New York). Among those filling out the Philadelphia roster were fellow indoor select members George O'Neill and Barry Barto, along with Bobby Smith, Bill Straub, and Sports Illustrated cover boy goalkeeper, Bob Rigby. It was a lively atmosphere, with 11,790 people in attendance. Although the Russians won the game, 6–3, it was entertaining soccer. Who knew that a few years later I would be back in that same arena as a professional player living my dream in front of a sellout crowd of 16,259. What a journey!

A few weeks passed, and the Community College Indoor Tournament was around the corner. I had accepted Coach Vizvary's invitation to watch the Ulster team play at this annual event held at

Sullivan County Community College. Vizvary had called Coach Joe Famellette at Rockland County Community College and organized a ride for me in the Rockland team van. Coach Famellette saw it as an opportunity for me to get to know him and his players, so it was a win-win for everyone. It was a two-hour drive and I remember pulling out in the RCC van in the dark of early morning. I knew some of the Rockland guys, as I had played against them the last two years when they were still in high school. They remembered me too and we got on well with lots of soccer talk.

When we arrived, we stepped into a commotion. All the coaches had gathered by the scorer's table. Rumor was that Dutchess Community College had a transportation issue and had only three players. The field house was big, and the tournament was set up in a six versus six format. No one wanted to see a forfeited game. Every team wants to play all its scheduled games, and having one team out ruins the flow. The Dutchess guys had a coach, a goalkeeper, and two field players. Vizvary looked at me and asked if I had brought sneakers. I felt a grin spread from cheek to cheek. Did I have my sneakers? I went to every New York Cosmos game with my soccer shoes in a bag, praying that a beam of light would hit me and take me down to the field to play. "Yes, I have my shoes with me," I said. Vizvary turned to the Dutchess coach and said, "Now you have four, all we need is two more."

Minutes later I took to the turf in a college soccer tournament, even though I was still in high school. I think Vizvary had pulled the Duchess coach to the side and let him know that I could play. You would think a college coach would have been cautious about showcasing a prospective recruit. Not Vizvary. He had some flaws but insecurity was not one of them. The Dutchess coach asked me what position I wanted to play, and I said center midfield. Well, this rag-tag team of gypsies won all three of our group games. I scored at least once in each match, and I was in the hunt for the overall top scorer. Next was the sudden-death semifinals. We won that match and it was on to the final to play . . . Ulster County Community College. We were down one late when I scored to tie the game. Then Mario Oliva, the same guy whose All-American plaque I had seen on Vizvary's wall, scored the winner in overtime, and Ulster was champion. I was disappointed I was not the top scorer, and deep down, I was hoping to be Most Valuable Player, but both honors went to Ulster guys. I did make the all-tournament team, the icing on a wonderful day for me. At the end of the awards ceremony, the Ulster guys came over and told me we would have a great team next year and they looked forward to me being part of it.

CHAPTER TWENTY-EIGHT

IT WAS LIKE A BOMB SCARE

As I headed into the last few months of my last year in high school, things were breaking my way. Our soccer team had won the Rockland County championship, and it looked like I was going to graduate. I had plenty of good friends all over the county, as well as my New York City buddies. Come the fall, I would start my college soccer career at Ulster County Community College. I was riding high.

I wish I could say the same for my poor mom. Agnes was working two jobs, walking almost two miles to her day job every morning and working as a waitress on the weekends. Working 50 or 60-hour weeks wasn't her biggest challenge, nor was her wage of $1.40 per hour, which meant she was raising us on about $60 a week. Mom had no problem with hard work, and she had enough money to put food on the table and clothes in the closet. It was my older brother, John, who weighed heavy on her heart. Over the past few years, somehow John had become angrier and angrier. For every good soccer moment that my mom could celebrate with me, she had to deal with trouble in my brother's life. I'm not talking about cutting school, or staying out late. I'm talking about episodes that make a mom's heart stop.

For example, we had a Thursday night catechism class at the Saint Joseph church school on Route 45. One night, yelling erupted in the room down the hall. That was my brother, John, cursing out Father Reynolds, the two of them one push away from a fistfight. My brother had dropped out of school when he was 15. The only reason they didn't put him in a reform school for juveniles was his job at the Hillcrest Pub. Because my mom had such a low income, the family court judge had ruled that as long as John kept his job, he wouldn't be sent to reform school upstate. Court appearances were how my poor mom had to spend her days off from work.

I remember one evening when the neighborhood kids were playing our usual pickup game on my front lawn. A police car with flashing lights turned the corner on East Hickory Street onto Pascack Road and roared up our driveway. We all froze as the car stopped on the edge of the lawn. An officer got out and opened the back door. Out stepped my brother, John, smiling and waving to everyone. He took a few steps and fell flat on his face. He was two sheets to the wind, drunk or high or both. Uncle Frank opened the front door of the house, stepped out, and said, "Okay, the game's over; everyone go home."

It was like a bomb scare. The kids snapped out of their trances and sprinted across the lawn toward their houses. As for John, at that point we hoped he had hit bottom. But John kept spiraling down, and it got to the point where my mom had to kick my brother out of the house. She felt that unless she did something drastic, he would become more and more self-destructive. It was bad enough for mom and me, but my Uncle Frank and Aunt Nancy were raising the first four of their five kids next door. Thankfully, all of my cousins turned out to be upstanding citizens: Frankie, Kathleen, Danny, Bonnie, and Jenny.

Getting kicked out of the house didn't help my brother. Now he needed a place to live. He loved working on cars, so he went out and got a van, and that became his home. Most mornings after my mom and my uncle had gone to work, John would pull the van into our driveway and sleep off a night of partying. My mom and my uncle seemed to be cool with that. Mom at least knew where he was, and he was safe. That was fine and dandy, until we found out that John was running hookers out of the back of the van. I remember him introducing me to two girls who he said were his friends; they couldn't have been much older than 18. When my mother and Uncle Frank got wind of it, John was no longer able to use the driveway as his safe haven. John and I didn't always get along, but when push came to shove, I really loved my brother. He always had my back. There wasn't much I could do to help my mom, other than be a good kid and stay out of trouble. My devotion to soccer and my awesome coaches kept me on the right track.

That spring, my Clarkstown Sports Club team was near the top of the table, as usual. Sadly, we got knocked out of the State Cup a few rounds in. Now it was on my to-do list to win the State Cup and win the McGuire Cup National Championship the next season. That would be my last chance, since it would be my last year as a junior player before moving up to the adult division.

As high school wound down, everyone was talking about college. All of my classmates were running around getting their friends to write snappy quotes and love notes in their yearbooks. This was an awful time for me. While I had lots of wonderful things to tell my friends, my writing was an embarrassment. I couldn't even spell half my friends' first names correctly, never mind jot a memorable snippet. I did everything I could do to avoid signing yearbooks. That meant I didn't get my book signed by anyone either. I have every yearbook from my time at Ramapo, sophomore, junior, and senior books, and I enjoy seeing the soccer pictures in the sports section.

Yearbook woes aside, I held tight to the fact that I was on track to graduate. I am sure more than a few teachers who knew me over the years thought this would never happen. But now I would be the first one in my family to earn a high school diploma. For most high school kids and their families, the high school graduation ceremony was a big deal. It was a big deal to me too, until I found out that the ceremony would be held on a Saturday afternoon and my club team had a game scheduled that day at the Metropolitan Oval. I'm sure it was a nice ceremony.

The last Mulroy family photo together

CHAPTER TWENTY-NINE

BIG-TIME SUMMER SOCCER

High school was over. Summer was here. Time to focus on soccer, get ready to play at the college level. Our Clarkstown club junior team was prepping for Oneonta 74, the first international youth soccer tournament ever held in the U.S. This event would serve as the forerunner to other huge youth tournaments of today, such as the Dallas Cup, Disney's Soccer Showcase, San Diego Surf Cup, and the adidas Potomac Memorial Tournament. The tournament format was 16 teams, with four groups of four teams. There would be eight international teams and eight teams from the U.S. Each group of four would have two international teams and two U.S. teams. The international teams came from Germany, England, Mexico, Scotland, and Canada. The domestic teams came from Los Angeles, St. Louis (a Midwest soccer hotbed), and teams from around the northeast. Coach Rottenbucher set out to beef up our roster with a few stars from around metropolitan New York. We added Nick Megaloudis, my Greek buddy from Astoria Queens; Sepp Gantenhammer, the best goalkeeper in NY; and Joe Ryan and Sean O'Donnell from the New Jersey state team.

At that time, Hartwick College, located in Oneonta, had emerged as a top collegiate program. Their coach, Timo Liekoski, had teamed with soccer entrepreneur Francisco Marcos to create Oneonta 74. Clarkstown was drawn into a group with an English team from Liverpool, a German team from Frankfurt, and an American team, Delaware United. We lost our first game to Liverpool and then drew against the Germans. We beat Delaware and made the round of eight on goal difference. Be careful what you wish for. Our quarterfinal bracket of four teams featured what many thought were the best two teams in the tournament. One was Possilpark from Scotland, and the other was Mexico's Club America, the youth team from one of Mexico's top First Division professional clubs. Rumor was that two or three players on the Mexican team had signed professional contracts for next season. The other American team in our group was from Springfield, Massachusetts, a good side but one we felt we could beat.

Before the next round of games would be played, the organizers set up an all-star match between top U.S. players and the best international players, the first such match held in the U.S. Coaches, referees, and tournament officials selected the players for both rosters. Three players were selected from our club: goalkeeper Sepp Gantenhammer, defender Kenny Fisher, and I, as a midfielder. It was a thrill to be selected to play alongside some of the best amateur players in the country. Several guys on that roster went on to play professionally at big clubs around the world. Others played for the U.S. National Team and the U.S. Olympic team. In addition to the three Clarkstown guys, here was the rest of the U.S. roster: David Stones, Frank Molina, Paul Torrentes, and Ken Street of

Los Angeles; Larry Hulcer (Tournament MVP), Dave Brcic, Ty Keough, Don Abuchon, and Don Huber of St. Louis; and reserves Bill Klauberg and Pat Veale of Springfield. The coaches were Bob Huber of St. Louis and Lee Kenworthy of Springfield.

This would be the biggest game of my life to that point. The match was being played at Hartwick's Elmore Field, cut out of a hill looking down on the campus. It was an ideal setting, a place where you say, *Of course they built a soccer field here*. We entered the field FIFA style, the bleachers full, a standing-room-only throng encircling the field. I played the whole match in midfield, next to Ty Keough, who would be one of the best American professional players of my time. Ty came from a family of U.S. soccer royalty at a time when there was little soccer royalty in the U.S. He was the son of Harry Keough, who played on the United States national team that upset England, 1–0, at the 1950 FIFA World Cup in Brazil. Ty would later play for his dad at St. Louis University before turning pro. We would face each other many times in the professional ranks. He was a good guy, very humble, a true leader of all the guys from St. Louis. The game ended in a 1–1 draw. This game was a perfect halfway point for me in the tournament. It was my fourth game in as many days, but I had that soccer high, that feeling I could only get from soccer.

Now the round-of-eight games were kicking off. In our opener, the team from Springfield, Massachusetts, gave us trouble. In the first few minutes, our keeper, Sepp Gantenhammer, got knocked out and was taken to the hospital. Without a back-up keeper, we were sunk and we lost. In the next match against Possilpark, we played well but lost to a better team. We had no chance to advance, and our last game would be against Mexico's Club America Junior team. This would be our last shot to prove that we could play with the best of the best. Our task had grown taller because Nick Megaloudis had badly sprained his ankle in the last game and was on crutches.

Turns out that the Ulster Coach, George Vizvary, was at the tournament. He was recruiting for the upcoming season and hoping that he might reel Nicky in. Little did I know that Coach Vizvary was a bit of a Hungarian witch doctor. A day before the game, we were having lunch in the cafeteria at Hartwick when George came to our table. When he saw Nicky's crutches, he asked him what had happened. Nicky lifted his foot, and his ankle was three times the size of his other ankle. Coach looked at it, looked Nicky in the eyes, and said, "Son, the only thing standing between you and playing tomorrow is the fluids stopping you from having full motion in your ankle."

Nicky was a bit of a wise guy, and he said, "Yeah, it would take a miracle."

Coach Vizvary replied, "Okay, let's make a miracle, my son. Let's go back to the dorm; we start now."

Coach wrapped Nicky's ankle in a way that prevented the fluids from gathering in the front of his foot. It was uncomfortable, but Nicky was a warrior. Then Coach made Nicky stick his foot and shin into a bucket of ice water for 15 minutes or so. Then he had Nicky put his foot in hot water for another 15 minutes, then back to the ice for 15 minutes. Finally, he had Nicky elevate his foot, then he retaped it with a little more pressure to push the fluids up his leg and away from his ankle. Coach was also giving Nicky some type of anti-inflammatory, maybe ibuprofen.

Every hour on the hour, Vizvary came back to Nicky's room. They did this straight through the night. We brought Nicky breakfast in bed while his foot was still elevated. It was working. His ankle was still black and blue, but it had shrunk back to nearly its normal size. The fluids had moved away from the ankle. By the time we piled into Coach Rottenbucher's van to head to the game, Nicky was off his crutches and his tightly taped ankle could finally fit into his cleat. We were about to play one of the best and most physical teams we would ever face. As we drove to the field, most of us didn't think Nicky would be able to play. When we got to the field, Nicky started to warm up, slowly at first, then a little harder. He told Coach he would try. Coach decided to put Nicky on defense and have him cover Francisco Tagango, the Club America superstar who had a pro contract waiting for him when he got back to Mexico City.

Nicky was one of the best players on the field. He stuck to Francisco like a second shirt, rarely letting him touch the ball. Nicky's grit and dogged marking inspired us all. We notched the biggest upset of the tournament, winning, 2–1, behind goals from Joe Ryan and Sean O'Donnell, our guest players from New Jersey. The newspaper headline read, "A Mexican Hat Dance." Our win put Possilpark of Scotland through to the final against St. Louis United. More importantly, Clarkstown was the buzz of the tournament for the day.

Most teams that had been eliminated would have headed home that night, but not us. Our entire team stayed to watch the final. It was a game to remember, one that raged through regulation and 30 minutes of overtime before ending in a 2–2 draw that saw both teams crowned as co-champions. After the game, we packed into Coach's van for our three-hour journey back to Rockland County. Looking back, I realize that this was before pay-to-play, and Coach Rottenbucher was only a volunteer. He earned no coaching income, and he provided financial support to half the kids on the team. This tournament was a two-week commitment, running from Monday,

July 15th, to Sunday, July 28th. Coach paid for his room and board and covered the fuel expenses both ways. He had missed two full weeks of work and the income he could have earned to feed his family. We love you, Coach Rottenbucher, thank you!

CHAPTER THIRTY

A HISTORIC WIN FOR THE US NATIONAL YOUTH TEAM

Soon after I got home from Oneonta, a letter came in the mail. It was from the United States Soccer Federation. The letter read, "Dear Tom, It is my pleasure to inform you that you have been selected as a player for the USSF National Youth Team. This team will play in the CONCACAF (North, Central American, and Caribbean Soccer Confederation) tournament that will be held in Ontario, Canada, from August 17th through September 1st, 1974." Bullet points followed with the details. The letter ended with: "I want to congratulate you on your selection and I know that you will represent our country to the very best of your ability." I read that last line twice. Now, that sounded important. The letter was signed by Vice President Donald Greer, with copies to the State and Regional Commissioner Kurt Lamm, Assistant Team Manager Gene Chyzowych, Head Coach George Logan, and Assistant Coach Timo Liekoski.

I read the letter with my mom. It was a bit confusing, littered with alphabet soup of the soccer industry. At the time, we didn't even know what FIFA stood for (*Federation Internationale de Football Association*). Bottom line, I would be heading to Canada to play soccer for three weeks, and it was going to be free of charge. Free, that was a figure my mom could afford.

Once I got to training camp in Oneonta, New York, I realized I had been picked to represent the U.S. in one of the first CONCACAF youth tournaments. This was a big step closer to reaching my dream. I checked into the Hartwick College dormitories. The first practice was scheduled for Friday evening, August 9th. Players had arrived from points around the country: California, Missouri, Texas. As I made my way up the hill to the team's first training session, coming down the path were a few older men dressed in soccer kits. They didn't look like a team, as no one wore matching gear. And then I heard, "Hello, son, aren't you going to say hi?" To my shock, there stood George Vizvary, soon to be my coach at Ulster County Community College. As we shook hands, I asked, "Coach, what are you doing here?" He said, "Son, I am here taking my United States Soccer Federation "A" Coaching License course." This was the first I had ever heard of a coaching license. By now I had coached the U-10 boys' team for my Clarkstown club, and I was intrigued.

The first training session that evening was a casual kick-around, as some players had flown in that day from California. It ended with a brief scrimmage and then we went to the dorms for pizza. The next few days were made-to-order for me: wake up, eat breakfast with the guys, take in a classroom tactical session, and go to the field for technical training. Then back to the dorms for lunch and a little afternoon down time. Finally, back to the fields for a team tactical session, then dinner, then back out for a controlled scrimmage.

What did I do during the afternoon downtime? I watched the coaching candidates work toward their coaching licenses. Sometimes I would listen as the instructors, Walter Chyzowych and Bill Muse, interacted with the coaches. Later in the week, I got to see coaches being tested on the topics they had to master. I couldn't get enough. By the second evening of training, our entire team had arrived, and we would hold our first full scrimmage. As we reached the field, I saw the coaching candidates kicking a ball around. Coach Logan announced that we would be playing against those coaches. Many of them had played at a high level, some of them were former pros.

In the opening minutes of the match, they attacked hard and had us pinned in our defensive third. In time we hit our stride, and we began to wear them down. We were in our late teens, while most of our foes were past their prime. We found holes in their defense and managed to post a 5–0 win. The result was a surprise to most of the coaches and perhaps a small dent in a few egos. No one is young forever.

On the last night of camp, we would play a second scrimmage against the coaching candidates. This would be an important game for us, our last tune-up before we got on the bus for the seven-hour ride to Canada. When we reached the field, the coaches were already warming up. This was a big game for them too, because part of their curriculum was devoted to game performance.

This was no ordinary coaching school, nor ordinary group of coaches. This was a special group in the history of U.S. Soccer. A short time before this school, Coach Walter Chyzowych and a handful of coaches had taken the first-ever USSF coaching course. The course was led by FIFA Coach Dettmar Cramer, who had been hired by the USSF to become the head coach of the U.S. Men's National Team. Cramer was also charged with starting a coaching education program. He designed the original USSF coaching school curriculum for the A, B, and C national licenses, before handing the program to Chyzowych, a participant in Cramer's first course when Cramer accepted an offer from Beckenbauer to coach at Bayern Munich. As the director of coaching for the USSF, Chyzowych recruited instructors to teach the national coaching license courses.

Chyzowych was among the first of many coaches who played leading roles in advancing and teaching the USSF coaching curriculum. Others include Bob Gansler, coach of the U.S. National Team at the 1990 World Cup; Joe Machnik, a goalkeeper specialist and US Soccer National Soccer Hall of Fame Inductee and coach; Nick Zlatar, recipient of the Dr. Thomas Fleck US Youth Soccer Excellence in Coaching Education Award; Jim Lennox, coach of Hartwick College, where he won a national title in 1977; Arnie Ramirez, coach of the Puerto Rico National Football Team; Timo Liekoski, U.S. National Team assistant coach and head coach in both the NASL and MLS; and George Vizvary, a player for the Hungarian National Team, coach at Ulster County Community College, and a member of the NJCAA Soccer Coaches National Hall of Fame.

It turned out to be a scrappy game, with the kids edging the veterans, 1–0. Almost 50 years later, the coaches still argue over who was to blame for the goal they allowed. Joe Machnik was in goal, Bob Gansler and George Vizvary were playing center back. All three of them stood six feet or taller. Tony Graham outjumped them all to head in the winning goal. Tony was 5 feet, 6 inches.

We headed off to Canada for what would be the biggest tournament of our lives. We had heard that Pelé would be at the tournament to do a ceremonial kick-off. I was hoping to meet him in person. Wasn't that every soccer person's dream, to meet the king? The tournament was being played in four different cities. The U.S. team got drawn into Group 3 and would be playing matches in London, Ontario. The other cities were Sudbury, Ottawa, and Toronto. Pelé did the tournament kickoff in Toronto, so I would have to wait to meet my idol.

This was the first time I had played on a team where I was not one of the best players. I had to fight for a position, and played very little in central midfield. Ahead of me were Ty Keough and Larry Hulcer. I did, however, start at left-back, so I was on the field and that is what really mattered. I was slotted at left back because I had a reliable left foot. All that time kicking a ball off the wall at Cinema 45 was paying another dividend. Our captain was Neil Cohen, who was already playing with the Dallas Tornados of the NASL. It was cool to be playing alongside a pro.

This was only the second time a U.S. team had competed in a CONCACAF youth tournament. The first came in 1964 in Guatemala, where the team failed to win a game. So, when we beat Guatemala 2–1, in our opening game, it was a historic win. We then edged Jamaica, 2–1, and played to a scoreless draw with Cuba. We sat at the top of the group. In the playoffs, we drew with Trinidad and Tobago, only to lose on penalties, 5–4. The next day, Thursday, August 29th, I boarded the first flight of my life, accompanied by my coach, Timo Liekoski. It was an American Airlines flight from Toronto to LaGuardia Airport in New York City. The ticket cost $46.44. I remember looking at it and thinking, *God, this is expensive, how cool that I don't have to pay for it.* Today, I have about 3 million miles on American Airlines and usually the tax on my tickets is more than $46.44. This was the first airborne leg of a lifetime of soccer adventures that would take me around the globe.

US Youth National Team CONCACAF Tournament 1974

**Standing L-R: Coach Logan, Bernhard Mattheis,
Neil Cohen, Tommy Mulroy, Mark Riedel, Joseph Heights,
Greg Makowski, Jim McKeow, Michael Wall, Coach Timo Liekoski,
Donald Greer VP USSF**

**Front L-R: Don Huber, Tony Graham, Don Aubuchon,
Dan Payne, Ty Keough, Tony Bellenger, Douglas Spaunagle,
Larry Hulcer, Richard Emmel.**

United States Soccer Federation Coaching Candidates
Oneonta, New York 1974

Front: L- R: Alex Bernstein, Lee Kenworthy, George Vizvary, Bob Gansler

Middle: L- R: Timo Liekoski, Guy St. Vil, Garth Stam, Arnold Ramirez, Nick Zlatar, Ron Jabusch,

Back: L- R: Jimmy Lennox, Roy Pfeil, Joseph Machnik, N/A

CHAPTER THIRTY-ONE

THE COLLEGE JOURNEY BEGINS

I had been home from Canada for only a few days when Ricky swung his maroon '67 Grand Prix into my driveway on Pascack Road. I hopped in with my bag and we headed north up the New York State Thruway, a 60-mile ride to our new apartment on Main Street in New Paltz. This is where we would live for the entire time that we attended Ulster. What a spot, on the main drag, home to all the bars and action. It was a two-bedroom apartment, nothing fancy. Ricky and I shared one room, and in the other were two of our teammates, Aldo Sergovich from Croatia, and Simon Curanaj from Albania. They were damn good players, and they were straight out of the movie, Saturday Night Fever. There was a pizza place next door. You could get a slice for 35 cents. Ricky and I ate a lot of pizza. There was only one downside. The drive to campus, along the backroads of Ulster County, ate up thirty minutes. On a snowy morning, it could take a lot longer.

Coach Vizvary had the players report a week before school started. He wanted to be sure we had housing and had met with our guidance counselors to select classes. Most importantly, he had set up a robust preseason training program. Each day that first week, we held three training sessions. The morning session, from 7:30am to 9:00am, focused on ball fitness, conditioning and strength training. The second session, from 1 p.m. to 3 p.m., was devoted to ball skills, both individual and small group drills. In the third session, from 6 p.m. to 8 p.m., we covered team tactics and then played a full-field scrimmage. Once school started, we practiced twice a day, once before school and once after. This was the most comprehensive training camp I had ever experienced. Every activity was designed to make us better players, to hone an edge, be it technical, tactical, physical, or psychological.

Later, when I was playing professionally, in the off-seasons I would return to Ulster to work as an assistant coach to help George train the teams. There was no better place for me to train. George had learned the game from Hungarian coach Gustav Sebes, who had an unbeaten run from 1950–54, won the 1952 Olympics, and finished runner-up in the 1954 World Cup. Coach played alongside Hungarian legends Puskas, Kocsis, Hidegkuti, Czibor, Bozsik, and Grocsis. He would speak about these guys as if he had shared a beer with them the day before.

After the 1954 World Cup, Coach had emerged as one of Hungary's bright young prospects. During the 1956 Hungarian Revolution, he fled the country and came to the U.S. Viz had a profound influence on every soccer person he met, both his players at Ulster and his students in coaching classes he taught for the USSF. I cannot measure his influence on me. He was like a father. He shaped me as a player, coach, and person. Today, whenever I step onto the field, I realize that how I look at the game traces back to my time on the field at Ulster, both while a college player and during my later visits. From 1968 to 2010, Vizvary's record at SUNY Ulster was 534-159-28. At the time of his retirement in 2010, Coach had set the record for most wins in junior college history. He led Ulster to back-to-back NJCAA national titles in 1977 and 1978. He turned out many players who became pros. In the 1979 NASL draft, three Ulster players were picked in the first round including the first over-all pick, Njego Pesa of the Dallas Tornados; Johnny Lignos of the New England Tea Men; and Niels Guldbjerg of the Detroit Express. So many success stories were written at Ulster. Kevin Clinton of the Tampa Bay Rowdies. Let us not forget Joe Ulrich, the captain of Duke and the 1982 Hermann Trophy winner; Tom Byer, who became a worldwide soccer icon with his *SOCCER STARTS AT HOME* program; and my cousin Frank Fuchs, who later played for the Detroit Express. Ulster, that little school in Stone Ridge, was a soccer powerhouse.

Every Ulster season began with the First Official Team Meeting. Only the players and coaches could attend. No other school staff, no athletic trainers, no parents, and no guests. Only the inner family. Whatever was said in that locker room, no matter who said it, died there amongst the family. It was a sacred space. This is where each pregame and halftime talk would take place. It is where the warriors would celebrate their wins after each home game. That first meeting set the tone.

I remember my first meeting like it was yesterday. I was a 17-year-old freshman, a bit cocky, but in that room, I was intim-idated, even a little scared. The room was packed with 45 players, including some walk-ons who would not make the final roster. The average age was mid-20s. Rick Derella and I were the only two Americans. We were the youngest guys in the room, probably the only teenagers. The meeting would start with Viz shutting the door leading to the main locker room. He would then saunter from one end of the blackboard to the other. Next, he would make eye contact with each person in the room. George was tall, broad-shouldered, big-boned. He was a presence. He could intimidate; he could charm. He was a polished public speaker. His first words were something like, "Gentlemen, welcome to the Ulster County Community College soccer team. For many of you, this experience will be brief, because not everyone in this room has what it takes to play on this team." One of his catch phrases was, "You come here as boys, but you will leave here as men." Here's another: "Gentlemen, anyone can piss on the floor, but my players can piss on the ceiling." Then he would turn to the blackboard and speak these words as he wrote them on the board:

- Ulster will have 20 Wins 0 Losses 0 Ties
- Ulster will have 60 Goals For and 0 Goals Against
- Ulster will be Mid-Hudson Conference Champions
- Ulster will be Region 15 Champions
- Ulster will be NJCAA National Champions

When he was done, we knew what he expected. He would then pause, clasp his hands behind his back, and pace. He had this stare, like he was looking into everyone's souls. Then, in a loud, hard voice, he would ask, "Is there anyone here who has any doubt, any doubt at all, about our team reaching these goals?" He would scan each set of eyes, letting another quiet moment pass. Then he would point to the door and say, "You can leave now. Leave and don't come back, because you're either with us one hundred percent or you're against us. There is the door now and this is your last chance."

At this point, I was mesmerized. Then Coach would lay out the team rules. One was, "English, speak English." It was funny to hear him say that in his thick Hungarian accent. We had guys from Italy, Argentina, Honduras, Yugoslavia, Greece, and Jamaica, among other places. Coach wanted all his players to master English; he did not want the cliques that would form if every guy spoke his native language. We had black guys, white guys, and every shade in between. What bonded us was our love for soccer and our shared roots of growing up in poor, hardworking families. All but a few of us were ghetto kids. Coach was a builder. He took kids from different cultures and wove them into a family. This is not a talent you can learn out of a book. He would tell you his biggest wins were helping many boys grow into responsible citizens.

In shorthand, Coach's other rules were no drinking, no drugs, no women, only studying and soccer. He drilled into us that we were at Ulster for two things: education and soccer. Everything else was a distraction. Setting goals, making priorities, living a life of discipline. As I grow old and look back, these attributes that I learned at Ulster are among the most important gifts that soccer gave me. Once we got through that meeting, the fun began. We went out the door, down the hill, and onto the field for the first kick of my college soccer career.

By the time our NJCAA season began, we had a bunch of preseason games under our belt. Whether we played the Kingston Kickers, NYU, Columbia University, Hunter College, or local clubs from the German American League, or touring international teams, Coach always had us tuned up for the regular season. For one of those preseason games, we drove to SUNY Cobleskill. This is an agricultural school, somewhere in central New York, and the van ride seemed to last forever. As we warmed up before the game, I was surprised to see Ron Hauser, a good friend of mine from Ramapo High School, standing on the sidelines. I popped over for a quick chat. Ronald asked if I was starting. I said I didn't think so, because our coach wanted to give time to some reserves. I remember my man Ronnie giving me a grin that said, "Sure, Tom." I wanted to say something, but let it go. About ten minutes into the game, Cobleskill scored. Bang, Vizvary subbed out the entire second team and put in the starting lineup. Coach said not a word, he just signaled to the referees and he ran out eleven guys, including me. Well, by halftime, I was pretty sure that Ronald knew that I was, in fact, on the first team. The score was now 6–1, Ulster. It is funny how, after all these years, you remember a little episode like that.

Soon our Region 15 schedule began and we were a juggernaut. We ran our ranking up to #1 in the country. We were averaging three goals for and zero against. Oh, and we were playing home games on our new, beautiful, FIFA-sized field. The field had been built next to the athletic building, right outside our locker room door. It was a perfect place to start a dynasty. And a dynasty we became.

Before our new field was built, Ulster had played its home games at Dietz Stadium in Kingston. At our first game on our new field, against Manhattan, the school scheduled a ribbon cutting and dedication of the field. The sun lit the grass on a Saturday afternoon, and our college president, Robert Brown, kicked out the ceremonial first ball. A high school marching band played and local youth soccer teams and media joined in the celebration. A few hundred fans were sitting on the hill overlooking the field.

For whatever reason, big games would bring out the beast in me. As a midfielder, my focus was on my overall play, not on scoring goals. That said, every goal scored brought its own kind of high. Well, I rang in this special day by hitting the net four times. You could chalk it up to a bit of luck and an inferior opponent. Whatever, I was in the zone.

Coach Vizvary occupies a lot of space in my memory bank. The first time I met him, in my driveway, he had told me that none of his players could beat him in foot tennis. I just nodded. I knew that many exceptional players had played under Coach, guys like Mario Oliva and Kurt "Lion" Kedrick, a Jamaican whose nickname derived from his dreadlocks. Back in that moment on my driveway, I remember looking at Viz, standing there in his tight slacks and Sunday shoes, and wondering, *How could he beat his college players in foot tennis?*

One day early in the season, I walked out of the locker room toward the makeshift foot tennis field at the bottom of the hill. A bunch of my teammates had lined up to have a crack at Viz. Many games were close, but Coach always prevailed. Viz looked a lot different in a sweatsuit and adidas soccer shoes. This old guy was still a baller.

The first time I faced him, Coach schooled me. It took me a few games to figure out his strategy. Here were some of his secrets: Number one, he was the referee, and if it was close, it was his call. Number two, Coach would identify your weakness, and he would play to it hard. For example, most players were one-footed, and Coach would play everything to the weak foot. This is how he became king of the Ulster foot tennis court. Eventually, I had his number. I became the one Ulster County Community College player that George Vizvary will admit beat him in foot tennis. During my two years at Ulster, more days than not a player would come early to practice or stay late in a bid to take down Viz. Word is this foot tennis tradition began in 1968 and continued until 2010 when he retired from coaching.

Why was I able to beat Coach? I did not have a weak foot. A big thanks to Coach Rottenbucher for advising me to train more with my left foot than my natural right foot. And thanks to the wall at Cinema 45, for always being there for me.

As our season progressed, every day we would check the Kingston Freeman newspaper to see if there was any coverage of our team, or of soccer in general. One day that fall, I read a story that Pelé was considering coming out of retirement to play for the New York Cosmos. *I'll keep an eye on that*, I thought.

CHAPTER THIRTY-TWO

UNFORTUNATELY, I DID HAVE TO GO TO CLASS

It's the same old song, but as well as soccer was going, I was struggling in school. My strategic plan for academics was simple: do whatever I had to do to stay eligible. That meant I would take the easiest courses I could find. My major was Parks and Recreation, but I also had to take English, math, and all the core courses. I also took classes like golf, outdoor recreation, and cross-country skiing, which was one of my favorites. The good news was that the college had no classes designated as "BA" (below average), so I did not have to hide on my way in or out of any classrooms. That said, my learning disabilities continued to hound me.

My English 101 teacher was named Mr. Meyerhof. He would assign us a few chapters to read, and the next day in class we would discuss, debate, and dissect what we had read. He engaged everyone in lively group discussion, and I was enjoying the class. He was trying to get us to think, which is something I could do. I had no problem absorbing spoken content. I felt like I knew what was going on.

Then reality hit me. Mr. Meyerhof gave us a homework assignment where we had to read a few chapters and then write a paper summarizing what had happened. I knew that when I read, I did not absorb the material as well as I did in the classroom discussions. That night at home, it took me a long time to read the chapters. I forced myself to reread it until I thought I understood the content. Reading was hard enough, and now I had to put my thoughts on paper. What a nightmare!

The next day I handed in my paper and didn't think much about it afterward. A few days later, toward the end of class, Mr. Meyerhof said, "Well, class, I've marked your papers, and as usual, I can tell some people devoted more time to this than others." He grabbed up the stack of papers and stood in front of his desk, which was in front of me because I always sat in the seat closest to the teacher's desk. He would read off the name on each paper, say, "Karen Smith," and then he would look to see which student had a hand up. This was his way to remember names and match them to faces.

Finally, from the back of the room, Mr. Meyerhof said my name. I put up my hand and said, "Here." He walked toward me and put the paper on my desk. He looked me straight in the eyes, bent down, and said in a low voice, "Please see me after class." I looked at the paper and saw a big red F circled on the top. Red scrawl littered the page. I knew this would not be a fun meeting. I could write a five-page paper that had only three or four sentences, no commas, no punctuation. I guess that wouldn't cut it.

Class ended and the students started leaving. I waited until every kid was gone and then stood up and went to his desk, my paper in hand. Mr. Meyerhof was of average size. He had bushy long hair and a beard. He looked like a hippie who had hung out just up the road at Woodstock. He sat back in his chair, looked at me, and said, "Let me see that paper." I handed it to him. He threw it on his desk, and said, "What the fuck is that?"

I took a deep breath, looked him right in the eye, and said, "That paper took me three hours, and that is the best you are going to get because that is the best I got."

He asked, "So how do you think you are going to pass my class?"

I said, "I am going to have perfect attendance. I am going to be on time every morning. I am going to sit right there in that chair in the front row and pay attention to every word you say, as I have done up to now. I am going to complete every assignment you give, on time. I am going to participate in all class discussions, and if you offer extra credit, I will do that as well. Then you are going to give me a 'D' so I can pass the class."

He looked at me, shock on his face. Then he asked what high school I had attended. I said Ramapo High School. He said, "Ramapo High School, what the hell are you doing here?"

"I play on the soccer team," I said.

He slapped his forehead, sat back, and said, "Oh my God, you are one of George's kids." Mr. Meyerhof and I got along fine. I did everything I said I would do, and I did pass his class.

As much as I struggled to read and write, I think these learning challenges gave me strengths in other ways. For example, I focused on being able to read people. I learned to sense what people meant, rather than what they said. I think this helped me hone my people skills over my entire life.

CHAPTER THIRTY-THREE

CONTINUING THE PURSUIT OF THE AMERICAN DREAM

The more time I spent with my teammates, the more respect I had for each one. I was learning about each member in my new family and, most importantly, about the unique nature of every being. These guys had different backgrounds, ate different foods, listened to different music. They all looked different, from Jamaican dreadlocks to crew-cuts, from the Retro Disco Danny shirt to the casual blue jeans and white T-shirt. It was as if we were at the star station in the Star Wars movie where aliens from different planets came to socialize. There were also many different personalities, some quiet and religious, some loud and wild. The better I got to know them, the more my world grew.

Each player had a different story but, in some ways, our journeys were similar. Most guys had a long and complicated immigration journey. Their families had come to the USA to survive. Most of us came from low-income families and many grew up in a one-parent household. Many guys had come from some of the worst neighborhoods in New York City. How did these inner-city kids find their way to the picturesque little town of Stone Ridge, in the middle of apple orchard country in upstate New York? The answer was simple: Coach Viz was a relentless recruiter. From his house in Saugerties, New York, he would get in his little Karmann Ghia and take the almost 100-mile trip to the city to watch high school teams play on fields of dirt. Each year he would attend the annual New York City high school all-star game. This is where you could find the best of the best. Most college coaches were either afraid to drive into those neighborhoods or knew that they had little chance to get these ethnic ghetto kids admitted to their school.

For Viz, the 200-mile round trip ride to watch the games was the easy part. By the way, costs for these trips came out of Coach's pocket and were not reimbursed. I would say that Viz's entire coaching salary would not cover what he put into the team. He *paid* to coach the team. The most time-consuming part of recruiting was when Coach would visit each player's house to meet the family. He would shake hands with his firm grip, look the parents straight in the eye, and, with his Hungarian charm, and tell them that their son would be safe with him. He assured them that he would watch over his players as if they were his own children. He stressed that Ulster was the best choice for their son's future and that Ulster was the place for them to continue their family's pursuit of the American Dream. Ulster would provide a good education for their son and Coach would then help the boy navigate his next step in life. He would help find a four-year school for the boy, where he could continue his education and his soccer career.

Many of these conversations were carried out through a translator. Often it was the recruited player who had to take the coach's

English, salted with his heavy Hungarian accent, and put those words into his family's native language, whether Spanish, Greek, Yugoslavian, or Italian. For most families, these players were the first members of the family to get a high school diploma, let alone go to college. Once the head of the household was convinced that the son's future would be safe in Viz's hands, the next question was how much would this cost and how would it get paid. Most families could hardly keep the lights on in their own houses. Vizvary was the master of the "ghetto scholarship," better known as financial aid. I would estimate that 90 percent of his players qualified for some form of financial aid. For eligible families for whom English was not the first language, the biggest challenge was filling out the paperwork. Needless to say, Coach Viz kept the Ulster Financial Aid Office very busy.

One night, about halfway through my first season, Ricky and I had stopped by the apartment where some of our teammates lived. As we sat around talking, it started to get dark. John Bertuna, our goalkeeper from Argentina, got up from the couch and started unwinding a long extension cord. I was thinking to myself, *What the hell are you going to do with that?* They lived on the bottom floor of the apartment complex, and they had not paid the electricity bill, so Central Hudson Gas and Electric had turned off their electricity. They did not have any money, but they were survivors, so they figured it out. Each evening, after the building manager had left to go home, they passed the extension cord out their apartment window and into the public laundry room window just a few yards away. Then they would plug the cord in, and voila, electricity again. Early each morning they would unplug the cord before they left for school. The building manager never saw the cord.

CHAPTER THIRTY-FOUR

THEY WERE SURVIVORS!

Franklin Hill was one of our top players and one of the toughest defenders I ever met. His nickname was "the executioner," and with good reason. He was a great guy, much older than me, and not someone you wanted to be on the wrong side of. One day after practice, he invited me back to his house for dinner. After we left campus, we stopped at the A&P Supermarket. Franklin said he did not have much at the house and he wanted to pick up dinner on the way home. I offered to help pay, but he told me to not worry, that he had it.

As we walked around the supermarket, he would pick something up and ask me if I liked it. I was not very choosy and didn't want to be a pain, so I just said yes, whatever he wanted was cool with me. "Do you eat meat?" he asked.

I said, "Sure, I love steak."

Well, after a tour around the supermarket, we got to the checkout counter. I saw that he had a long loaf of baguette bread, a bag of rice and a can of beans, and not much more. I did not care what we ate. He was a leader on the team, and I was happy to be hanging out with him.

Back at his car, I jumped into the copilot seat and looked over at him as he was getting into the driver's seat. He passed me the grocery bag. Then he hunched between the car and his still-open door and reached down his pants. At first, I wondered, *Does he have an itch? What the hell is he doing?* Then he began taking things out of his pants: steak, chicken, and even some frozen shrimp. While we were in the store, I was at his side the entire time, but I never saw him or even suspected him of stealing anything. He had more stuff in his pants than we had in the grocery bag. He looked at me with his big eyes and said, "We are going to eat good tonight, my friend." He smiled, jumped in, and off we went. The way he looked at it, he had no money, so shoplifting for dinner was a survival tactic.

Later in the season, I learned that some of my teammates had befriended a few girls who worked checkout at that supermarket. The girls would often slip items by the register and not charge the guys. Many of these guys dated and hung out with upstate girls. The girls would take them out to dinner and buy them drinks at the clubs, and even lend them money. For the most part, the guys saw it as another form of survival.

Many of our African-American players lived in the dorms on the SUNY New Paltz campus. As I look back now, it was probably hard if not impossible for African-American kids to find housing in upstate New York, whether it be a room in a private house or an apartment. At that time, I thought that our players liked the dorms because the girls' dorm was nearby and some of the girls had meal plans at the college cafeteria. In hindsight, there was more to it than that. The term "systemic racism" was not yet in anybody's vocabulary, but it was real, even if, at the time, most of us had our heads buried.

Here's one story I will never forget. It was early October, and we had a game scheduled at Staten Island Community College. We would have a two-hour-plus ride, and that was if we hit no traffic. As a standard protocol for a weekday game that far away, the players got dismissed early from class. Everyone met in the parking lot by the gym, where the school vans were parked. Both vans were full; the team equipment was loaded, and we were all ready to go. Coach Viz did a headcount and when he was one short, he did the roll call. Mario Isaac was missing.

Coach thought Mario may have forgotten to leave class early, so he sent one of our players to run across campus and check his class. When the player returned alone, Coach was lathered up. Viz kept looking at his watch and pacing. Finally, he got in the van, and we started to drive off. Just then Coach DiBernardo, the athletic director, ran out of the gymnasium, waving his arms and chasing after us. We pulled over, and Viz got out. As they were talking, I remember looking out the window and saying to myself, *This is not good*. When Viz got back in the van, someone said, "Hey Coach, what's up with Mario?" Coach raised a dismissive hand and without a word, off we went.

It was not uncommon for us to take the back roads from Stone Ridge to reach the New York State Thruway at the New Paltz exit. So, none of us were thinking about our route. Then, right before the thruway entrance, Coach pulled onto Main Street in New Paltz. He turned onto a side street and rolled into a space at the New Paltz Police Station. Coach got out and went inside, leaving us all to wonder, *What the hell is going on?*

About 20 minutes later, Coach came out with Mario at his side. They got in and there was silence the entire two-hour ride to Staten Island. Once we arrived at the fields, we got out and started to warm up. Coach called us into a huddle and addressed the elephant in the room. He said that the night before, Mario had been accused of robbing a young lady at knifepoint in New Paltz. Viz said, "I have spoken with Mario, and I have looked into his eyes, and he swears that it was not him. I believe him. Now the only thing I want anyone to think about is the game we are about to win." Viz looked at Mario and said, "Mario, your family is behind you. Do you feel like you can play?"

Mario looked around the huddle and said, "Yes, Coach, I cannot wait to play."

As usual, Viz found a way to turn a negative into a positive. Coach had Mario's back; we all did. Staten Island rarely touched the ball that afternoon, and we won, 4–0.

The ride home was a lot more upbeat than the ride there. Looking back, I am amazed that Coach Vizvary could walk into a police station he had never been in before, and, in 20 minutes, convince officers to release into his custody a young Black man whom they were holding for armed robbery so we could make our soccer game. Remember this was the early '70s, and we were not a Division 1 college football team.

A few days later, the New Paltz Police Department got a positive identification and arrested another Black man who did not even fit Mario's description. They were both African American; that was all they had in common. To paraphrase Vizvary, he said something like, "These hillbillies are not used to seeing Black people and cannot tell one from another." Looking back, it was unfair for Mario to have to endure such a harrowing situation. Let me be clear: that would have never happened to me or Ricky or any of our white players. Systemic racism, another hurdle my teammates had to clear to survive.

CHAPTER THIRTY-FIVE

BRONX COMMUNITY COLLEGE: WHEN SOCCER BECOMES WAR

It was a typical mid-autumn day, cloudy and cool, as we prepared to play host to Bronx Community College. Bronx was 6-3-2 and still battling for a spot in the playoffs. We knew we were in for a dog-fight. When you are ranked in the top five in the nation all season long, in every match, the other team has it out for you. They do not care how they win; they just want to be able to say they beat Ulster. On top of that, Viz had warned us that Bronx was known for hitting off the ball and any other manner of cheap shots. He said that we must stay calm and focus on putting the ball in the net.

We were not a dirty team; we did not have to be. Most of the time we had the ball. Besides, when you stepped onto Viz's field, discipline was a must. At the same time, we were not going to be easy prey. Every guy on our team had grown up in the trenches. Each guy knew how to stand up for himself. If you got knocked, you knocked back a little harder.

The Bronx team pulled up in a real bus, which was unusual. All our other opponents traveled in team vans, as we did. From the opening whistle, Bronx played as if they were in a hurry to create chances, sending long, aimless balls into our back third. As a scoreless game unfolded, they became more desperate. Their tackles were cynical, even reckless. They were playing to win at all costs. On this day, the referees would earn their money. Or would they?

Back in the early 1970s, quality referees were hard to come by. Few refs could officiate at the same level we could play. They lagged a step behind the action, and in nearly every game, there was at least one debacle. Whenever that happened, we saw the true character of Coach Viz. He would never raise his voice at the referees. He believed that refs were like the weather and you had no control over them. On occasion, one of our players would make a hard but clean tackle, ball first, and the referee would still blow his whistle. Coach would yell to the player, "Aldo, do not worry; it was a good tackle; you got the whole ball."

Viz acted like the referee had never seen a tackle like that before, and that's why he had called a foul. It was not the ref's fault. How did Viz remain so calm? He was an instructor for USSF coaching schools, and he understood that a coach has to set the correct tone on the sideline. Viz knew that if a coach is aggressive or unruly, the game can unravel fast. He would smile at the refs, pay them an occasional compliment. More often than not, he earned their respect. He never gave the ref a reason to favor the other team. That's a victory in itself.

In our game with Bronx, the refs were in over their heads. For starters, there were only two refs, both roaming the field, both with equal power. Both had a whistle and often both whistles would sound at once and both referees would point, but not always in the same direction. Ideally, we would have three referees, one on the field with a whistle and two assistants using flags on the touchlines. But for this game, only two. Worse yet, most of our referees had never played soccer. They officiated other sports at the high school or college level, and had read a soccer rulebook and thus called soccer games for side income. Okay, back to the action.

Thirty minutes in, Rick Derella scored to put us on top. Now Bronx became even more desperate. When Kurt Nedrick dribbled free near the Bronx box, their center back wrestled him to the ground with an American football tackle. Kurt kept his cool, but the kindling had been lit. A few minutes later, as our center back Franklin Hill stepped into a clearance, their striker spilled him with a hard, late tackle. The referee stood nearby but did not make a call. Franklin got up and stepped over to his opponent. With a smile, he said, "Okay, so that is how you want to play."

A bit later that same Bronx striker ran onto a ball near midfield, not far from the team benches. As he built speed, Franklin closed in. Franklin's timing was perfect. He stuck a two-legged tackle on the guy, cleats up, just above the knees. The player hit the ground, bounced up, and went chest-to-chest with Franklin. Then he flinched his arm, as if he were about to throw a punch. But it was only a flinch. Well, if you are going to throw a punch at Franklin, you better make it count. Throwing a phantom punch at Franklin was like poking a bear in the eye. Now you must deal with what you woke up.

Franklin saw the flinch. While most people might have ducked, Franklin had a different reaction. He punched the guy in the face, knocking him over, right there in front of the team benches. As the Bronx player hit the ground, a man in a long winter coat jumped off the Bronx bench and headed toward Franklin. Meanwhile, Kurt and their center back were trading blows. Soon Willie, Maximo, Aldo, Simon, and Segundo had all squared off with Bronx players. Our goalkeeper, John Bertuna, and the Bronx keeper had each sprinted 50 yards to midfield. First, they went head-to-head like two sumo wrestlers. Then they were throwing punches, pulling shirts, and kicking each other like they were two hockey goalies at the Stanley Cup Final.

When the brawl had started, I was on the far side of the field near the woods. I was forty yards from the fray, but close enough to get ambushed. Fearful of getting blindsided, I backed into the woods and picked up some rocks. Ricky and I were the only two guys who were not fighting. Sure, Ricky and I had seen fights before, but it was usually two guys and it would get broken up quickly. This was a melee. As I looked over at the benches, I could see Coach Vizvary standing right where he was when this started. He had not moved an inch. I remember what he wore; an all-white adidas training suit with light blue trim. His arms were crossed as he watched a New York City gang war break out in the quiet hamlet of Stone Ridge, New York.

I looked over at the man in the coat who had jumped off the bench. He had pulled a knife, and he was only a few yards from Franklin, who was standing over his dazed combatant. Franklin saw the knife and bolted for the woods. He disappeared into the trees, and a few seconds later, so did the guy with the knife. My eyes swung back to Kurt, who had his foe pinned to the ground.

Just when I thought things were about to calm down, another Bronx player grabbed a wooden corner flag and ran toward Kurt. The stake was five feet long with a four-inch metal tip, and this dude was running like a warrior in a movie. Now, it took a lot to unnerve Kurt. He was built like a hunk of marble, and having grown up in the streets of Jamaica and later Brooklyn, he knew how to fend. But when Kurt saw the guy with the corner post bearing down, he stood and broke into a sprint. The player Kurt had been holding down got up and chased after Kurt. I'm sure the guy thought Kurt was running away from him; he didn't know that 20 yards behind him was a guy carrying a serious weapon.

Kurt had forged a lead on his two pursuers; that was the good news. The bad news was he was heading toward me. Kurt ran by me and headed for an old ramshackle barn that stood another 30 yards away, just off campus. He reached the front door of the barn, which had fallen to the ground. The door still held six large windows, about three feet square. Kurt stepped on a pane and picked up a big hunk of glass. He turned to see his foe running at him. Kurt cracked him over the head, the glass breaking on contact. The blow did not cut the guy's head, no blood. But the guy kept coming and Kirk swung the remaining piece. This time he opened a gash above the guy's knee, blood everywhere. The player fell to his other knee and tried to hold the gash closed. The guy with the corner flag arrived and stood over his teammate, who clearly needed medical attention.

After a standoff that lasted maybe 30 seconds, the two Bronx teammates turned and made their way back toward their bus. Kurt threw the glass down and started jogging toward the locker room. About 80 yards in the other direction, Franklin had been chased into the woods by the guy with the switchblade. At that moment they came running out of the trees, only this time the guy with the knife was being chased by Franklin. Franklin carried a long oak branch, maybe six inches thick, which he could barely hold with two hands. He was swinging it over his head and screaming as he chased the knife guy.

Even in his long coat, the knife guy could motor. Not far behind him, Franklin looked like a samurai warrior holding that branch over his head. As the knife guy neared his bench, the Bronx coach was trying to gather his players. They all had their backs to the field, so they had not seen the knife guy or Franklin coming. At the last minute, the players saw their guy being hunted down by Franklin. They started screaming and scattering. Franklin started swinging the branch, trying to inflict damage on anyone who got in his way. He was at war. Luckily, the coach ducked out of one of Franklin's swings, and their players started making a beeline toward the bus in the parking lot.

At this point, almost all the Bronx players had made their way back to the bus. Some of the Ulster players were headed into our locker room. Among the last players not to make it back to our locker room were Willie and Maximo, who continued to batter their foes. I saw one guy retreat from Maximo and scurry toward his bus. Willie got off the other guy and stepped away, but as the guy started to get up, Willie turned and lashed at him with a kick that sent him back to the ground. Willie smiled and jogged to the locker room.

When I arrived in the locker room, I was still shaking. Coach took a headcount to make sure we did not lose anyone. Then one of the players asked, "So, Coach, are we going to finish the game?"

Right about then people began to wonder, *What happened to the referees?* The answer was easy. Once the referees realized what was going on, they had run off to their cars. So no, we were not going to finish that game. From a political standpoint, this game was a disaster. Our Athletic Director, Coach DiBernardo, was on hand, as was the college president. Yes, President Brown had stopped by to watch. So having Coach DiBernardo and President Brown there did not bode well for Coach Vizvary and his Ulster soccer program. Never mind that we were just a bunch of underserved guys trying to survive.

A sidebar to that crazy day. In attendance was a high school player, Dave Farrell, who was from the nearby hamlet of Port Ewen, home to fewer than 1,000 people. Later in life, Dave became best friends and business partners with Rick Derella and myself. He was at this game with his mom, Marge, to see the campus and get a look at the team he hoped to play for next season. Dave knew that it was highly improbable that a local player would make the Ulster soccer team. But he and his mom thought this would be a nice afternoon to enjoy a friendly college soccer game. They saw anything but that. In fact, before the melee broke out, Mario Oliva and a Bronx player clashed in a hard tackle. The ball flew into the crowd, where it ripped the strap off Marge's handbag and bruised her arm. Mario did run over and apologize, but the rest of what Dave and Marge witnessed that day was unforgivable. It was not until a year later when Dave showed up for tryouts that he realized that the brawl he had seen was a stroke of incredibly good fortune. The fallout of that fight would open the door for Dave to make our team as a local player, an event that defined the path of his life.

CHAPTER THIRTY-SIX

POSTSEASON: WIN OR GO HOME

Our regular season had ended with 11 wins, one loss, and one tie. We scored 46 goals and allowed seven. Most people would call that a successful season. Coach George Vizvary was not like most people. Deep down, I think he was proud of us. But no way would he let us think it was okay to have lost a game and tied another.

In his bid to make us better, Coach employed some unusual tactics. When a player was underperforming, Coach would yank him off the field. No big deal, right? Well, when Viz removed a player, he often did not replace him. When the player would come off, the bench guys would look toward Viz like hungry puppies waiting for a treat. In a stern voice, Coach would say that the player taken off had played like shit, and the bench player had not earned the spot so they will not go in. It did not matter who you were, you had a standard to meet. If 11 players had not met the standard, Coach played with fewer than 11. In some cases, we played eight versus 11. This was one way Coach prepared us to win in the postseason.

While Coach's substitution pattern may seem extreme, I believe it had the desired effect. Here is an example. We had a player named George who tended to hold the ball, taking the extra dribble instead of making the pass. We were playing in a home match, early in the season. Most fans had chosen to spread blankets on the hill behind our bench, close enough to hear Coach Viz's colorful comments. On this day you could hear Coach calling out, *George, release the ball; you must play the ball quicker.* At one point the ball went out of bounds, and Viz signaled to the ref and off came George. Viz did not send in a replacement.

Coach thought George had to learn the hard way. Viz called him over. He grabbed a practice ball, handed it to George and said, "So, you want to dribble? Well, here is a ball; you seem to need your own ball; you do not want to share it with your teammates. Now you can dribble right here behind the bench. You want to dribble for the spectators. Here is your chance to dribble; show them your beautiful moves, and show them how well George holds the ball."

George hung his head and headed toward the bench. Viz called him back and said, "George, I am not kidding; you will dribble or you will go to the locker room and return your uniform." With tears in his eyes, George dribbled in little circles behind the team bench. He did so until halftime. In the second half, Coach put George back in and he played one of the best forty-five minutes of his Ulster career.

CHAPTER THIRTY-SEVEN

THE TABLE WAS SET

Our postseason would begin in a few days, and our opponent would be Dutchess Community College. This game was huge for three reasons. First, it was a revenge match, as we had tied 2–2 in the first game of the regular season. Second, the winner of this game would claim the mid-Hudson conference championship. And third, the winner would move one step closer to the national championship, while the loser would be eliminated.

Our first training session for the postseason tournament was an eye-opener for me. Normally, the players would arrive at the field before Coach. I was usually the first one there and the last one to leave. When Coach would reach the field, he would greet us with a smile and say, "How are you today, my son?" Coach loved being out there as much as we did; it was his life's calling. On this day, when the first group of players arrived, Coach was already there. His greeting was more formal, his look more serious. Was he still upset over our last game against the Bronx, played just a few days prior?

Training started with our usual warm-up, everyone with a ball. After that Coach covered some tactical adjustments for our coming game. He was louder and more animated than usual. His message was clear: I demand total concentration. I noticed that he was wearing this big winter hat. Granted, it was mid-November and starting to get cold, but I had never seen him wear a hat before. Here's why I remember the hat. A few minutes into our tactical session, Viz stopped practice, threw his hat down, and started jumping on it. Trust me, he had everyone's attention. You could have heard a deer fart on the other side of the woods. By the time that session was over, that hat had taken a beating.

On every day leading up to the playoffs, when Coach stopped training to make a point, he had a rapt audience. We were on high alert. All that said, Viz still made it fun. We left the field feeling good about ourselves. Coach had us confident in ourselves and our team. We were ready to go after the national title.

The game against Dutchess went exactly how Coach planned, except for the goal we conceded. Viz loved his shutouts, but he also wanted us to score at least three goals and we hit that mark. We earned a 3–1 win against one of only two teams that we did not beat in the regular season. Our next game would be the semifinal of Region 15, and our opponent would be New York City Community College. NYCCC was the only team to beat us in the regular season. That game was on their field and we lost, 2–0. We wanted payback.

As Coach liked to say, it is important to peak at the right time. This mentality was a keystone in the Ulster soccer culture. Peaking is not just physical; it is tactical and most importantly, psychological. Peaking is something most coaches never talk about. That's because they do not see what Viz sees when he looks out on the field. Most coaches are too busy sweating the X's and O's. Viz could not only see the forest through the trees; he knew where each tree was planted and how that tree would grow. Coach could control when and how his team would play at their best. He saw the little things, like a player becoming too cocky. Coach would bring that player back down. His knack for using individual and team psychology cannot be taught in any book; it was something only life can teach.

How did Viz get us to peak? It might be as simple as a lineup change for a particular game. On that day, that change may not have been optimal for the player or the team. However, that 30-minute rest gave that player the energy he needed for the next game. Coach also knew when to give a role player an important assignment as a way to instill confidence.

To play to your full potential, as individuals and as a team, in the biggest moments, that is the ultimate team-athlete experience. Coach knew how to create this high. I think that is why his Ulster teams won two national championships and earned a berth in 17 national tournaments. Viz's record was 534-159-28, the most wins by any coach in junior college history.

Under Coach's lead, we thumped NYCCC 4–0 in the Region 15 semifinal. Mario Oliva, our All-American left-footed wonder, bagged a hat trick. Now the one team standing between us and going to the national championships was Queensborough Community College, who had beat Suffolk Community College 3–2 in overtime. Ulster had not faced Queensborough this season. We last met them a year earlier in the first round of the Region 15 playoffs, when they eliminated us.

The headline in the paper read, "**Ulster Ousted, 2 to 1, in last four seconds.**" The Ulster train had been derailed. The game had been played at Westchester Community College, a neutral site, and the ride home was miserable. I was in the van that Viz was driving, and no one spoke the entire trip. Viz was an engineering professor, and the rumor was that when his soccer team lost a game, his classes would get a quiz the next day. Some people thought Coach did this to encourage his students to follow the team. At that moment, I felt sorry for his students.

We were barely out of the vans when we heard the rumor that Queensborough had fielded an ineligible player against us. Less than 48 hours later the newspaper headline read: **"Another Chance for Ulster Booters."** The player from Queensborough who was ruled ineligible was a friend of mine, Eddie Mauser, the younger brother of Arnie Mauser, the U.S. National Team goalkeeper. Coach had read an article in a German paper that indicated Eddie had played in a league game for which he was not eligible.

Now we would meet Suffolk County Community College, who had lost in overtime to Queensborough, 3–2. The Region 15 executive committee had decided that since Queensborough had beaten both Suffolk and Ulster, a match between these two teams would be the fairest way to determine the Region 15 champion. We were given a new life and we ran with it. The game ended 6–1, and we were heading to Baltimore for the national championships. Or were we? By the time we got back to Ulster after the Suffolk match, another rumor had surfaced about more ineligible players, and this time they were our players. Ulster had been accused of having three players who had played a match in New York City's Honduras league. They were Mario Oliva, Willie Navas, and Rigoberto Maximo. They all denied that they played. Still, off we went to Baltimore under a dark cloud.

It was the first time Ulster had ever made it to the NJCAA National Tournament. We checked into the hotel and headed for bed. The last thing Coach said was that curfew was in 30 minutes and breakfast was at 8 a.m. and we'd better not be late. The next morning, we were in the hotel restaurant when the dark cloud turned into a hurricane. Gathered at the entrance was the Suffolk team that we had knocked off two days earlier. The place went quiet. Coach Viz got up from his table and went over to the group. In addition to the Suffolk team, there were a few men in suits, who we would learn were officials from Region 15. After their investigation, they had declared Mario, Willie, and Rigoberto ineligible. That meant that Suffolk, not Ulster, would represent Region 15 in the tournament that afternoon. Coach had turned pale. He walked back to us and said, "Gentlemen, we have been disqualified from the tournament; we are going home. Now go to your rooms, and get your things. The vans will be leaving as soon as possible."

I packed my bag quickly and stepped out to the hall. That's when I saw Mario, Willie, and Rigoberto in an altercation with Franklin Hill and Kurt Nedrick. Franklin and Kurt told the three guys that they had ruined our future, robbed us of opportunities to get scholarships and to play in front of pro coaches and scouts. When it started to get physical, Coach Viz stepped in and screamed, "Get in the van, now!" That hall was evacuated like it was a bomb scare.

As we got outside, I noticed that Coach, along with Mario, Willie, and Rigoberto, had already boarded one van. That van was running but only the back door was open, so guys could place their bags in the back. Coach was keeping the three offenders separate from the rest of the team. He was not doing it as punishment; he was protecting them from the other players. The five-hour ride back to Ulster would be miserable, with 17 depressed and angry guys packed into a 15-seat van. Once we got on the road, each time our van got close to Coach's van, Franklin or another guy would bang on the window and give the finger to their former teammates. Just part of surviving.

As I reflected on my first year at Ulster County Community College, on balance it was a positive soccer experience. The team did not play in the national championship, and I did not play in front of any pro scouts. However, we had many successful moments, and many of our players went on to play at four-year colleges, as Viz promised. I was voted the Most Valuable Player in the Mid-Hudson Conference, and Most Valuable Player in Region 15. I also was the first Ulster player to become a first-team double All-American, for both the NJCAA and NSCAA. For the first time in school history, a soccer player was named The Outstanding Male Athlete for the 1974–75 academic year.

My first college season was behind me. It was late in the semester and most players were focusing on their finals. I was focused on soccer. The leaves had fallen, snow had blanketed our field, and most days were too cold to train outside, so each day after my classes ended, I went to the gym. If the basketball team was not training, I would work out with my ball off the gym wall. One section of the gym was once used to teach racquetball, and with all those walls it was a perfect spot for ball work. When that section was in use, I would go to the wrestling room, small with low ceilings, another ideal place for me to hone my ball skills. Cardio workouts were a challenge, as the snow and cold kept me from running outside. Thankfully, Coach DiBernardo, who taught most of my recreation classes, allowed me to use the school's cross-country skis. I would go for several miles. I later learned that it was not uncommon for professional players in Europe to cross-country ski in the off-season.

Before long, our spring semester was under way. There were rules barring teams from training in the offseason, and every weekend most guys went back to the city to play in their native neighborhoods. We would always play in a late winter indoor tournament, the same one that I had played in the year before as a high school guest player. It was held at Sullivan County Community College in a field house ideal for indoor soccer. Ulster came away champions. I was voted Most Valuable Player, which was the prize I had my eyes on the year before.

Ulster County Community College
Freshman Year Fall 1974
"This was my most talented team" George Vizvary

Back (L-R) George Vizvary, Tom Mulroy, Segundo Zapatier, Renato Hill, Oscar Rendon, Franklin Hill, Alvaro Rendón, Aldo Sergovich, Rodrigo Maximo, Willie Navas, Jim Studley Asst Coach

Front (L-R) Simon Curanaj, Rick Derella, Mario Olivia, John Bertuna, Kurt Nedrick, Tom Rontiris, Juan Diaz, Mario Isaac

CHAPTER THIRTY-EIGHT

THE MCGUIRE CUP

Spring had arrived, and this would be my last season playing in the junior division of the German American League. That league is where I first learned to play, on my Clarkstown Sports Club team, and later with the German American League All Star team and the New York State team. I was about to write the final chapter of my time as a junior player.

Our Clarkstown junior team was always ranked near the top of the first division. We talked about winning the State Cup and usually went deep in that single-elimination competition. But we never brought the cup home. At that time, every serious soccer player dreamed of winning not only the State Cup, but then the regional tournament, and then the national McGuire Cup. US Soccer's most prestigious youth trophy is the McGuire Cup, which brought together the best youth teams from across the U.S. In 1975, the McGuire Cup was the only national youth soccer competition in the country. If your team won the McGuire Cup, your team was the best in the country.

At Clarkstown, we never talked about winning the McGuire Cup. That was a bridge too far. But now I believed we had the talent to win it. I had put that on my list of goals, right next to winning the NJCAA National Championship and becoming a professional player and even the best in the world. Ever since I was in junior high school, I was never afraid to say my personal goals aloud. The way I saw it, as long as you set goals and were willing to sacrifice everything to achieve them, then you should not be afraid to share them.

The path was now much clearer to me. I was 18 years old, living away from home for the first time. I had a coach who set goals and laid out a clear plan to reach them. I had just spent the past few months living out our Ulster team plan. It was a step-by-step blueprint to take us all to our dream. We did not win the national championship, but Coach's plan took us far. Learning to create a life map was a transcendent lesson for me, one that I still use to this day.

Every time my Clarkstown team played in the State Cup, we had a dream but we did not have a plan. My plan to win the McGuire Cup was simple. Clarkstown had talented players and we had a very good leader, Coach Rottenbucher. All we had to do was get everybody fully committed to working hard and making the sacrifices needed to execute the plan. We would have to practice harder and more often than we ever did before. That was going to be a challenge, because Ricky and I and a few other players were away at college. Herve Guillioid was at SUNY Fredonia, about six hours away, and Richie Murray and Kenny Fisher were at the University of Connecticut, more than two hours away. Those guys could not be expected to get back to Rockland for training.

I thought it would not be unreasonable for everyone to get back for weekend games, especially the big ones. **That was in the plan.** Most of the players still lived in Rockland County, so training for them should be no problem. **That was in the plan.** Our players away at college would train on their own. **That was in the plan.** I was the leader, and I did not care how long it took to get to training. I would be there because I lead by example. **That was in the plan**.

Our German American Junior Division was ready to kick off its spring season. After I had spent most of the winter training alone at Ulster, I was excited to get back outside and train with our Clarkstown Junior team. We trained on Tuesday and Thursday evenings at Clarkstown Junior High. Getting back for training from Ulster was a good 90-minute drive, and that was if you had a direct ride without traffic. When you had to hitchhike, as I did, it could take four hours. Most days, either Ricky or another guy with a car would drop me at the Thruway entrance in New Paltz. Then I would hold up my sign that said "Exit 14, Spring Valley," so as not to be mixed up with Exit 14A, which took you to New Jersey via the Garden State Parkway.

Once I made the Spring Valley exit, I still had to hitchhike another two miles on back roads to reach my house. The plan was to get to my house, say hello to the family, and grab a bite. Then my Aunt Nancy would give me and my cousins, Franky and Danny, a ride to the school. The next morning, I would get up at 5 a.m. and my Uncle Frank, who always went to work early, would drop me back at Exit 14. I would try to get to New Paltz before Ricky or the other guys with cars left for the campus in Stone Ridge. Reaching New Paltz on time was key, because it could take longer to hitchhike from New Paltz to Stone Ridge than from Spring Valley to New Paltz. This commute was not fun, but I was committed to doing it twice a week. **This was part of the plan.** Oh, and I would ride back with Ricky for games on either Friday night or Saturday morning.

"A Dream Without a Plan is Just a Wish"

As the spring season unfolded, Ricky was the only 'commuter' that showed up regularly for our weekend games. The other players who were away at school were not so committed. That was understandable, as these guys had academic commitments. I believed they would be there for the state cup games. We were like family. Our problem was closer to home. We had a core group of 14 to 16 local players. These guys should have made every session. Instead, I would show up and there might be six guys. At first, they said when it was raining or cold, they figured we weren't going to train. Then they had to study for a test. One bullshit excuse after another. What really irked me was when someone said they didn't have a ride. I responded that I had hitchhiked 75 miles to get here, and I'll be hitchhiking back at dawn so I could make my classes.

Too many guys were not all-in. I had worked too hard and sacrificed too much to let anything impede me. By now, the deadline to submit rosters for the state cup was only a few weeks away. I approached Coach Rottenbucher and told him that I wanted to move to another team that had players who shared my commitment. This was not easy for me, as Coach was as committed as I was. He was open-minded and fair. He asked to have a team meeting and to give everybody one more chance. We had that meeting, but when I showed up for training the next Tuesday after hitchhiking for three and a half hours, we barely had enough guys to play 4v4.

Coach agreed that he would give me my release so I could play with Blau Weis Gottschee (Gottschee). However, he had one stipulation: if Clarkstown met Gottschee in the state cup, I would not be able to play. We shook hands, and that was worth more than anything you could put on paper. Next, I called Ben Bohem, Gottschee youth director, who had had me on his radar for years. Gottschee would invite me to participate in their international games whenever a touring German team would be in New York. Mr. Bohem put me in touch with Martin Petschauer, the coach of the junior team. Coach Petschauer had seen me play many times, and I got signed immediately. I was set to train that Thursday and play my first game that weekend.

Back at Ulster, my best friend and roommate Ricky Derella was not speaking to me. I mean he was acting like I was not alive. If he needed to tell me something, he would leave a note. It was like we were going through an ugly divorce, where someone cheated and they were still living together. Looking back, I do not think Ricky was as mad as he was hurt. I know my Clarkstown teammates felt much the same. It was a tough time for us all. I was upfront, and I think I managed it as best I could. I loved those guys. I still do, we were, and still are, family.

Think about this. Ricky would still drive me to school and home, but he would not talk to me in the car. If we stopped at a gas station, he would ask the other players to ask me for my share of the gas money. The guy used to check my homework, and we did everything together. It hurt me knowing I was hurting him. Ricky was as committed to winning that McGuire Cup as I was. But for my plan to work, everyone had to be all-in.

Changing teams meant my commute got tougher. Instead of my twice-weekly, 150-mile round-trip hitchhike between Stone Ridge and Rockland County, I was now facing this itinerary: hitchhike from Stone Ridge to Spring Valley (1.5–3 hours); take a bus from Spring Valley Transit Center to the Port Authority in Manhattan (1–1.5 hours); walk to the M train and take it to the last stop, which was Metropolitan Ave. (45 min.–1 hour); meet my new Gottschee teammates, and then walk 10 minutes to Brennan Field where we trained. Give or take, a five-hour commute.

That Thursday, I was on my way to my first training session with my new team in Queens. That first day I had only two things on my mind. One, would I get on and off the M train at the correct stops? Two, was this team committed to doing what it took to win the McGuire Cup? The next thing I know, I am leaving the M train at the Metropolitan Ave. station. As I step onto the sidewalk, I see half the team waiting to greet me. They made me feel like a celebrity, handshakes and hugs all around. I was getting welcomed in "Willkommen" and "Bienvenidos Gringo." I felt like every guy was happy to have me as a teammate.

After a wonderful training session, the plan was for Coach Petschauer or his assistant coach Bobby Sprague to drop me at the Port Authority on 8th Avenue in Manhattan. It was at least a 45-minute drive each way for them, but it spared me from having to take the train alone through some suspect neighborhoods at night. They would reimburse me for the round-trip bus ride and give me a little cash for dinner. On that first day, I got dropped off at the Port Authority and I arrived at the bus station in Spring Valley after 11 p.m. My Uncle Frank met me, thank God, because there were few cars at that time of night to pick me up hitchhiking. I would have had to walk the whole way.

The next morning, I rose at 5 a.m., and Uncle Frank, who always went to work early, dropped me back at Exit 14. I hitchhiked back to New Paltz in time to make it to my classes. This routine would happen twice a week, and Uncle Frank was heroic. To top it off, all my weekend games with Gottschee were in the city, so I had to make this commute on weekends as well. All good because a little traveling was not going to hamper my quest for the McGuire Cup.

My Gottschee journey would take me through the Port Authority countless times, and that ritual was not without incident. One hot summer afternoon, I was on my way home from a game at the Met Oval. Coach Petschauer had dropped me at the Port Authority bus station. I was exhausted, and I did not have time to shower off the dirt. Dust stuck in my hair and even coated my eyelids. I bought my ticket to Spring Valley and had nearly an hour to kill. I took a seat and put my soccer bag under my legs and closed my eyes. I had my hand on my bag strap and my feet on top of the bag. In the Port Authority, a wallet could disappear out of your pocket like a magic trick in Las Vegas.

I had nearly dozed off when I heard, "Hello, where are you going today?" I was a little startled, and I looked up at this middle-aged man sitting next to me. There were plenty of open seats, so why was this dude right next to me? I told him I was going upstate. He asked where, and I said Rockland County. He asked where in Rockland County. I asked where he was going, and he said he lived in the city. I thought, *This is getting weird.* I told him I was thirsty and I was going to get a Coke. Then I got up and walked to a restaurant and got in line. As I was paying, I noticed this same guy in line about two people behind me. It was creepy, but I thought maybe it's a coincidence. After I paid, I hurried out and walked quickly through the terminal, up an escalator and toward the other side of the building. I stood for a few minutes, drinking my Coke. I did not see the guy and I thought it was all in my imagination.

I started walking toward where my bus would be. I took a seat on the platform and started dozing off again. This time I heard, "You look very tired; my place is not far from here. Would you like to take a nap?" I opened my eyes and saw the guy sitting next to me, plenty of open seats around us. Now I was scared and pissed. I jumped up and said loudly, "Why are you following me? I am not coming back to your house. Now stop following me." Now I had everyone's attention. The guy stood and said, "You misunderstood me," and he walked quickly away. A few minutes later, the bus pulled up. I usually sat in the back, but this time I sat up front by the driver. The minute he shut the door I fell asleep.

Hitchhiking could be even creepier and more dangerous than public transportation. Many of my friends who hitchhiked had stories that were mostly about weird men. Here is one of my memorable hitchhiking adventures: I was hitchhiking to Clarkstown Junior High, standing near the corner of Pascack Road and Eckerson Road, and I got an early ride. I ran up and jumped in the front of this big sports car. I am dressed in my soccer shorts, and I have my soccer bag with me. I said something like, "Thanks a lot for your help."

The guy asked, "Where are you heading?"

I said, "To Clarkstown Junior High."

He said, "Oh fantastic, I am going right by there; I can take you all the way."

It usually takes at least two rides, sometimes three, and a lot of walking to get to Clarkstown Junior High. In fact, this was the only time my first ride took me all the way from my starting point to the school. As I settled into the ride, we swapped the usual small talk. The driver, an older guy, looked normal. He asked if I had a girlfriend. I thought maybe he was making conversation. My answer was, "Not really."

Then he asked, "Do you like girls?" Okay, now my caution lights were on.

I said, "Sure, I like girls."

With a creepy smile he said, "Have a look in the glove compartment, right there in front of you."

I opened the compartment and there was a stack of porn magazines, weird but nothing I had not seen before. Then I realized that some of the magazines had nude men on the covers. At this point, I knew this guy was not only weird but trouble. Right about then we were slowing up for a traffic light on the corner of Germonds Road and Route 304.

I said, "Hey I got to get out here."

He said, "But the school is just up the road and I'm going right past it." As the car eased to a stop, I opened the door and got out. The guy rolled down the window and tried to talk me back into the car. I started to jog. It was only a half-mile from that intersection, and it would not be my first run from there. Another bizarre experience that makes you a survivor. Whatever doesn't kill you makes you stronger, I guess.

My new team still had a few league games left on the German American League schedule. That would give us time to settle on a revamped lineup and get a few games under our belt before we would play our first state cup game. Days later, I was about to play my first game in a Gottschee uniform. We were playing at the Metro and Coach Petschauer was giving us a few final words. I heard, "Captains, captains." It was the referee summoning the team captains to do the coin toss and pick sides. My reflex was to jog out to meet the referee and the opposing captains. Then I caught myself as Gary Kresse and Gustavo Cerri made their way out.

Gary and Gustavo were tremendous captains who always put the team before themselves. Gustavo spoke Spanish, and not only did we have a few players who spoke only Spanish; that went for some referees as well. Gary was big and soft-spoken, and he had a way of uniting the diverse cultures among the group. Still, this was an odd moment for me. I had been captain of every team I had played on, dating to when Mr. Sautner gave me the armband for the boys' team. I committed to supporting Gary and Gustavo and do all I could to lead us forward.

I also learned that the Gottschee club ran like a Swiss watch. Every detail was carefully planned, all masterminded by Mr. Bohem. The club had a youth pyramid, the junior U19 team at the top. Most youth clubs look at their teams one year at a time, based on the soccer calendar that runs from late August to early June. Not Gottschee. They planned for players and teams years in advance. All of their youth teams worked together; the better players from the younger teams would train up and guest-play at the higher levels. The team I had just joined was no random collection; it was years in the making.

On our roster, we had a few really young players. Earhart Kapp was at least three years younger than me, but tough beyond words. I will never forget one game at the Met Oval. Earhart went in for a tackle with this huge guy. They both hit the ground and Earhart sprang up, blood dripping off his face. I ran over. He had a huge gash on the side of his nose. He wiped his face, looked at the blood on his hand, and said, "Wow, that is a lot of blood."

I thought he would come off, but then he grabbed a handful of sandy dirt and pressed it to his face. After a few seconds, he leaned into me and asked if the bleeding had stopped. My face was blank; I said nothing. He smiled and said, "Good to go; let's get these guys." Years later, Earhart starred at UConn and played for the New York Cosmos and the U.S. National Team.

The club also had communication down cold. Most of it was face to face. Much of it took place at the clubhouse, known as Gottscheer Hall in Ridgewood, Queens, where we would gather two hours before our games. Being late at Gottschee? There was no such thing. We would get dressed in the locker room at the club and then head together to the games, whether we played at the Met Oval or elsewhere in the city.

Back then, all teams owned the uniforms. Our junior team guys would come into the locker room and find each uniform laid out on the seats in front of each locker. After each game, we would return to the clubhouse and toss the uniforms in a pile. A coach or a team mom would collect them and wash them. When we returned for our next game, our uniforms had that clean scent. You would often get the shirt with the number of your position, say, the center forward would get #9, and the goalkeeper always had #1. Everyone wanted #10, Pelé's number. And today everybody still wants #10, Messi's number.

After having one game and a full week of training sessions behind me, I was feeling better about my decision. For one, we had had nearly perfect attendance. Granted, these guys went to St. Francis College, Columbia University, LIU, and other nearby schools, so it was much easier for them to make training. No wonder they had won the Junior League eight straight years, and to date have won the New York State Cup a record 15 times. They also had groomed many players into pros, and I was confident that Gottschee could help me get there.

How did Gottschee come to be? The club was formed in 1951 when Austrian immigrants who had settled in the Ridgewood and Glendale sections of Queens sought to recreate the spirit of their homeland. Many Americans will struggle to understand this because they have never picked up a newspaper printed in a foreign language. They don't have to go to a certain neighborhood to find a newspaper they can read, or buy a car in a different community because they knew a dealer there spoke their native language.

Other immigrants, whether they spoke Yugoslavian, German, Hungarian, or Greek, created ethnic strongholds within neighborhoods across New York City and the U.S. Gottscheer Hall was much more than a place where soccer players went to take showers and drink beer. It was where you made friends with your compatriots, dined, and socialized. If you wanted food from back home, they had the best. This is where people went to Christmas parties and celebrated New Year's. Often, your sons and daughters would get married at your clubhouse. It was a safe haven in big, crazy New York City. This is a world apart for the average American, who is surrounded by millions of people who speak the same language, eat the same foods, and watch the NFL and the NBA together.

Just as Gottschee has their clubhouse and their tight-knit community in Ridgewood, the New York Greek Americans have their clubhouse in Astoria, Queens, which has one of the largest populations of Greeks outside of Greece. The Brooklyn Italians have their clubhouse in the middle of that borough. The New York HOTA Bavarian Soccer Club has a wonderful clubhouse overlooking two beautiful soccer fields in Franklin Square out in Nassau County. Across the Hudson River, the Kearny Scots play in the Gunnell Oval in Kearny, New Jersey. These rivalries exist not only in and around New York City, but in other urban areas across the country.

CHAPTER THIRTY-NINE

SOCCER RIVALRIES: WHERE IT ALL BEGAN

Soccer rivalries run deep around the world. **Rivalry by Religion**, for example. In Glasgow, Scotland, the two big football clubs are founded on the religious divide between Catholicism and Protestantism. Traditionally, Rangers' supporters are Protestant, while Celtic fans support the Catholic Church. Soccer in Glasgow has become a public stage for sectarianism, the religious bigotry that has plagued Scotland for hundreds of years. Some of the worst riots in sporting history have taken place there. Sadly, this is only one of many examples of Rivalry by Religion that play out around the world.

Rivalry by Economics. In Buenos Aires, Argentina, a fierce rivalry exists between two first-division soccer teams. River Plate and Boca Juniors reflect economic and class division. Because of its location in a working-class neighborhood, the Boca Juniors are known as the "people's club." River Plate, because of their upper-class support base, are known as Los Millonarios, or the millionaires. This is but one of many examples of Rivalry by Economics.

Rivalry by Race: Lima, Peru, is home to one of the world's oldest football derbies between Alianza Lima and Universitario El Clásico Peruano (the Peruvian Classic). For decades, Alianza Lima, with roots in a working-class neighborhood, was a symbol of prestige for Black people in Peru. Universitario, founded by a group of university students, produced many white players. Therefore, this rivalry is known as "Negros contra Blancos." It is one of many such rivalries around the world.

As an aside, Alianza Lima has developed many exceptional Black players. One is my former teammate with the Fort Lauderdale Sun, Teófilo "El Nene" Cubillas. Nene was among the best South American players ever and one of the top performers in the history of the World Cup. *Sports Illustrated* included him in the ideal eleven of the past 50 years of South American footballers, along with Pelé, Maradona, Garrincha, and other continental legends. One of my greatest thrills was playing in Nene's farewell game in 1986, when his club team, Alianza Lima, played against Team Rest of The World. Nene asked me to play, not because I was a world all-star, but because we had become good friends playing together in U.S. He thought that people around the world should know Americans can play this game. This was a huge honor and one of my most memorable experiences. Thank you, Nene; I love you, brother.

CHAPTER FORTY

LET THE STATE CUP BEGIN

The early rounds of the 1975 State Cup were good tune-ups for my Gottschee team. We eased through group play and into the semi-finals of the southern New York region. We were about to meet our first real test against New York Eintracht, our biggest rival. This matchup always brought epic clashes on the field and bitter exchanges between fans. This would be a home game for both teams, since we both played our home matches at the Metropolitan Oval.

Coach Petschauer had told us that all parents had to be at the pregame meeting at Gothscheer Hall. When I told him that my mom would not be able to get off work, he gave me a smile. "Tommy," he said, "we're not worried about your mother running onto the field after the referee, or fighting with the other parents and spectators." People knew that I had grown up in a gringo household far removed from the fire and fury of ethnic soccer. Yet I fit in like a missing piece to a puzzle, and not just because I could play. People saw that I had a genuine passion for the game. My friends and team-mates knew that I loved this sport as much as anyone. That is why I was accepted in every community: European, Hispanic, or Haitian. I loved them all.

It was game day and we were laced up and ready to go. At our team meeting, Coach stressed the need to show discipline and civility. I knew there was animosity between the teams, but I had nothing against Eintracht. In fact, I had some pals on that team, like Sepp Gantenhammer, Vlado Sergovich, and one of my best friends, Nicky Megaloudis. Once the whistle blew, I would play hard and fair like I always did.

It was a fast and physical battle, the marking tight and the chances few. The game was scoreless at halftime and stayed that way through regulation and two 10-minute extra times. When the second extra time ended, players hugged their teammates and opponents and then we went to penalty kicks. I sent the first one low into the netting on my right side, my go-to spot. We made all five of our kicks. Eintracht missed their last kick, and the Gottschee community went crazy. We were through to the southern New York State Cup final, one step closer to making the McGuire Cup national finals.

There was just one hitch. My nightmare scenario had played out. That's right: Gottschee would play Clarkstown SC. When Coach Rottenbucher had agreed to let me go to another club, the one caveat was that I could not play against Clarkstown. At the time I had thought, *What are the odds of that?* We shook on it and that was it. Back then I thought Coach had taken this stance because he didn't want me on the other side of the ball. But Coach loved me like one of his own kids, and I loved him like he was my dad. Now I believed he asked for that caveat because he knew the game would be highly emotional, maybe even dangerous. He was protecting me.

The week before that game, my apartment in New Paltz simmered with tension. Ricky went from not talking to me to not looking at me. My friendships with all my former Clarkstown teammates had been strained. Finally, game day arrived, and Clarkstown had to come to the Metropolitan Oval. The word was out: Gottschee versus Clarkstown would be good soccer. When people in the ethnic neighborhoods heard "good soccer," they would show up, rain or shine. Ethnic newspapers like the German Stock and the Greek Paper would have reporters on site.

When I arrived at Gottscheer Hall my uniform was not laid out, and I went straight to Coach Petschauer. He told me he knew that I had agreed with Mr. Rottenbucher to not play against Clarkstown. Mr. Petschauer had told Rottenbucher that he would not let me play. He said, "Tommy, you must know that when I give my word and when our club gives its word, we always keep that word."

I told him I had no intention of going back on my word to Coach Rottenbucher. What I did want to do was wear my Gottschee uniform to show my teammates I was all-in for them. Truth is, I had more at stake than any of the guys who would play that day. I had walked away from people I loved and cast my lot with a new team. I had no regrets. Sometimes, you have to stand alone. Sometimes, you must make hard sacrifices. To lead others, you must first lead yourself.

The game started with both teams a bit tense. In a single-elimination tournament, there is no room for error. Guys get conservative and don't take chances they might otherwise take. Mid-way through the first half, Gottschee went ahead 1–0, firing up the 1,000-plus fans. The half ended 1–0. When the second half started, my former teammates became more physical. At one point, Gottschee wingback Helmut Gspurning was attacking up the north flank near the railroad tracks side of the field. Eddy St. Cloud bodychecked

Helmut, his ribs slamming into the iron bar that separated the field from the stands. Helmut's feet flew over his head and he landed on the other side of the bar in front of the bleachers.

The referee blew a foul but showed no card, and now the game took on a combustible air. Up until then, I had sat quietly. Now I was off the bench, screaming. Our guys could dish it hard. At every clash on the ball, we gave as good as we got. But as the second half elapsed, it was fitness, not physicality, that made the difference. Clarkstown seemed to tire, while the Gottschee boys still had plenty of spring. That was all part of the Gottschee plan. During long, hard training sessions, with balls at our feet we would run laps in a line around the park. Coach Bobby would ride a bicycle alongside us, screaming, "Next," a cue to the player at the back to sprint to the front. Now came the dividend. We had taken over midfield, and we were in control. With 25 minutes left, Gustavo scored to make it 2–0.

In the waning moments, our captain Gary Kresse fired in a third goal, lighting up the Oval. As Gary jogged back toward midfield, he gave us a little wave and a smile. Gerard Guilliod, who had been covering Gary, was jogging up behind him. As Gerard got closer, he started to speed up. When he drew up to Gary, he wrapped his left arm around Gary's neck and swung his right fist into his face. Gary staggered, blood pouring out of his broken nose.

The referee was documenting the goal and missed the punch. When he heard the screams from fans, he ran out to Gary. Gerard was long gone. The closest Clarkstown player was Coach Rottenbucher's son, Frankie Jr., the gentle giant, his head hung in disbelief. When the referee saw Gary's nose, he turned around and gave Frankie the first and only red card of his life.

At this point fans were streaming onto the field from all sides. Coach Rottenbucher was in the ref's face, complaining that he carded the wrong player. The match was nearly over and Gottschee had a safe lead, so the ref blew the final whistle and bolted out. Coach Rottenbucher knew he had to get his team out. He and his players, about half of them Haitian, hustled toward the east end of the stadium. As they climbed the railroad ties toward their van, you could hear a chant of "N*****s, go home; N*****s, go home," at first soft but growing louder. Thankfully, my former teammates made it to Coach's van and got back to Rockland unharmed.

To that point, this was the most emotional game of my career, and I didn't even play in it. I was hoping that time would heal the wounds that my decision had opened among the guys in my Clarkstown fraternity. Eventually, time was my ally. To this day we all keep in touch and we love each other like we did fifty years ago. We even get together once a year to celebrate Coach Rottenbucher's life and give an award in his name.

CHAPTER FORTY-ONE

THE NEW YORK STATE CUP FINAL, SOUTH VS. WEST

The southern New York State Cup was now ours. Our next opponent would be from Penfield, a suburb of Rochester in western New York. The game would be played in the Metropolitan Oval, or the Met Oval, as locals call it. Home field is always an advantage, but when a team from the sticks plays at the Met Oval for the first time, it is an unnerving experience. First, no one can get to the stadium on their first visit without getting lost, not even in today's world with GPS. The one-way streets could confuse a bloodhound tracking a rabbit. Even when you're at the front gate, you cannot convince yourself there is a stadium behind that gate. When you finally reach the stadium, you realize there is no parking, so you drop the team off. If you are lucky to find a spot anywhere near the stadium, you cannot find your way back to the field. As longtime soccer leader Jim Vogt once said, when a team enters the Met Oval for the first time and you see the look on their faces, that is called the "you're already losing, 1–0" look.

The Met Oval was built in 1925 by German and Hungarian immigrants. It is a full-sized, FIFA field squeezed into a residential neighborhood in Maspeth, Queens. When you first enter, you think, *How the hell did they put this here; it is part of some lost city?* Here's what it looked like in 1975. On the west side of the stadium, behind one goal line stood a 30-foot-high chain link fence. The fence stood about 10 feet beyond the endline. In the fence was a small door leading out to the street, where balls often flew. If the door was locked, as it often was, there was a hole in the fence that a kid or a fit adult could squeeze through so they could retrieve the ball.

To this day railroad tracks border the northern sideline of the field. That would be the Long Island Railroad—one of the busiest commuter lines. A brick wall runs between the field and the railroad tracks. Many balls have cleared that wall and been lost to the railroad grounds. Bleachers, five or six rows high, sit in front of the wall, stretching corner flag to corner flag. Across the field on the south sideline, the stadium wall was the only thing between the field and a row of neighborhood homes. This sideline also had bleachers three or four rows high. A roof ran from penalty area to penalty area.

On the east side of the stadium was the main entrance. When you entered here, you could not tell there was a stadium until you walked through a big gate that looked like an entrance to a parking lot. Then you would reach the door, where on most days someone would collect a fee.

Once you pass through that door and stand atop the grandstand facing west, there is a magnificent view of midtown Manhattan, including the Empire State Building and the Chrysler Building. This is one of the city's most dramatic views, especially at night. The field itself is almost hiding in plain sight. Once you enter and are on top of the hill, you can look down on the field from behind the closest goal. From corner flag to corner flag, the hill has been shaped in tiers that are reinforced with railroad ties. This section has the feel of the back of a European stadium where fans stand behind the goals. To your right, stairs lead you down to the field. At the bottom of the stairs, you can see the facilities.

The clubhouse, really a cinderblock shack, held two small locker rooms. It also had a men's room with a piss pot that ran along an entire wall. There was a little room with a toilet in case someone had to go bad, I mean bad. You never had to ask where the restrooms were because you could smell them as you walked down the stairs to enter the stadium at the field level. I think there was a ladies' room there somewhere. Women did not play soccer at that time, so only a few ladies or moms with their kids might need a restroom. The shack also held a snack bar, serving knockwurst and Bratwurst. At one point they even sold beer, and on a frosty winter day you could get a German Glühwein, like back in the old country.

Once first-time visitors arrived at field level, two things stood out. The first was an iron fence that stood about four feet back from the out-of-bounds lines. It circled the entire field and was more of a boundary than a fence. It was four feet high and made with a four-inch pipe. It kept the spectators away from the field and was good to lean on when you were watching a game. The second thing that catches your eye is the absence of grass. The field was dirt. On dry summer days, the groundskeeper "Pop" had to water the dirt before games and at halftime, especially if it was windy. Otherwise, you'd think you were playing in a dust storm in the Sahara Desert.

Now it was an hour before the kickoff on a wonderful spring day. We were juggling the ball in a team circle, waiting for the game being played before us to reach halftime so we could kick it around on the field. Then we saw a team entering the stadium at the top of the grandstand. We knew it was our opponent because we had never seen those uniforms before, and the New York City soccer community was like a cult. We knew all the uniforms.

When game time arrived, The Met Oval had filled up. Our foes were big and physical, but could not match us on the ball. Ricky Kren scored before the break, and then we dominated the second half. Our Romanian wonder Sima made several brilliant runs down the right side and scored twice. Johnny Roros, our Greek defender, and our Italian rock Sal Bommarito stood out in the back. The game ended 3–0 and we were moving on to the semifinal of the Eastern Region, the next stop on our road to the McGuire Cup.

The Historical Metropolitan Oval - Maspeth, Queens NYC

CHAPTER FORTY-TWO

THE REGION CUP SEMIFINAL, CONNECTICUT

Our next opponent was Westport from Connecticut. As usual, Coach Petschauer had a detailed plan. Even for road games, we would hold our team meeting at Gottscheer Hall. Coach wanted no surprises. He liked us to leave early for games outside the city, especially if we had not played there before. This was a challenge for me. If I had to travel from Rockland into Queens and then to Westport, that was a big ask. To my delight, Gary Kresse invited me to stay overnight at his house in Ridgewood in Queens. I would get a good night's sleep, travel with the team, and not have crazy travel before the game. Gary was a talented player, a great leader, and an even better person. His dad made every big game. His mom treated me like family and she was a wonderful cook. As always, the Gottschee plan was working like a Swiss watch.

Westport had a big, beautiful field, the grass just the right height. It was a big change from playing on dirt, rocks, and glass in New York City, and it took us a while to get used to the surface. Man for man, we were more technical and we had a higher collective soccer IQ. Late in the half we carried play but we went to halftime in a scoreless draw.

Early in the second half, Ricky Kren put us ahead 1–0. With 10 minutes left, they tied it up. Our goalkeeper quickly retrieved the ball from the net and we rushed it up to midfield for kick-off. When you are the better team, the last thing you want is to go to penalties. We believed in each other; no one put his head down. We were pressuring high, and even our keeper had roamed out of his penalty area.

With five minutes left, I got the ball twenty-five yards out near the arc. I struck it pure. It sailed past the keeper's outstretched arms and punched the net just under the bar. My brothers piled on top of me. We were one step closer and more confident than ever.

CHAPTER FORTY-THREE

THE REGION CUP FINAL, MARYLAND

We were now set to play St. Elizabeth SC of Baltimore for the Eastern Region championship. This game would be played in Baltimore. St. Elizabeth would be the toughest team we had faced all year. They had won the McGuire Cup just two years prior in 1973. We knew little about them, but it was no secret that they had an outstanding scorer in John "Sonny" Askew. He was gifted on the ball and dangerous anywhere near goal.

The night before, I headed to Gary's house for an Austrian-Bavarian dinner. Very early the next morning, we met at Gottscheer Hall. We had chartered a bus for the four-hour ride down Route 95. We arrived two hours before kickoff. The field sat in the middle of a large park. There was only one small bleacher, and by kickoff, the fans had ringed the entire field, five or six deep. I had never played before a crowd that was so big, so close, and so hostile. I had always thought the iron fence that ran around the Met Oval was a little odd. Now, I could see why that fence made sense.

Every time the ball went over the sideline, fans would have to step back to make room for the guy throwing it in. Each time I jogged out to take a corner, a spectator tried to rattle me, usually in another language. I didn't know what was said but I knew it wasn't good. Still, I loved the smack talk. The crowd had energy and I was feeding off it.

From the start this was a tactical, technical battle, no kick-and-run. Guys clashed over 50-50 balls like it was life or death. Neither team could forge a good chance until late in the first half when Helmut made a long run and was taken down inches outside the penalty area. I stepped up as their keeper scrambled to set the wall. The referee set the ball and I asked for my ten yards. As he walked them off, I calculated where to place my shot. When I take free kicks, I size up my options. Once I decide, I turn everything off. It's like turning down the music on the radio. I take one last look at my target and visualize the shot going in. From that moment, I never take my eye off the ball. The referee blew his whistle. I took my approach and lashed a bolt past the diving keeper and into the upper corner at the far post.

As my brothers ran to me to celebrate, most fans had gone quiet. A few applauded my goal. The half ended with us up, 1–0. We could now hold the ball, no need to take risks. They would have to come at us. As the second half rolled out, Gustavo and I kept close tabs on Sonny Askew. Time was ticking down, and I could hear our coaches yelling to the referee to blow the final whistle. With less than a minute left, Gary Kresse smashed home a rocket to settle it. We were Eastern Region champions. Next stop, Milwaukee.

CHAPTER FORTY-FOUR

THE TRUE NATIONAL CHAMPIONSHIP, MCGUIRE CUP FINAL

I boarded the second flight of my life, and after we landed in Milwaukee, we rode a charter bus to a hotel near the Bavarian Soccer Stadium. We arrived a day early so we could acclimate and train on the field. Our opponent would be Livermore of California. Livermore sits in a valley framed by vineyards, ranches, and farmland. This kind of matchup—teams from totally different worlds—is what I love about soccer. In the other semifinal, Imo's Pizza of St. Louis would face the Dallas Pirate Club.

The Bavarian club had lots of land and beautiful fields. Their clubhouse was much like Gottscheer Hall, and the food was great as well. I was learning more and more about what a small but connected world the ethnic soccer community was. I also learned that Bob Gansler was a main figure and a significant part of the identity of the Bavarian Soccer Club. Coach Gansler had been one of the coaches from the coaching school the prior summer at Hartwick, the guy who played center back with Coach Vizvary. In the future, my path would cross many times with Coach Gansler. I always had profound respect for him. He would eventually coach the U.S. National team in the 1990 World Cup.

Let the games begin. In the first half, we outplayed Livermore, but at the break we trailed 1–0. Early in the second half, one of our young players, Ricky Kren, spotted their keeper off his line. Ricky floated a ball beyond the keeper's reach and under the bar. Minutes later, Ricky struck again, and that one proved to be the winner. This game was vintage Ricky. This blonde-haired, blue-eyed kid was not overly fast, strong, or technical. What my boy could do was score goals. Most prolific scorers have a defining attribute; some are deadly shooters, others excel in the air. Ricky had something else, some kind of extra-sensory perception. He seemed to know where the ball would go next. He also knew where the keeper was. When he prepared to shoot, he thought first about location, second about how hard to hit it. He was what every team needs: a finisher.

We were on our way to the McGuire Cup final. On the other side of the bracket, Imo's Pizza of St. Louis drubbed the Dallas Pirate Club, 3–0.

CHAPTER FORTY-FIVE

JUNE 15TH, 1975 – A SPECIAL DAY FOR SOCCER IN THE U.S.

The McGuire Cup would be a huge event, but not the biggest soccer event of the day.

Back home in New York City, Pelé would play his first game for the New York Cosmos. He had come out of retirement and signed a two-and-a half-year $7 million deal, making him the highest paid athlete in the world at that time. Yes, at the same time we would kick off in Milwaukee, Pelé would play his first game as a Cosmo. The game would be played in the Randall's Island stadium, where my mother took me to see him play five years earlier.

Pelé and the Cosmos would play an exhibition match against the Dallas Tornado with Kyle Rote Jr., the American superstar. Some 21,278 fans would pack the stadium. Ten million Americans watched CBS' live broadcast, which was a record American TV audience for a soccer game. The game aired in 20 countries and drew 300 journalists from across the world.

Pelé brought instant credibility for the Cosmos and the league. Home attendance tripled over the second half of the season, when Pelé was there. Our Gottschee team had an alumnus on the Cosmos, Joey Fink. I had another personal connection to the Cosmos, John Kerr Sr. I had befriended John a few summers prior when he was my coach at Cosmos soccer camp. I wondered, could Joey or Johnny get me back into the Cosmos locker room, so I could meet the King?

CHAPTER FORTY-SIX

MCGUIRE CUP FINAL: THE POT OF GOLD

Blau Weiss Gottschee versus Imo's Pizza for the McGuire Cup, at the Bavarian Soccer Stadium in Milwaukee. Kickoff at 3 p.m., Central Time. Both teams were staying at the same hotel. The night before the final, as we arrived back from our team dinner, some players from the Imo's Pizza team were hanging out in the lobby. My friends and former teammates from the U.S. Junior National Team, Ty Keough and Don Aubuchon, were among the group. I had first met them at the Oneonta '74 tournament last summer. We swapped friendly banter and wished each other good luck. In soccer, an unwritten code holds that, no matter how big the game, before and after you can still be friends. Over my life, my opponents have become some of my best friends. Soccer is remarkable in that way.

In soccer, finals are often dull because both teams play like they are trying not to lose rather than to win. Not this game, this was a barnburner from the opening tap, good chances created at both ends, excellent goalkeeping. I was in that zone. I scored our first goal on a free kick from thirty yards out, a sizzler right in the upper

90. It was the kind of goal that causes opponents to think, *We can't foul in our third of the field.* Our second goal came when I curled in a corner kick. We played two 45-minute halves and two 10-minute overtimes before the game ended in a 2–2 tie. When the second overtime ended, we all dropped to the turf in exhaustion. Penalty kicks awaited.

The hardest pill to swallow in soccer is when two teams go full-throttle for 110 minutes, only to have to decide it on penalties. We won the flip and I buried our first shot in the corner. Ty Keough answered with a goal, and we were knotted at 1–1. Next up for us was Ricky Kren. His shot veered wide left and he sank to his knees. I jogged over and told him we were still in it. Next up for Imo's was Chris Cacciatore. He fired at the left corner, and our keeper Dragon dove and parried the shot. We flipped from sad to ecstatic. Gary Kresse stepped up. He fired toward his left post but Brcic lunged and batted it away. It was still 1–1, but Imo's had one shot left. Up stepped Don Aubuchon, probably the cockiest kid I ever met on a field. Don blasted the ball toward the upper-right corner. Dragon guessed correctly but could get only a finger on the ball as it punched the corner.

I swept away a few tears. We shook hands with our opponents and then we embraced as teammates. At moments like this, there is a sense of kinship known only to teammates who have shared a rugged, soulful journey. It is a feeling that stays with you for the rest of your life.

Both keepers in that game went on to professional careers. Our keeper, Dragon Radovich, a Croatian-American kid, played for three NASL teams. Our rival, David Brcic, played for the New York Cosmos for eight years and for the U.S. National Team. Several field players also turned pro.

As I boarded the plane in Milwaukee, I asked myself, *Did I work my hardest and sacrifice everything for it?* I believed I could answer yes. Now, on to my next goal, to become a pro and be the best player in the world.

Blau Weiss Gottschee U19 McGuire Cup runners up 1975

Top L to R Bill Easteadt, Reinhold Shaukat, Richard Kren, Kenny Fisher, Sal Bommarito, Edie Mausser, Gerhard Weber, Tommy Mulroy, Sima Stancu, Gary Kresse, Coach Martin Petschauer

Bottom L to R Rick Derella, Helmut Gspurning, Frank Lachner, Dragan Radovic, Erhardt Kapp, John Sautner, Gustoavo Cerri, Willy Becker, Emil Rudic

CHAPTER FORTY-SEVEN

MY FIRST NATIONAL COACHING LICENSE

Upon my return from Milwaukee, I had a break in my soccer schedule. My next big event was the Amsterdam 700 International tournament, being held in Holland to celebrate the 700th birthday of the city of Amsterdam. I would not be leaving until mid-August. After the grueling schedule I had just endured, you might think I would want to hit the beach. Not me. I could not get enough of the round ball.

Training on my own was fine, but where would I get my competitive fix? Club ball was on hiatus. The New York State and German American League All-Star teams did little training over the summer. I was too old to go to camp. I even tried to find games on TV but mostly struck out.

While pacing in the house one afternoon, I saw a brochure that I had picked up in Coach Viz's office. It promoted coaching license courses being held that summer by the U.S. Soccer Federation. This was the same coaching school that had taken place at Hartwick last summer when I was at the youth national training camp. I scanned the list of courses. The only one I could get to would be held at St. Andrews School in Delaware. This was about 170 miles away, a three-hour car ride, if you had a car. Getting there would be the first hurdle, though I knew I could hitchhike. The next obstacle was how to pay for the course. This weeklong camp included room and board at a ritzy private school. The camp would give me an opportunity to earn a USSF National C license. The cost: $295. Today that fee looks laughably low. At the time, $295 wasn't laughable to me. That was roughly three or four weeks of my mother's salary.

When I told my mom about my interest in the camp, I struggled to define the value of a USSF National Coaching license. At that time almost no one knew about these licenses. Only members of the ethnic soccer cults knew about them. I sold the camp as educational. Like everything else that I needed in life, Mom found a way to make it happen. Whether she would walk to work rather than take a cab, or negotiate an advance from her boss, or put a portion on her credit card, Mom always came through. If I needed it, I got it. She was the best, and in my life, I am constantly reminded of her generosity and love.

People couldn't understand why I chose to pursue my first USSF coaching license at age 18. My friends asked, "You're a player, not a coach, why do you need a coaching license?" I would reply that learning to coach helped to satisfy my appetite for the game. The further I got into my playing career, the more I saw the benefit of seeing the game from a coach's perspective. The more you know, the better you can play. I learned that early in my soccer life.

The first leg of my journey to Delaware was a bus ride from Spring Valley to the Port Authority in Manhattan, a little more than an hour's trip. From there, I took a bus to Wilmington, which ate about four hours. In Wilmington, I found my way to Delaware

Route 13. At that point I was about a 30-minute car ride from the school. Relying on my thumb, I figured it would take between one and two hours. I got my first ride pretty fast, and the guy took me more than halfway before he dropped me off.

Five minutes later, my thumb out, a state trooper hit his lights and siren and pulled over on the shoulder in front of me. A big guy with a big hat stepped out. I started to walk toward him, but he told me to stay where I was. As he approached, he said in a stern voice, "It's illegal to hitchhike on Route 13." I said that I was sorry, I didn't know, and I wasn't from around there. Now picture this: I am wearing tight bell-bottom jeans, and my long hair is in a mullet. It is the '70s, a time known for sex, drugs, and rock and roll. Now sex and rock and roll weren't illegal, but drugs were, and sure enough, Big Hat asked if he could check my bag. I smiled and said sure. He asked where I was headed. I told him and asked if I was far away. He said I wasn't close, maybe 20 minutes up the road. "What are you doing at St. Andrews School?" he asked.

I tried to tell him about the camp and the license, confused the hell out of him, I'm sure. Once he checked my bag, he knew that I was an athlete, not a druggie. He told me to get in his car and he drove me to the station. Another trooper gave me a ride to the school. I remember getting out in front of the gym where guys were registering for the course. I think everybody was wondering, *Who the hell is this kid and why is he getting an escort from a state trooper?*

The course began on a Sunday evening. During orientation that night, the meeting was kicked off by Walter Chyzowych, who would become the guru of soccer education in our country. He introduced the national coaching staff, many of whom I recognized from the prior summer at Hartwick, where they took a course to become national instructors. As Walter described what we would do to earn the coaching licenses, I became more excited. At that time, they held camps for all three USSF National Coaching licenses at the same time and site. That means "A," "B," or "C" licenses would be given to whoever earned them that week.

As Coach Chyzowych laid out his expectations, I was surprised to learn that everyone would be graded on their ability to play. I thought, *Let's go, I can't wait to get on the field.* Then I looked around. There was not a woman in the room. Most of these guys were older men, and in many cases not so physically fit. In fact, I was sure I was by far the youngest person in the room and certainly the only teenager.

Coach Chyzowych said that in the morning everyone would take a Cooper test as their first field session. I knew what that was; you would run for 12 minutes and were expected to cover at least two miles. It was a challenge, even if you were fit. Coach Bill Muse spoke next, outlining the classroom sessions. He told us that we would be graded on an on-field coaching test, as well as on a written test. I thought, *Oh shit, not a written test.* I knew I could absorb everything they could throw at me, but writing it down gave me fits.

A hot sun beat down the next morning as we gathered for the Cooper test. Most of the guys in my group finished the two miles, but none in under 12 minutes. A few never finished. My sense is the camp leaders did not expect everyone to hit two miles, or even run for 12 minutes. Rather, I thought this was more about mental toughness, a way to determine who was serious about committing to the course. After lunch, we had a classroom session and then went back on the field. I loved the field sessions. They would ask for volunteers to demonstrate what they were teaching. Heading or chipping or shielding, I volunteered for everything.

It was at this camp where I began to realize that I learned much better when I was physically engaged. In one classroom session, I remember the instructor saying that sometimes even the best players don't quite get it when it's on the board. But when they have a ball at their feet, it all becomes clear. Wow, I felt like I finally had a teacher who understood how I absorbed information. That mentor was describing exactly how I learned. After dinner, we had another classroom session and then hit the field. By the time we went to our rooms to turn in, I thought, *Wow, I'm super tired and I am 18, and I came here pretty fit. These old and not-so-fit guys must be hurting.*

The next morning, there were many empty seats in our first classroom session. I thought that some of the guys must have slept in. I found out later that they hadn't slept in and they weren't injured or sick. After experiencing one demanding day, they packed their bags and left in the middle of the night. As these courses evolved over the years, leaders realized that physical performance was not crucial to being an effective coach. Back then they did not even allow a candidate to wear a hat while coaching. After many coaches got skin cancer, coaches were allowed to wear hats during their testing and other on-field sessions.

Bill Killen was the main instructor of my group. He made several points that stuck with me, among them: *No one has all the answers. You can learn as much from the coach next to you as you can from this course. To be a good coach, you must always be a student of the game.* The more experienced I became, the more I realized how true this is. You can never stop learning.

The U.S. Soccer Federation courses focused on the four basic pillars of soccer: technical, tactical, physical, and psychological. In one session, we heard from Dr. John McKeon of East Stroudsburg State University, who spoke on sports psychology and its effect on young players. To this day, I share his insights about the impact a coach can have on a young child's self-esteem. He told us that how a player feels about himself when leaving a training session could affect them in ways you might never realize. That sense of self spills over into every facet of their lives. Always find a way to be positive!

Let me come back to Killen's comment about learning from other coaches. What better way to be a student of the game than to learn from others on the same journey? Over my career, I played for many coaches and I attended many coaching schools run by legendary coaches. Today I realize how fortunate I was to learn and grow while collaborating with so many great players and coaches. People like Horst Bertl, a German who played in 174 Bundesliga games and was a highly accomplished developer of young talent. Schellas Hyndman coached at Southern Methodist University, where he became one of the most successful college soccer coaches in history. Bob Bradley, who played and then coached at Princeton University, was head coach of the U.S. Men's National Team and later became the first American to coach in the Premiership at Swansea City.

Here are a few coaching stories I think are worth sharing. It was January 1978 and I was attending the NSCAA Coaches Convention. At the time, many coaches would finance their soccer careers by working summer camps, moving from city to city like a circus worker. There were not too many places where someone could draw a soccer income. Aside from referees, college soccer coaches, and a sprinkling of professional players, back then few people got paid in the U.S. soccer industry. It's not like the billion-dollar industry it is today.

One morning, I was having coffee with a bunch of other coaches. One was my good friend John Cossaboon, a native of Rochester, New York, who had emerged as an outstanding collegiate coach. We knew each other from the national coaching schools and from doing summer camp tours across the country. John told us that he had a new job: a soccer job. Our ears perked up. *What the hell is a soccer job,* we thought. John had been hired by the North Texas State Soccer Association as the director of coaching. He would train Olympic development players and design and implement the state's coaching education program. Another coach asked John about the pay. John said he was getting $2,000 a month, along with health insurance and a car so he could travel the state running clinics and camps. We were thrilled for John. We could not believe that someone could get paid a decent buck to do what everybody had been volunteering to do. This was the onset of pay-to-play, before it got out of hand.

Another guy, Mike Berticelli, and I had crossed paths at various soccer events before we ever took a coaching course together. Mike grew up in Lewiston, Maine, where he had played goalkeeper but not at a high level. In fact, when it came to playing, Mike couldn't trap a bag of cement. But this guy could coach. I thought his main attribute was his people skills. He could look at a kid across the room and know the kid's mood. Mike had a wonderful college coaching career, winning the Division III championship at UNC Greensboro and competing at the highest level with Division I Notre Dame. Mike also taught coaches. He was the national director of Coaching for the NSCAA before his passing in 2000. The organization still honors him with the annual *Mike Berticelli Excellence in Coaching Education Award.*

As my mentor, Mike changed how I looked at coaching and developing players. By now, you know I was a self-motivated, intense, and at times overbearing athlete. Mike helped me realize that most young players were not like me. Our goal as youth coaches was to help every player reach their potential, but more importantly, to help them use soccer as a vehicle to become upstanding citizens. He believed that soccer was the perfect vehicle to nurture each child's success. He thought if he could get youth coaches to provide a fun and healthy environment, the U.S. soccer community could produce great players and great people.

At one coaching school, Mike and I were hanging around the dorm when he pulled out a piece of paper and said, "I wrote a poem." Mike was the most macho guy you would ever meet. He would drink beer through his nose and then spit it out through his mouth like a statue in a fountain. Now he wants to read me his poem. You can see why I was skeptical. Well, this poem speaks to what an exceptional person and visionary Mike was. I'd like to share it here.

The Youth Soccer Coach
By Mike Berticelli

You donate your time for the good of our youth.

But you scream, and you yell and are often uncouth.

The ref is just twelve and still learning the game,

But you call him a jerk and say he's not sane.

The parents are screaming and follow your lead,

As you spring up the sideline at uncontrollable speed.

You jump as you yell, "Pass, pass the ball!"

You turn red as you bellow, "Ref, make the call!"

"You're the left back now, get in your position.

If you don't, we might lose and ruin our tradition!"

Positions are needed so we look like a team,

'cause they're miniature pros, or so it does seem.

The fullback is bored; he picks at his nose,

While the others run wild and kick with their toes.

You scream for a goal, no matter how it goes in,

The skill doesn't matter, just as long as we win!

The parents go crazy as the ball nears the goal,

Their advice and instructions will soon take their toll.

You see, "Junior" feels pressure; he's not having much fun,

We tell him to pass, when to shoot, and to run.

He came here to play and to use his own mind,

'cause soccer's the most creative game that you'll find.

Imagination is needed on the part of each child,

Solving problems on the field is what makes them go wild.

A week of long practice, while just standing in line,

Waiting to shoot, using one ball at a time.

This just doesn't cut it, and for some, it's too late.

Make your practices fun, don't be the coach that they hate.

They come to "play" soccer, not to "work" at the game.

Their excitement is something we don't want to tame.

Maradona has moves that are beyond comprehension.

No coach taught those moves while threatening detention!

He learned from his friends, and tried copying others,

While playing games, without coaches and mothers.

Soccer is different, not like baseball at all,

We don't need positions, just give them the ball.

They first must learn skill; it's the meat of the game,

If they can't dribble or shoot then who should we blame?

Skill must be learned through repeated trials.

If motivation is present, you will see teams run miles.

"Fun games" are the answer to encourage repetition.

They laugh and they scream and enjoy competition.

Without the skill to dribble past an opponent at will,

Your players may win, but their growth will stand still.

I dream of the day when the parents just cheer,

And losing the game doesn't bring out a tear.

When practice is fun, not dull and so boring,

And playing the game means more than just scoring.

I know you mean well, and you donate your time,

But bury your ego, and try something sublime.

Call all the parents, and ask for their aid,

You're teaching their kids and not getting paid.

Your goal is to develop a youngster with skill,

Not a team that must win, or some fancy new drill!

You see players are not judged by their wins and their losses,

Instead, they are judged by their shots, headers, and crosses!

Scholarships are given to players with great names.

Not to those on youth teams who never lost games.

A pro player gets paid because his skills are real fine,

Not because his team never lost when he was just nine.

It's time to bring soccer to new heights in this nation.

The future's in players, not a coaching citation!

Let's start to say "dribble," and stop yelling "Pass!"

You'll then see our players go to the head of the class.

I hope you're concerned, but not really offended,

It's the need for more skill that I have defended.

You're giving your all, from the good of your heart,

Why not make sure the kids get the right start?

I am very proud to say that he was a very dear friend. Love always for Mike Berticelli.

My first coaching license course was coming to an end. I had found a ride back to Wilmington, where I would catch a bus to New York. This was a great week. I loved the class sessions, the field sessions, and the field testing. I even liked the written test. I'm not sure anybody could read what I wrote but I did know the answers. The other benefit was the networking. I met people from all over the country; many are still friends, almost 50 years later.

One guy, Dave Amsler, was a coach from Virginia. He was getting his USSF "A" License, becoming one of only 50 coaches who had it in 1975. We had hit it off. At that time, Dave and his partner Helmut Werner ran an overnight soccer camp that took place at Randolph-Macon, a private college located 15 miles north of Richmond in Ashland. The night before we were going to check out of St. Andrews School and head home, Dave offered me my first-ever paid coaching job. He and I would ride back to his house and spend a day with his family. The next day we would head to Randolph-Macon where I would work camp for two weeks. He offered me $150 per week, then the going rate for a "C" license coach. That was enough to pay my mom back for the coaching license, plus he would drop me off at a bus terminal in Richmond where I could get a bus to New York and avoid hitchhiking.

As an 18-year-old American kid, I had more soccer coaching experience than most people did. At 16, I became the U10 coach for my Clarkstown club, so I had two years under my belt. Now that I had my USSF National "C" License, I understood what instructor Bill Killen meant when he said the license puts parts of the game you may already know into a sequence that makes things clearer for you as a coach. Just a few days later, I was using what I learned.

After being on the field all day with the kids, the camp coaches played games each night. This was a great training environment for me before I would head to the Netherlands with my Gottschee team. As Dave handed me the first soccer paycheck of my life, I remember thinking, *How cool would it be if I never had to work a day in my life, and I could get paid for doing soccer stuff?* Thanks, Dave. Here I am almost half of a century later, and during that time I have never worked a day outside of my soccer dream. How lucky can you get?

By the time I got back home, my USSF National "C" Coaching license had arrived. It had #318 stamped on it.

CHAPTER FORTY-EIGHT

HOLLAND: THE LAND OF JOHAN CRUYFF

It was late summer 1975 and my Gottschee team had been invited to play in a huge international tournament, the Amsterdam 700. This would be my last appearance as a youth player. Gottschee would be graduating many junior players, so taking our team abroad would be a nice reward for the players who rose through its ranks. It would also be an opportunity to show the European soccer community that young Americans could play the game.

In addition to the youth tournament, this event featured a four-team professional tournament that included two Dutch teams, Ajax Amsterdam and Feyenoord Rotterdam, and two international teams, R.W.D. Molenbeek, from Belgium, and the world-famous Barcelona, from Catalonia, Spain. Barcelona featured Dutchman Johan Cruyff, the former Ajax player and three-time winner of the Ballon d'Or. He was the player we all wanted to see. The 1974 World Cup was still fresh in our mind, and no one played better in that event than Cruyff. In 1974, the only way you could watch the World Cup in the U.S. was on closed-circuit television. In the New York metropolitan area, there was only one place fans could watch the games live: Madison Square Garden and the adjacent Felt Forum. My Clarkstown boys Rick Derella, Rich Murray, and others would travel into Manhattan to watch games on a big screen. My non-soccer friends thought we were psychos.

In Holland, Gottschee was intent on winning. Our roster had all the key guys from this year's team, and we added two players who had starred on the 1974 McGuire Cup team, Eddie Mauser and Billy Eastedt. To give us depth at every position, Gottschee also invited three players from Clarkstown: Rick Derella, Kenny Fisher, and Johnny Sautner. We flew out of JFK airport in New York on a direct flight to Amsterdam. Once we arrived, we boarded a team bus that took us to the Blauw-Wit Amsterdam clubhouse, where we were treated to lunch. Then we were introduced to the Blauw-Wit families that would host our players. Only a few players would stay at the Hotel Columbus Amsterdam with the coaches.

I was matched up with the wonderful Schouten family. Mr. Schouten was an executive on the board at The Blauw-Wit Amsterdam Club, so he loved talking about soccer and how it worked in the states. They had a son, Ralph, about 14, a skinny lad with blonde hair and really cool. They also had a girl, about 10, and the mother was very nurturing. They lived on Surinameplein, smack in the middle of Amsterdam and right across from the Metro. When we sat down for our first dinner together, I was amazed to see that even the little girl was speaking English. I asked, "How come you all can speak English?"

The mom said, "For the same reason we speak German and Spanish."

My jaw dropped. Are you kidding? Dutch, German, Spanish, and English? I was feeling a bit inadequate.

I asked how they learned so many languages. The mom said each night when they ate dinner, they put on the table a dictionary of the language to be practiced that evening, kind of like a game. For example, in Dutch we would say "Geef me de aardap," and then someone else would say, "Pass me the potatoes." She added that on the first try it would come out a little funny, and they would rib each other. If they needed help, they went to the dictionary. Ralph added that in school, everyone had to take English in addition to Dutch, as well as another language that they chose, such as Spanish, French, or Chinese. Mr. Schouten explained that this was part of the Dutch culture for hundreds of years. The city of Amsterdam had been an international shipping hub. In order for the Dutch to do business globally, they learned many languages. I left that table with a better understanding of how different and big the world is.

I knew that Holland was known for developing soccer players. Well, the Dutch underestimated what American kids could do on a soccer field. In our first game we faced our host Blauw-Wit Amsterdam, and they did not send their best team. We won 5–0, even as we were trying to be gracious guests. We thought, *Now they know we are not here to fool around.* Next up was ASV Arsenal Amsterdam. We gave it to them, 9–0.

Off the field, we were having a blast. Between the city tours and hanging together, it was like a vacation on steroids. We even went to the Olympic Stadium, where we marched in with passionate fans to see Ajax play Barcelona. We saw Johan Cruyff play in person, which was way better than on closed-circuit television. We even toured the Cruyff Brothers Soccer Store, where we were like a bunch of big kids in a candy shop.

One afternoon, the team had eaten at an outdoor restaurant overlooking a lovely canal. As we got up to do a little sightseeing, Coach Petschauer told us to follow him. He said, "I know a wonderful museum, not far from here." We were following him when Gary Kresse signaled the guys to start slowing down. As Coach Petschauer turned right to head to the museum, Gary led the team around the corner and out of Coach's sight. The next thing I know, we were roaming the red-light district. After all, it was a big tourist destination.

The next day we played local club Odid Amsterdam, and it was embarrassing. As I tell the coaches and kids in my club today, if you win by more than five, it does not mean you are so good, nor does it mean the other team is so bad. It is because someone erred in organizing the game. The score was 15–0. No wonder I don't remember playing these games. They were meaningless. Once we reached the semifinals, the competition ramped up. I cannot be sure, but I believe we beat a good Venezuela side and then lost to Mexico in the final.

All in, the trip was a wonderful experience. At age 18, I had spent two wonderful weeks in one of my favorite cities, with a group of guys I enjoyed on and off the field. I have been back many times and hope to have a few more trips in me.

CHAPTER FORTY-NINE

ULSTER COUNTY COMMUNITY COLLEGE, SEASON II

It was late summer 1975, time to return to Ulster for my second year. Ricky pulled into my driveway on Pascack Road. He had a different car, a 1963 green Chevrolet Corvair. I am not much into cars, but this one was special. It remains the only American-designed passenger car with a rear-mounted, air-cooled engine. Yes, a rear-mounted, air-cooled engine, remember that! We were heading back to the same apartment on Main Street in New Paltz. One of our roommates, Simon Curanaj, had graduated and was now playing at Albany State. He was one of many Ulster players to go onto higher education and continue playing soccer. Others include Kurt Nedrick (Oneonta State), Mario Isaac (Florida Tech), James Jepburn (Stetson), and our former keeper, John Bertuna (Keene State), to name a few. Coach Viz had kept his promises.

As usual, the players reported a week before school started, so we could settle into our housing and get the first shot at classes.

It was our sophomore year, so we were ready for Coach's rigorous preseason training program. We had gathered in the locker room for the first team meeting. Viz had shut the door and started to pace in front of his blackboard. Last year I was anxious, even a bit scared, but now I felt like a disciple of the program he was about to lay out. I was all-in, especially when it came to Coach's last bullet point: "Ulster will be NJCAA national champions." I knew that if I was going to go pro, my best chance was to be scouted at the national championships.

When the meeting ended, I stepped out and ran down the hill to the field. We had many talented players coming back, like Segundo Zapatier, Rick Derella, Aldo Sergovich, and Oscar Rendon. I could not wait to see the new guys who would replace the players who had graduated. The big question was who would replace Mario Oliva and Franklin Hill, our All-Americans, as well as our top scorer, Kurt Nedrick. We were not worried, because Coach Viz was a resourceful and dogged recruiter.

As training started, I noticed that we had several players from local schools like Kingston High and Rondout Valley. The only freshman I knew was Paul Rocker, my Clarkstown teammates who could play any position. On the second day we played a scrimmage, and I could see something was missing. What was missing was good players. It hit me like a bag of cement. I thought, *How the hell are we going to get to the nationals with second-class players?*

When training ended that night, I went to Coach Viz's locker room. He called me in and I got straight to it. "Where are the players you recruited?" I asked.

Coach nodded, as if he agreed with me. He said, "My son, you've seen the players for this season's team."

I said, "Coach, you gotta be kidding; you recruited those guys?" Coach hesitated to answer. He knew these guys would not replace Mario and the other stars. He just didn't want to say it.

I said, "That blonde guy, Dave from Kingston High School, he cannot do five juggles. When he has the ball, it's more dangerous for us than for the other team." I asked Coach how we were going to make the nationals with players like that. By now, many coaches might have shooed off a cocky punk with attitude. Not Coach Viz; he was a master of psychology. He knew that we both wanted the same thing, an NJCAA national championship. We needed each other and we needed the players who were not yet ready for the big stage. Starting with that guy Dave Farrell, who would later turn out to be a good player, a lifelong friend and a brilliant soccer coach and mentor.

Coach asked me to sit. He told me that school leaders were so upset about last year's Bronx game that they had considered dropping the soccer program. Coach was told that he could not recruit outside Ulster County until the legal issues from the Bronx game were settled. Viz said, "My son, we have no other choice. We must take this group of players and make it happen. Together as a family we need to believe, and we need to make them believe we can do it."

Coach Vizvary had weaknesses, but self-doubt was not one of them. He believed that he could take us to the national championship. By the time I left his room that night, he had me believing it too. Some of the freshmen were decent players. They were not Mario Oliva or Franklin Hill or even Kurt Nedrick, but they could play. I had to get on board. I could not make excuses, point fingers, or fret over things I did not control. It was time to focus on the prize.

A lot had changed in a year. As a freshman, I was a young punk, a gringo no one ever heard of, no pressure or expectations. Now I was Mister All-American and everyone knew me. Every opposing coach spoke my name in his pregame talk. There were high expectations, but none higher than those I set for myself. I didn't care what other people thought. I didn't feel pressure. I also knew that I would have to step up and lead, and so would guys like Segundo and Aldo. And Viz would have to coach his ass off. I knew he was up for it.

We started the 1975 season ranked sixth in the country, and we got off to a good start. While we were not as talented as last year, we were a closer group with fewer large egos. Off the field, we were adapting to living on our own again. My roomies and I were learning to cook, but doing dishes was not our strength. "I did them yesterday." "Those are your dishes, not mine!" Finally, we came up with a plan. We took a soccer ball into the living room and moved the coffee table against the wall. Sitting juggles would decide dish-washing duty. You sit on the floor, toss the ball up and start juggling. Each guy got two chances. The guy with the fewest juggles washed the dishes. The guy with the second-fewest dried the dishes. The guy with the third-fewest put the dishes away. The guy with the most juggles got to watch television every night. That would be me. Later in life, I told this story as part of my juggling demonstrations while promoting the sport across the country.

Now back to Ricky's car. Remember I mentioned the Corvair with the rear-mounted, air-cooled engine? In his 1965 book, *Unsafe at Any Speed*, activist Ralph Nader called the Corvair "the one-car accident." He wrote that a design flaw in the rear suspension made the car likely to flip. He felt the car was dangerous off the production line, let alone a 12-year-old model being driven by college kids on twisting country roads glazed in snow and ice.

Rick got the car from his uncle who taught in the South Bronx. It had been broken into so many times that the door locks no longer worked. The passenger door window was shattered and the top hinge on that door was destroyed. To this day Ricky swears it was the fault of a telephone pole. Many of us relied on Ricky to get from New Paltz to Stone Ridge. On any given morning, six or eight of us piled into that Corvair.

One morning we were on State Road 32, Ricky doing about 50 miles per hour. Bang, the hood popped straight up! It was like a blackout. None of us could see out the front windshield. Ricky hit the brakes and stuck his head out his window. I was in the passenger seat, better known as the "death seat." I put my feet on the dashboard, bracing for impact. We could see and hear the hood banging against the roof above the windshield. Another bang followed and the hinges snapped off the hood and the hood flew off behind us. Now we had a clear view out the windshield. Ricky was still hitting the brakes. I had my eyes closed for a second. I opened them and glanced back and saw that the hood had not hit any cars. Ricky brought the car to a stop.

I am sure that Ralph Nader was right about the Chevrolet Corvair. The hood had flipped off because one of our guys, after putting his bag in the hood, had forgotten to make sure it was shut properly. Had the trunk been in the back like every other car, that 75-pound steel hood would have never gone flying through the air on a busy street. Speaking of Ralph Nader, years later, my mom Agnes won the Ralph Nader Whistleblower Protection Award, and they flew her to Washington, D.C., to accept the honor. She had spoken up against Becton, Dickinson and Company, where she worked. They had used dangerous chemicals in their factory and didn't protect their employees. In fact, later in life Mom was crippled from the chemicals and won a worker's compensation case. What a brave lady!

Once we had pulled over, we jumped out and two of us pulled the hood out of the road. We tried to fit it back in, but the hinges were bent. We had no other way to get to school, so Ricky drove on. Once we reached the college grounds, he drove very slowly. Later, in a burst of creativity, Ricky used hangers to hold the hood back in place. We couldn't use the front as a trunk anymore but at least the hood wasn't flying up and off like a torpedo.

Toward the end of our season, it was getting cold. One morning we piled into the Corvair to make our first-period classes. Ricky started her up, put her in gear, and hit the gas. The engine revved but the car didn't move. Ricky got out and opened the rear hood to check the engine.

Everyone was snuggled together trying to stay warm. A light freezing rain fell. Ricky opened the door and said it didn't look like we were going anywhere. He said the gas-pedal cable to the rear engine carburetor had snapped. Our other teammates with cars had already left so we were up the creek. We got out and looked under the hood. Ricky pointed to this little spring-like thing and showed us the broken cable connection. I asked if I could lay across the back of the engine with my head sticking out enough to see. I got under the back hood and laid next to the engine. My feet were up against the passenger side of the engine. My left hand gripped the inside of the engine and my right hand held the little spring-like thing.

I could look straight up the side of the car to see oncoming traffic, but I was not long enough to see where we were going. How would I know when to speed up, or slow down, or stop? I needed more vision or it was a suicide mission. I was lying in the back of the engine area (see photo) when Ricky got in the driver's seat and said, "Hey, can you see my hand?" His left hand was extended out the window.

I said, "Sure, I see your entire arm."

Ricky suggested we use hand signals. He said that when he held up his hand, fingers pointed to the sky, I would hit the gas. If he put his hand down, I would let off. Rick put the car in neutral so we could give it a test run. He started with his hand down, so I wasn't pulling the spring at all. When he moved his hand up, I slowly pulled the spring and we heard the engine rev. After a few minutes, Rick said, "Okay, guys, get in. Ulster, here we come."

As we drove off, a cold rain stung my face. Driving along Main Street in New Paltz was scary. There were always a lot of police, and if they saw this, we would get pulled over. We took the back roads to school, and it took a little longer than usual, but it worked. Once we arrived, my shirt was soaking wet and so was Ricky's left arm. Everybody got out of the car high-fiving and laughing. We did this for two weeks before Ricky was able to get it fixed. Ricky and I have been joined at the hip since we first met. This endeavor was proof that we trusted each other with our lives. By the way, do not try this at home!

When our soccer season ended, we were ranked 10th in the nation. Our Region 15 quarterfinal game would be against Westchester Community College. We had edged them, 2–1, in the regular season. As I left the locker room for our first post-season training session, I spied Coach Viz already on the field. He wore that "let's get down to business" face under his winter hat, and I wondered if that hat would take another beating. I was thinking that our freshmen had no idea what they were in for. Coach knew how to prepare his boys for the playoffs and this would be an intense two hours.

Viz was a master coach. He could design a training session that would bring out our competitive best. This talent was especially evident when our team had already played against our opponent. His tactical adjustments were sheer brilliance. Coach also knew how to use individual and team psychology to control when his team would peak.

Once I had earned my first coaching license, I would try to understand not only *what* Coach was saying but *why* he was saying it. It was like I was absorbing his words as two separate messages. For example, if Coach said, "We need to high pressure them in their third of the field," that meant that we had to put more pressure on our marks and do it deep in their side of the field. That was the *what*, a simple message that players could carry out together as a team.

But *why* did Coach tell us to apply high pressure? What intel supported the decision? Did he see that their defenders were not technically advanced? Did they lack the endurance to withstand that pressure? Was it the score? The size of the field? Was the sun in their eyes? What about the wind? Was it based on their formation? That was the *why*. The coaching schools taught me to see the game through the eyes of a coach. I learned to think beyond my own view, a skill that has served me well throughout my life.

CHAPTER FIFTY

REGION 15: THE QUARTERFINAL

Ulster against Westchester Community College, Region 15 Tournament. Win and advance, or lose and go home. In the first minute, two Clarkstown alumni clicked. Rick Derella curled a cross into the box, when Paul Rocker outjumped two defenders and nodded it home. We controlled the first half, creating a few good chances to extend our lead. Here's how the article in the next day's Kingston Freeman newspaper described one such chance: "Mulroy fired a bullet that nearly snapped the crossbar in half." But close didn't cut it, and Westchester struck back to even the game at halftime.

After regulation, the score stood 1–1, two 10-minute overtime periods to come. Coach Viz pulled Segundo and me to the side and said, "It's up to you, guys. If we win back the midfield, we will win the game. I know you can do this, my sons." Segundo was a former youth national team player from Ecuador. Fast and strong, he had a high soccer IQ and was our top scorer. Under his lead, we took control in overtime. We had them pinned in their back third, but we could not score, and penalties loomed.

With the clock ticking down, the ref called a foul, giving us a free kick from 45 yards out. I chipped it into the mixer near the far post, and in the ensuing scramble Oscar Random tucked it home. Westchester played an aimless ball into our half, and we responded with a quick counter. Rick Derella threaded a beautiful through-ball to Oscar, who buried it for his second goal. We were through to the semifinals.

CHAPTER FIFTY-ONE

REGION 15: THE SEMIFINAL

The Region 15 semifinal matchups were set—Ulster versus New York City and Dutchess versus Bronx. We had faced New York City earlier in the year, a 1–1 draw. I had hit a penalty in the second half to pull us level. Since we had played them before, I was excited to see what Viz was cooking up.

Two days before the game, I was hurrying from campus to the locker room when it started to rain ice cubes. As I arrived, I heard that a few players had asked Coach about practicing in the gym. On one hand, I had empathy for my brothers from South and Central America or the Caribbean, who felt that anything below 60 degrees is winter. Still, I was pissed and started to argue with the guys who wanted to train indoors two days before the big game. It turned into a screaming match and Coach gave in to keep guys happy. I didn't care about happy. I knew that we needed to run through Viz's tactical training to be fully prepared. While my teammates gathered in the gym, I grabbed the bag of balls and lugged it out and down the hill. I took out a ball and started to warm up, alone. I could not feel the clammy air because I was too pissed off. I was thinking, *What a bunch of pussies.*

Then the locker room door opened and out came Aldo, Ricky, Segundo, and Dave. Soon everyone was on the field. A few minutes later, Coach Viz emerged, wearing that hat and a big grin. He warmed us up and then went into team tactics. After practice, I left the field, knowing that we were prepared.

Two days later, it was game on. It was raw and damp, the wind up. Twenty-nine seconds into the game, New York City scored. I looked at our keeper Leo and said, "Pick your head up; we'll get it back." That goal woke us up. As the subhead read in the paper the next day, "All Hell Broke Loose." We seized control, pinging it around and forcing them to chase. Later in the half, Rick Derella played a sweet through-ball that Oscar Rendon buried to knot the game, 1–1. Just before the halftime whistle, I got onto a ball 25 yards out, took one touch and let it fly. As the Kingston Freedman reporter wrote the next day, "Tom Mulroy unleashed one of his patented rockets into the upper left-hand corner of the cage." After the game, Coach Viz said, "They are still repairing the net." I had hit that ball so well it had no spin or curve. A minute later we went to halftime on a high and ahead, 2–1.

As we began the five-minute walk to the locker room on the neutral New Paltz campus, Coach Viz redirected us to our passenger vans parked near the field. Coach knew we were amped; he wanted to bottle that high and use it to our advantage. He piled all 20-some guys into a 15-seat van. Coach sat in the driver's seat and shut his door. His eyes went from player to player, then he made a fist, held it up, and asked, "How do you feel?" The boys howled and we banged the roof and stomped our feet. I have never experienced a collective high like this with teammates.

Coach said, "My sons, in the second half, they will try to take this feeling away from you." We went crazy. Coach had control of our emotions. He said nothing about tactics; he did not need to. This master of psychology had us stepping out of the van ready to take on the world. I hit another bullet from 20 yards and we went on to a 5–2 win.

That night, as I reflected on the game, I thought back to the meeting that I had had with Coach at the start of the season. He wanted me to lead, and I think I did that when I stepped out to train in that ice storm. In three days, we would face Dutchess in the final.

**Coach George Vizvary and Tommy Pose for the
Ulster CCC Athlete of the year Award**

CHAPTER FIFTY-TWO

REGION 15: THE FINAL

Ulster and Dutchess had played to a 2–2 draw in the first game of the season. Since that was the only blemish for both teams in the regular season, this game would decide who won the conference title. What's more, Dutchess came into the game ranked #6 in the U.S. and Ulster ranked #10, so they had local bragging rights. This was our last hurdle to clear before the nationals.

This game would also be played at the neutral site SUNY New Paltz. From the opening kick, we took control and after 27 minutes, we had rolled to a 3–0 lead. As Dutchess coach Bill Holland said in the paper, "You can't give a team that good, the momentum." It ended 8–0. Paul Rocker had three, Segundo Zapatier had two, and Rick Derella, Oscar Rendon, and Mario Austin each had one. For the first time, Ulster was Region 15 Champion. We were one of eight teams on our way to Baltimore for the NJCAA national championships, where we would play in front of college and pro scouts.

CHAPTER FIFTY-THREE

NJCAA NATIONAL CHAMPIONSHIPS

Our quarterfinal game would be Wednesday, November 26th, versus the Dutchmen of Belleville, Illinois. We drove to Baltimore on Monday, trained that evening and had a light walkthrough on Tuesday. The next day, as the game unfolded, our technical ability won out. This was Oscar Rendon's day, as he converted a sweet dime from Ricky Derella and later buried a fine feed from Segundo to pace a 2–0 win. Among the crowd of over 3,000 were many college coaches, as well as some pro coaches. In the semifinals, we would face top seed Florissant Valley from St. Louis. Coached by the legendary Pete Sorber, this team had won the national title four times. Their top player, Steve Pecher, later played for the NASL Dallas Tornado.

We came out strong and Oscar was at it again, scoring on a pass from Paul to put us up in the 24th minute. In the 42nd minute, they converted a penalty kick to tie it up. The momentum swung, and we went on to lose, 3–1. They were a better and more experienced team. The loss stung hard, but before I left that field, I had made the most important contact of my life.

The next day, we lost the consolation game and headed back to Ulster with our fourth-place trophy. My Ulster career was over. I had played my last match for Coach Viz. Some 700 student athletes would go through the Ulster soccer program on his watch. Most went there "as boys and left as young men." Most went on to study and play at four-year colleges and became productive citizens. Many continued in the soccer industry, like Rick Derella, who graduated from Cornell, David Farrell, and me. It is quite something, that George Vizvary family tree.

Ulster County Community College - Sophomore Year Fall 1975

Back (L-R) Aldo Sergovich, Jack Sparacio, Oscar Rendon, Mario Austin, Andre Bailey "Huey", George Vasilaras, Tom Mulroy, Paul Rocker, Segundo Zapatier

Front (L-R) Louis Pratt, Dave Farrell, Leo Leopold, Chris Clinger, Rick Derella, Steve Mason, John Ivancovich, Coach George Vizvary

CHAPTER FIFTY-FOUR

THE CONTACTS OF A LIFETIME

As I walked off the field after our loss to Florissant Valley, Coach Sorber came up and told me I had played a great game. A sincere compliment like that from the opposing coach always feels good. Then this big blonde guy walked up, put his hand out, and said, "Hello, I am Bill Nuttall, the head coach at Florida International University. That was a tough loss, but you had a great game." Then he went into his sales pitch.

I had a folder of 50 or so letters from college soccer programs from all over the country, like UCLA, USF, Oneonta, Hartwick, Colgate, Cortland. These programs had no idea what kind of student I was, or they would have saved the postage. I was looking Nuttall in the eye but I had no interest in any college team. Two outdoor seasons and one indoor season of college was enough for me. I was looking for other horizons, ones without classrooms, as I had been tortured enough over 15 years in school. As Nuttall finished his pitch, I remembered what my mom always said: just be honest with people and they will respect you.

I said, "Coach Nuttall, thank you so much. Your school sounds great, but I am not really interested in continuing in college. I am trying to find my way to the pros." I figured he would think I was a cocky punk. Instead, he smiled. He told me that in addition to his post at FIU, he played goalkeeper for the Miami Toros of the NASL. I thought, *Wow this guy is even more cocky than I am.* He told me he was scouting, along with Greg Myers, the head coach of the Toros. Then he said, "Greg Myers is very interested in you. But as a professional team coach, he is not allowed to approach undergraduate college players." Then he added, "But players are allowed to contact him, and that is why I'm here." Nuttall nodded at the stands. "Greg is sitting over there, the guy in the red shirt with the glasses." I'm not sure I even said thank-you or goodbye to Bill before I stepped toward Coach Myers.

Seconds later, my heart banging around in my chest, I introduced myself to Greg Myers. He said, "Hello, Tommy, nice to meet you, have a seat. We have been doing our research on you, and we just saw you have a great tournament. Have you heard of the Miami Toros?"

I said, "Of course, you play against the New York Cosmos in the NASL."

Coach Myers told me that the Toros were owned by Joe and Elizabeth Robbie, the same family that owns the NFL's Miami Dolphins. Coach said he was looking for some young American players to add to his roster. Then he asked me to tell him a little about myself. I started to go through my soccer background when he stopped me and said he already knew about that. "Tell me about you, your family, what you like to do," he followed. I blurted out something like, "I like to play soccer. I have an older brother John and a great mom. I don't have a father. I live in Hillcrest, New York,

I am not a good student, and I am going to play professional soccer as soon as possible."

Coach said, "Do you mind if I ask if you are on financial aid?" I told him I was. "Well, that may be good news," he said. "Since you are only a sophomore, you are not eligible for the NASL draft. However, there is a hardship clause that allows a college student from a low-income household to leave school early. You may fall under that category. If so, we would not have to draft you and we may be able to make this happen sooner. Would you be willing to move to Miami?"

Little did he know I would have followed him home that day. "Miami sounds great," I said. We shook hands, and he said that he would be in touch. A minute later Nuttall walked up to me in the bleachers. He told me that he had played for Coach Myers at Davis & Elkins, where they won two NAIA National Championships, and that Myers was a great coach and a better person. He told me that if Myers offered me a spot, I should take it.

In time, Bill Nuttall would become my teammate and a life-long friend and mentor. He had coached in the NASL and later became the general manager for the U.S. Men's National Team leading up to the 1994 World Cup. Bill later moved to Miami to work with me at my Soccer Marketing and Promotions company, before moving on to become the CEO of Diadora, the Italian soccer brand for which he eventually became the sole owner. To this day, he has been like an older brother to me.

CHAPTER FIFTY-FIVE

I WILL NEVER DO THAT AGAIN

Our fall semester was winding down, and I was stressing over final exams. Every day I was hoping to get that call from the Toros. A few times a day, I would stop by Coach Vizvary's office to see if that call had come in. One day Viz did have some good news—I had been selected again as a first team All-American. But no, the Toros had not called. I even called my Uncle Frank's house to see if they had called my mom or sent anything in the mail. If I got the call early enough, I would not have to take the exams, and I could skirt that black cloud.

No call came, so I had to finish all my classes and exams. We headed home in Ricky's Corvair. A few weeks later, Ricky, Paul Rocker, and I headed back up to New Paltz to celebrate New Year's Eve. At that point, we had obeyed almost all of Coach Vizvary's team rules, especially during the season: no drugs, no drinking, no cutting class. The one rule that we ignored, in or out of season, was the no-women rule. The places to find girls were the bars on Main Street, or, if you were into the New York disco scene, at Joe's

Discotheque Nightclub, where our city guys would flash the latest disco moves. I am sure that place, which is still open today, has never seen a better dancer than my boy Aldo.

I did not drink often, and when I did, it was only a few beers. This night was different. Main Street was rocking, and the legal age for drinking in New York was only 18, so we did not even need a fake ID. If you have ever been to a college town on New Year's Eve, you know the scene: young adults running wild, hot college girls everywhere. Here, try a shot of this, now raise a toast to last year, now let's toast next year, now it's time to toast the toasts. The next thing I knew, I was toasted. As the bars closed, Ricky, our designated driver, was helping Paul and me into his car. On the way back to the apartment, the car started to spin like I was on a carnival ride. It got faster and faster and I was begging Ricky to pull over. We were slowing down when I could not take it anymore. I was hanging out the window, and the cold air felt good but it wasn't enough. My stomach was rumbling like a volcano, and before Ricky could come to a stop, I let loose.

By the time Ricky got out to help me, my entire side of the car had been coated with hot vomit, steaming in the cold air. It even covered the back tire. Ricky got us back to the apartment safely. The next day I was too ill to train. My head hurt, my stomach was still upset, and I was too weak to move, never mind train. Normally I trained every day, no matter the weather or how I felt. Not this day. I realized that there was no upside to drinking, that it was self-imposed destruction. My father had been an alcoholic and my brother was addicted to substances. Addiction ran in my family's DNA and put me at a higher risk. Making a career out of soccer will be hard enough without adding an unnecessary hurdle.

I knew that if I was going to be a professional player, never again could I put my body through that. So, I put abstinence on my list. I swore that I would never get drunk again and have upheld that pledge to this day. An occasional glass of wine before bed, that is it. I believe this has given me that little edge on my competitors. At the highest levels of competition, every little edge counts.

CHAPTER FIFTY-SIX

FINALLY, I GET THE CALL!

It was mid-January, and I had still not heard from the Toros. The plan was to head back to Ulster on Saturday and begin spring classes on Monday. I was disheartened. Had I misread Coach Myers? Then it happened, and it was one of those moments when you never forget where you were. Well, on Thursday night, January 15th, 1976, I was in my house watching one of the three channels on our black-and-white TV. The front door flew open and my cousin Frankie screamed that the pro coach was on the phone. It was a cold and snowy night. Clad in shorts and a T-shirt, I ran barefooted out my door and across the frozen ground up the cement steps and through the back door of my uncle's house. My Aunt Nancy was holding the phone toward me. With one hand over the receiver, she said it was the coach from Miami.

The phone had a long cord that could stretch 12 feet. As I took it, my whole family had piled into the kitchen. Uncle Frank was sitting at the table, a cigarette in hand, and my Aunt Nancy had one lit in the ashtray. Frankie, my oldest cousin, was behind me. My second-oldest cousin, Dee Dee, had left her homework to check on the commotion. Danny ran in from the living room and then Cousin Bonnie joined the party. Even Potsy, our beloved cocker spaniel, and a few of our many cats were all packed into the kitchen.

Now the room had gone quiet. I wished Coach Myers a Happy New Year. He asked if I was still thinking about playing with the Toros. I said, "Yes, sir, that would be awesome."

He said, "Well, Tommy, we'd like to offer you a contract. The season doesn't start until April 18th, and most players will not be in Miami until mid-March when we start preseason. Do you like to work with kids?"

I told him that I loved kids. He said they were thinking about bringing me in early to help out with some clinics. I told him I had my USSF National "C" coaching license, and I had worked camps last summer in Virginia. Coach told me he knew that, and that's why he thought I would be the perfect guy to bring in early. Coach asked if I could get there by Monday. I thought to myself, *Well, it's about 8 p.m. Thursday night. When I hang up the phone, I'll hurry back to my house and pack a bag.* I would also have to make a hitchhiking sign that said "MIAMI."

I figured Uncle Frank would drop me off on the New York Thruway South, where I could pick up the Garden State Parkway, then the New Jersey Turnpike, and then I-95 South the rest of the way. In a car, it would take maybe twenty hours. If I left now, I would have three full days plus. I guess my pause was a little long because Coach Myers asked, "Can you be here this next Monday?"

I answered, "Yes, I can."

He asked if I would be flying, in which case they could meet me at the airport. I said no. I had only been on a plane twice, and both times the teams organized the flights. No one in my family ever flew. I thought traveling by air was for rich people.

Coach responded, "So you have a car, and you will be driving yourself?" I said no again. He asked how I planned to get there. I told him that as soon as we hung up, I was going to run over to my house, pack my stuff, and leave my mom a note because she was still at work. Then I was going to get dropped off on the thruway, where I would begin to hitchhike. Coach Myers said, "Tommy, do not be ridiculous." He said he would have his secretary call me in the morning and she would book me a flight for that weekend.

When I hung up the phone, I said with a huge smile, "They are going to buy me a flight to Miami!" Everyone went crazy, big hugs all around. I was high on life again and sharing it with my family. As soon as we were done celebrating, I called Ricky to tell him that he did not have to pick me up that weekend because I was finished with school and the dark cloud had gone. That night I was the happiest soccer player in the world.

CHAPTER FIFTY-SEVEN

OFF TO MIAMI

On Saturday morning, January 17th, 1976, I was packed and ready for my next soccer journey. I was heading to JFK Airport to pick up a prepaid ticket and fly to Miami to sign my first professional contract. This trip would prove to a series of firsts: my first time flying alone, first time in Miami, first pro contract, and many more. I remember checking in at the Delta counter. When the lady handed me my ticket, I thought, *What a big shot I am, the Toros are picking up my airfare of $97.36.*

When I arrived at Miami International Airport, Coach Myers met me. As I was loading my bags into his car, he told me the players' apartments wouldn't be ready until February 1st, but I could stay at his house. Upon arrival, his wife Louise gave me a warm welcome. Their son Chris, age nine, loved to kick the ball around with me in the backyard. As we sat for dinner that first night, Coach said, "Tommy, I think I have a game for you. My friend Karl Kremser knows some guys that play in the local ethnic soccer league. They play at Curtis Park, the level is high, and the atmosphere can get a little crazy."

It sounded like the Met Oval, Miami style. Later, Coach reminded me that the owner of the Toros, Joe Robbie, also owned the Miami Dolphins. Coach pulled out two tickets to the Super Bowl to be played the next day at the Orange Bowl in Miami. I had a choice: play soccer or go to the Super Bowl. The next day Coach dropped me off at Curtis Park and he went to Super Bowl. I think Coach thought I was out of my mind. Once he reads this book and sees my American football experiences, I'm sure he will understand.

When I arrived at Curtis Park, I felt at home. The field was dirt, and no one spoke English. This time, however, instead of hearing German, Hungarian, or Creole, I heard only Spanish. The players were from many different countries, but they all spoke Spanish. As I was lacing my boots on the side of the field, I could tell there was some chatter about me. They were thinking, *Gringos do not play soccer.* After a few minutes, the boys knew I could play. When it ended, some Colombian guy came over to me and said something in Spanish. Then he handed me a $100 bill. *That is so Miami,* I thought.

That Monday would be my first day as an employee of a professional club. After breakfast, we left Coach's house for the Miami Toros' office. It was small with only a few people. The general manager was John Young, recently promoted after being named 1974 NASL coach of the year. A secretary, a receptionist, a public relations person, a marketing person, and a ticket/salesperson, that was about it. The Toros also shared some resources with the Miami Dolphins office, located elsewhere.

I wanted to know everything: how tickets are sold; how you work with the media; how marketing plans are created; how stadiums operate. Even then the game was still a bit of an ethnic cult, and I wanted to make it mainstream. This was another reason for me to be a student of the game. If I could learn the business side of soccer, I figured I could create a future in the sport. Like Coach Rottenbucher had said, some people only paint, some only do carpentry, and some only do plumbing. It is the guy that can do them all that always has a job. I hung around that office the first few weeks and soaked up all I could. Over time, I worked in a front-office capacity for each of the more than 10 pro teams I played for. It ranged from organizing clinics to eventually running a professional team franchise as the president. When I retired from playing, these experiences had prepared me to become an entrepreneur. I started my company, Soccer Marketing and Promotions & Se Habla Futbol, and have promoted my sport to millions of Americans who knew nothing about it.

Later that morning I met my first teammate, Trakoon Jirasuradet. Trakoon was from Thailand, where he played for the Olympic team. He had attended FIU and was drafted by the Toros in 1975. On this day, he would drive me to an elementary school where we would do a soccer clinic. When we arrived, we checked in at the principal's office and then went to the gym. I was expecting maybe 30 kids or so.

Soon, kids were streaming onto the field behind the gym. This clinic was not for one class; it was for the whole school. There had to be 500 kids in this huge semicircle, screaming and yelling. I was used to training 10 or 20 kids. An eerie memory sprang into my head. I was at a tournament in New Jersey that my youth team I was coaching had just won. I had to follow to the microphone the coach of the second-place team. The dude had spoken like he was running for office; he congratulated everybody he ever met. Then the tournament director called me up and gave me the microphone. I put it up to my mouth, and I froze. Thank God Coach Rottenbucher was there to step up and help me out. He gave the speech, and I handed out the trophies.

My senior year in high school, I had to take a public speaking class to graduate. My teacher would not let me talk about soccer. I got an F and had to retake the class in the spring. This time we could talk about any topic. I did all my speeches on soccer, and I passed with flying colors. There was no pressure talking in front of 15 or 20 friends and classmates. But 500 strangers?

So here I am in Florida, my first public-speaking gig as a pro. I was thinking, *I'm so glad Trakoon is going to lead the show.* Trakoon turns to me and says, "Normally I am with Ronnie Sharp or Steve Bauman. They are very good with kids." Wait a sec, is he hinting he wants me to lead? The principal stepped in front of the kids and the place went dead quiet. He introduced Trakoon and me and it was showtime. As Trakoon started to speak in his strong accent, I could barely understand him and I knew the kids were lost. Thankfully, he said that juggling was a great way to practice soccer. Then, he said, "Watch Tommy and me juggle." Once I touched the ball, my nerves calmed. As Trakoon talked, I kept juggling. The kids started to count each one. It got louder and louder, "Thirty-two, thirty-three." Then I threw in some tricks. First a few shoulder taps, then I caught the ball on the back of my neck and went down for a push up. The kids went bananas. Even Trakoon was impressed.

Half the kids had never seen a soccer ball before, never mind my tricks. A few teachers helped us get the kids under control. We did a little heading, then some dribbling. I had been talking more and more to help Trakoon out. I was not nervous. In fact, I was loving it so much that I forgot it was public speaking.

Then Trakoon told me we had to save some time for autographs. I almost asked him who was going to sign autographs. When I realized that would be Trakoon and me, I started to get that soccer high. The teachers organized the kids in a line. We signed Toros flyers that

Trakoon had brought from the office. As we got to the older grades, some kids asked us to write personal notes. Some names were tough for me to spell, and I had a flashback to high school yearbooks. Right then I decided I would write: "Keep Kicking, Tom Mulroy" with the Pelé swirl at the top of the "T" and then my uniform number, which was 14 for the Toros. Signing autographs was something I never tired of. Most pro athletes have a limit. The exception was Pelé. I heard he never turned down an autograph, especially to a kid. I would get to see how true that was later in life.

I had requested #14 because it was Johann Cruyff's number, as well as Bob Cousy's, the basketball player whose book is the only one I ever read cover to cover. There was no chance I would get #10, because Pelé wore #10 and even professional players would fight over that number.

Looking back, I don't know why I ever feared speaking in public. It became one of my favorite things to do. Since that first clinic in 1976, I have done over 5,000 live soccer clinics and or speaking engagements. All in, I have reached more than two million people in person. Hundreds of times I have promoted soccer in live and taped radio and television programming. My most memorable presentation came when I was the spokesperson for the 1994 World Cup, held in the U.S. I performed at the World Cup qualification draw on December 8, 1991, at Madison Square Garden in New York City. This event was held in front of a live audience of over 1,000 FIFA VIPs, and televised to 164 countries live.

For the Toros, I was doing at least one clinic a day, sometimes as many as three. I was meeting new players every day as the guys were starting to arrive in Miami for the preseason, right around the corner.

"Soccer Tom" Mulroy - First Professional Team Picture

Back Row L-R: Alan Hamlyn, Gordon Fearnley, Bob Wolf, Steve Mills, Nico Bodonczy

Middle Row L-R: Trainer Tom O'Neil , Steve Baumann, Ronnie Sharp, Roberto Aguirre, Denny Lee, Cliff Marshall, Emil Stoikovich, Coach Greg Myers

Front Row L-R: Bill Nuttall, Jim Holton, Tommy Mulroy, Rual Luzarraga, Steve David, John Shields, Van Taylor

CHAPTER FIFTY-EIGHT

WELCOME TO THE TOROS

I was meeting so many new teammates, and it was one character after another. My new roommate, Roman Rosul, was a bit of a cool hippie. Women loved his long hair. When we went out to a bar, women would just come up to him. It was not a bad thing. He liked his weed, but never tried to push it on me. That was a nice change after I had spent years warding off guys trying to get me to drink a beer or do a shot of booze.

In the early years, Brits dominated professional soccer in the U.S. Two of my British teammates were household names back home. Chris Lawler, the "Silent Knight," played for England and was a standout for Liverpool FC. Chris was terrific with the young American guys. Our second famous Brit was Jim Holton, who played for the rival Scottish national team. While playing for Manchester United, Jim was a favorite among fans. They would taunt opponents with this chant: "Six foot two, eyes of blue, Big Jim Holton's after you." Never mind that Holton was 6'1" with brown eyes. You gotta love those creative soccer fans.

I will never forget a moment with Jim in the locker room. Coach had given us our pep talk and we were about to head out to face the Cosmos in my first pro game. Jim was sitting next to me. He stood, threw both fists up, and screamed, "Let's go, boys; let's get this one." As he spoke, I realized he did not have any upper front teeth. I asked him what happened to his teeth, and he said, "I left them in the back of some bloke's head."

One thing that stands out about my English teammates is their skill in the air. I would stay after training to get tips. Even now, heading is not taught correctly in the U.S. The timing of the jump; how to use your arms to help elevate; how to protect yourself from injury; and how to hit your target, whether heading at goal or clearing a ball. These little details I could only learn from guys like Jim and Chris, and I became a much better header for it.

Another remarkable English teammate was Cliff Marshall. In 1975, Cliff became the first black footballer to make the first team at Everton Football Club. Cliff had told me it was not unusual for English fans to sing racist chants and sometimes even throw bananas on the pitch. "It didn't affect me; I just got on with the game," Cliff said. His courage helped open the door for others. Three years later, Viv Anderson became the first Black man to represent the England National Team.

Another British guy, our captain Ronnie Sharp, had a life story like no other. A flamboyant Scottish winger, Ronnie was known as "the pied piper of Miami" because of the countless clinics he put on for kids. He was also the team playboy, until he spent an off-season playing in the Mexican Primera División for San Luis Potosí. There he met his wife, Lupita. After my rookie season, Ronnie invited me to train with the San Luis Potosí team and stay at his house. It was all good until the time came for our return to the Toros. Ronnie wanted to drive his black Lincoln Continental 2,000 miles back to Miami. Anyone who has driven on the rutted roads of Mexico knows that was a poor idea. Ronnie told me he kept a gun in the glove compartment in case we broke down in a bad area. Did I mention that Ronnie's wife Lupita was along for the ride, and started going into early labor near Houston? We put her on a flight to Miami, where she had family waiting.

Ronnie was that rare player who would always tell you what he thought. One day in preseason training, we were on a long run. As I started to break from the pack, Ronnie caught up with me and said, "Tommy boy, two things you need to think about. First, running as fast as you can is not popular with some of the older guys. Second, if you go all out running, how will you play with rubber legs?" I eased off.

One day after practice, Ronnie shared more sound advice. During a scrimmage, I had played a few balls ahead of my older teammates, only to see them quit on the run and scream it was a bad pass. Ronnie said, "Lad, you can't let them take the piss out of you like that."

I said, "What do you mean?"

He said, "This morning you gave a few beautiful balls, and they were late to get on them, and they had a go at you. You need to stand up for yourself. If they scream at you and the coach wasn't looking, he'll assume you lost possession. Tommy, don't take any shit from anyone, get in their face, or it's going to get worse." I followed that advice throughout my playing career and beyond. Thank you, Ronnie.

Years later, Ronnie would return to Miami and buy the Fort Lauderdale Sun franchise of the United Soccer League. He recruited me to play and work as the team's community relations director. I had just finished an indoor season with the New York Arrows, so I moved to Miami. That season we averaged over 7,500 fans and won the USL championship. Then things took a dark turn. One morning I was listening to the news on the radio when I heard the anchor say that Ronnie Sharp had been arrested on the Mexican border for his alleged involvement in a marijuana smuggling operation.

Ronnie was jailed for 19 days in Laredo, Texas. He was accused of being a middle-man in a plan to smuggle 200,000 pounds of marijuana into the U.S. The DEA believed that he had put together the operation through contacts in Colombia, Mexico, and Texas. As part of a plea deal, Ronnie testified as a witness for the U.S. government.

All our Latin players were from South America, mostly from Argentina. Roberto "El Toro" Aguire had played for the Argentina national team. He could shield the ball until the sun went down and his touch was silk. After training, we often played a game called Crossbar. You place a ball on the penalty-box line, 18 yards from goal. The object is to hit the crossbar. One day after practice, I challenged Roberto to a game. He said, "Sure, and I will make it fair for you. My kicks will only count when I hit the crossbar and the ball takes one bounce back to me and with one touch I play the ball into the goal."

I noticed other players fighting off grins. I said, "So, you will chip the ball from the penalty line off the crossbar, and before it bounces twice you will one-touch it into the goal."

He nodded and said, "Would you like to be in goal so that after it hits the crossbar you can try to stop the shot?"

Was this guy pulling my leg? Well, I hit the bar four times on my ten kicks. One tipped the bar and went over, which did not count by our rules, so I had three, a decent score. Roberto hit seven out of ten shots. He not only hit the bar, but after one bounce, he one-touched each ball into the goal. He was just as deadly on penalty kicks. He could tell the keeper which corner he would shoot to, and he would still tuck it in. I never saw him miss one, in practice or in a game.

Roberto loved to play, but he did not like fitness training. He was 33 years old and I was 19 and he seemed ancient. In preseason training, in every fitness activity, Roberto was near the back. At one point we had lost a few games in a row and Coach Myers was hot. As we gathered for training, we knew we were in for a grind. Starting on the end line, we ran 10 yards out and back, then 20 yards out and back, then 30 and back. You had to complete each 120-yard series in 30 seconds, or be fined $50 per second. Poor, Roberto, I figured this would cost him a chunk. Coach blew the whistle. As I neared the second cone halfway through the drill, Roberto ran past me. By the time I finished, he was sitting there waiting for me. I realized that Roberto needed a reason to run. Without a carrot or a stick, running sprints in the Miami heat wasn't very motivating for this 16-year pro.

Another Argentinian teammate was defender Ricardo DeRienzo. Ricardo took pride in his tackling. He told me the most important moment of any game was the first time you and your mark battled for the ball. He believed that you must hit your foe hard. Many opponents would be intimidated and constantly look over the shoulder. Other foes would come back tough. Ricardo patted his chest and, in his Argentinian accent, said, "I like that. I am tough, too."

I can't buy that. My mom and my mentors made clear that you never hurt a player. During my professional career, several times I had players and coaches say, "I want you to take that guy out of the game," or "He needs to be hit hard." I would always give as good as I got, but I never crossed the line.

Fast forward to our game against the Hartford Bicentennials. In the early moments, Ricardo laid out Henry McCully. He had gone straight over the ball and almost broke Henry's leg. It happened near our bench and I could see Coach Myers cringe. Ricardo had said that a referee rarely gave a card for the first tackle of the game. In this case, the ref gave no card. I think it should have been a red card.

In the second half, Ricardo pushed up for a corner kick. When he jumped to head the ball, he was met by Charlie McCully, Henry's brother. Charlie had no interest in the ball. He arched back and snapped his forehead into Ricardo's temple. Ricardo went down like a bag of flour. He did not know that he was playing against Scottish brothers whose motto was, "You do my brother, I do you worse." The ref called for our trainer, and Ricardo was carried off with blood coming out of both his ears. That was his last game with the Toros. A few weeks later, he went back to Argentina. I am sorry to say it but, "You live by the sword; you die by the sword."

Our roster also featured two top players with Caribbean roots. Warren Archibald was born in Trinidad and Tobago with a ball on his foot. One time in preseason, he turned his ankle. It was so swollen that he could barely walk. The trainer had him icing it, elevating it, and he gave him anti-inflammatories as well. Nothing worked and Archibald, as he was called, grew frustrated. A few days later he got a package in the mail. As he opened it in the locker room, he said, "Now you will see how we do it in Trinidad."

I thought it was going to be a cake, but I was so wrong. It was a large bottle with about a dozen long slimy leeches in it. He took one out and put it on his swollen ankle. Soon the leech was growing bigger and bigger. As it became plump, Archibald took a knife and slit the leech off his ankle. He did this with each leech. By the time he left the locker room, the swelling was almost gone. So much for modern medicine.

I remember a story Archibald told me about a World Cup qualifier his Trinidad and Tobago side had played against Haiti in 1974. His team had five goals disallowed and did not qualify for a spot in Germany. He told me, "Just before that game kicked off, a huge black bird circled above our heads and then opened its wings. It glided very slowly. The stadium fell quiet and the players stopped warming up to watch. Then the bird landed in the middle of the field." Archibald was sure the bird was sent by Haitian voodoo men and that's how Haiti qualified. Who am I to doubt a guy that used leeches to heal his ankle?

One morning about a week before our opening game against the Cosmos, Roman and I were pulling into a lot on the FIU campus where we trained every day. Normally there were many open spots, but now the lot was full. We thought maybe the school was holding an event. A few players I didn't recognize were lacing their boots, and I thought they were just trying out.

I went around and shook everybody's hand, as I did every day. As I came to Archibald, he was talking to a lanky guy with long dreadlocks. Archibald said, "Tommy, this is my friend, Allan Cole. Everyone calls him 'Skill.' He is the Pelé of Jamaica."

Skill smiled and said, "Pleased to meet you, Wah Gwaan," which I later found out meant, "What's up?" I walked with Archibald and Skill toward our training field. As we drew near the sideline, a huge roar came out of the stands. There had to be close to 200

Rastafarians cheering, screaming, and banging drums and other instruments I didn't recognize. It was all for Skill Cole. He was Jamaica's most celebrated player, and he had played with pro teams in the U.S. and Brazil.

Every time Skill touched the ball, the fans went crazy. If someone tackled the ball from him, the crowd would shout "bomboclat," "bloodclaat," or "raasclaat." A large cloud of smoke billowed above their heads. You could smell the weed. This was 1976 and lots of people smoked, but usually not in public and not at 9 a.m.

I am not sure why we never signed Skill because he was a baller. I thought it was probably money. A few other guys thought Skill was turned off by the fitness workout that Coach Myers put us through on Skill's second day of training with us. Whatever it was, he never came back. Too bad, because I loved the way he played and his Jamaican entourage.

Steve David, another native of Trinidad and Tobago, was the fastest player I ever saw. Legend has it that before his football career, Steve had worked as a guard outside a prison in Trinidad. Whenever any prisoners on the work brigade would try to run, Steve was always sent to chase them down. He finished his NASL career as the league's 8th all-time leading scorer with 228 points in 175 games and was named league MVP in 1975.

In the early years of the NASL, most teams had only one American on the field, and it was often the goalkeeper. In 1976, the league introduced a mandate designed to help American players. Each team had to field at least one American player at all times, and carry at least five Americans on the gameday roster. In addition, teams would be allowed to carry a "taxi squad" of 14 players who had to be American or hold a resident green card.

Now, if the rule had required players to be born in the U.S., that would have been different. Teams would skirt this rule by securing green cards for foreign players, or permanent resident status. For example, many times the one "American" player on the field for the New York Cosmos was Giorgio Chinaglia. As much as I respect Chinaglia, if he is American, then I am Italian.

On my Toros team, one guy was a legit green card holder. Alan Hamlyn was born in London, England, and was always counted on our roster as an American. Alan played eight seasons in the NASL and earned four caps with the U.S. National Team. He was drafted into the U.S. Army and served in Vietnam, where he earned the Bronze Star. Alan still has scars on his back from bomb shrapnel. He represents America better than anyone I know.

Our roster included several other Americans, including goalkeepers Bill Nuttall and Van Taylor, plus forward Steve Baumann, who had starred at the University of Pennsylvania. Later in the season, we drafted Denny Lee, a St. Louis native. I didn't mention them all here, but each one of my Toros teammates contributed to my development on and off the field.

It was Monday, April 12th, 1976, the first day of our last week of training before our season-opening match against the New York Cosmos and Pelé. After practice, I started to do some extra ball work when Coach Myers approached me and said, "Tommy, hurry up and shower; you're coming with me to the office." On the ride, Coach said there was some paperwork we had not finished. When we got to the Toros office, I followed Coach into his room. He shut the door and we sat on opposite sides of his desk. He reached into a folder and pulled out two documents. He laid one in front of me and kept the other one. Coach asked, "Tommy, do you know what this is?" When I didn't answer right away, he said, "Son, that is your contract. That is the offer we are giving to you to be a member of the Miami Toros."

I was all smiles. Coach asked if I had any questions. I answered, "Yes, can I have your pen, and where do I sign?" He said I needed to read it and see if I had any questions. He waited while I read the whole thing. After I signed it, I was a professional player, seven-and-a-half years from the day I saw my first soccer ball. That would be the first of more than a dozen player contracts I would sign. That first contract was the only one I signed without understanding all the ins and outs. In fact, I became so experienced in this realm that I functioned as an agent for many of my younger teammates and friends.

Soon it was the day before my first pro game, when I would face my idol. At our team meeting, Coach Myers told us the game had sold out and would be televised nationally. I was pumped to hear that my friends back home could see me play. It never dawned on me that I might not play. In fact, up until that time, in my entire life, I had never sat on the bench, not even for an injury. The bench was for someone else, not me. That afternoon, my roommate Roman lent me his VW bug so I could pick up my cousin Frankie at the Greyhound station in Miami. Frankie was only 14, and he was like my little brother, so the family sent him on the forty-hour journey to see my first game. Few families would let a 14-year-old ride a bus alone from New York to Miami, but this was a big day for our clan.

When our team arrived at FIU the next day, the Cosmos' bus was parked in front of the locker rooms and the media swarmed all over. I was carrying my bag, which was heavier than usual because it held the scrapbook I began keeping when I saw Pelé play seven years earlier. The first three pages were dedicated to Pelé. The first page had a large, autographed black-and-white photo of Pelé standing in his Santos FC uniform with a ball at his feet. The book also had the ticket stubs from the Santos-West Ham United game that my Mom, Frankie, and I had attended. Truth be told, every guy on my team wanted Pelé to sign something.

A few hours before the game Pelé appeared in a small room between the two locker rooms. Here he was, signing autographs for his opponents. Coach Myers took me into the room, where it was only Coach, Pelé, myself, and a security guard. Pelé greeted me with a big smile, shook my hand, and said, "Good luck today." I looked into his big dark-brown eyes and felt as if I had met him before. He was familiar, from the way he smiled to his Brazilian accent. At first it was weird, then I thought, *Of course he is familiar; I have idolized him since I was 13 years old.* I had been running around dirt fields screaming his name. I watched his Pepsi instructional film, *The Master and His Method*, more times than any other sane person. Of course, to Pelé I was just one of the billion people who wanted to meet him. Yet he treated me like I was the most important person he ever met. That is what makes him the King. He signed my scrapbook, "Best Wishes, Pelé." I still have the scrapbook.

Minutes later we were dressed and ready to go. Coach read off the starting lineup and I wasn't in it. As we headed out the door, I thought back to when Coach had told me to be patient, that my time would come. This was our team's first official match at Tamiami Stadium. For the few exhibition matches we had played there, we would take the ten-minute walk across campus or jump in a player's car. Today was different; a sellout crowd meant there would be no parking available near the stadium. As we gathered in front of the building, up pulled a vintage cherry-red convertible antique fire truck, the bell ringing, the siren blaring. The driver wore a traditional white fireman's uniform and a little black fire hat.

Coach told us to hop on; this is how we would enter the stadium. I thought this was so cool. I jumped on the front and straddled the hood, a leg on each side. The guys started to pile in. Someone handed me a bright red helmet and said, "Here you go, Boy Wonder," a nickname given to me by a local reporter. As we reached the stadium gate, it swung open and we rode in and took a few laps around the field, the standing-room-only crowd cheering.

**My first professional game entrance on a fire truck!
They made me wear the hat!**

As we got off the truck at our bench, I looked over at the Cosmos bench and saw a familiar face. It was Coach Bradley, whom I had met at Cosmos camp a few summers before. He walked over and said, "Congratulations, Tommy, nice to see you made it."

I watched the game from the bench. In the 60th minute, David Clements took a feed from Pelé at 30 yards and lashed a dart into the corner. Minutes later, Pelé stepped up to take a penalty. My mentor and our goalkeeper Bill Nuttall made a diving save—a save he will always remember. We pushed hard for the equalizer but could not break through. I did not get off the bench.

Early in the season, I wasn't getting the time I wanted. I tried to stay positive but it was not easy. Coach Myers and my teammates reminded me that I was the youngest player on the team and in the league. When I did get on the field, I was feisty. I got my first yellow card against the Seattle Sounders in May. Two months later, I scored my first professional goal against the Chicago Sting. As the season wound down, I was getting regular time and had even started a few games. I had one upcoming game circled on my calendar.

CHAPTER FIFTY-NINE

MY LIFE'S ALTERNATIVE DARK ROAD

At age 19, I was living my dream. I wasn't rich, but when you grow up poor, you don't realize you are poor, and you don't miss what you never had. When I thought of my brother, I realized how lucky I was. It's hard to fathom that two brothers who grew up under the same loving mother could follow such divergent paths. My mother, Agnes, was proud to have a son who would become a professional athlete. At the same time, the pain and sorrow she felt for her other son is hard to describe.

A few days before my first professional game at Yankee Stadium, my older brother, John, was arrested for stealing a car. He kept sinking deeper into trouble, and soon after, he was caught up in a big heroin bust in Spring Valley. The police used him to turn over evidence, and John left New York and headed for Houston with his shotgun and whatever he could cram in the back of his hot rod.

My mom prayed that John's move would help him find peace. A skilled freehand tattooist, John had opened a tattoo shop called the Black Dragon on Westheimer Street in Montrose. That neighborhood featured topless bars, street hookers, drag-queen prostitutes, and oriental massage parlors. Hordes of people would cruise Westheimer every night. It was a happening place.

My first visit to the Black Dragon came in December 1979. I was playing with the Hartford Hellions indoor soccer team, and we had a game against the Houston Summit. We arrived in town the day before the game and Coach gave us the afternoon off. I rented a car and was looking forward to surprising my brother at his shop. Ron Atanasio, a Hellion teammate and lifelong friend, came along for the ride. There were no cell phones and no GPS. All I had was an address and a map from the car rental desk.

John's parlor was easy to find, a cute little house on the main drag of Westheimer. We parked on the street and started the short walk toward the front door. There were three motorcycles parked out front and a handful of biker guys hanging loose. We could smell a little reefer. As I put my hand on the front door, one guy said, "So, you here to get a tattoo?" I said no. That set off some bells and a few guys stepped between us and the door. My friend Ronnie wasn't so tall, even with his large afro, but he was a muscled Italian New Yorker. Ronnie never shied away from a good fight. His fists were clenched and he was ready to rumble.

On the other hand, I tried to make fighting the last resort. I was in clogs with bell-bottom jeans, a Members Only jacket, and a mullet haircut that hung over my shoulders. They certainly knew we weren't bikers. I said that I was there to see JT, which was my brother's street name. One guy said, "If you're not getting a tattoo, what do you want with JT?"

I said, "I'm his brother and I'm here to visit him."

They all turned to one guy and said, "Hey, Hinkel, you're JT's brother, so who's this guy?"

This Hinkel guy stepped up to me and said, "If you're his brother, where are you from?"

I said, "I'm Tom Mulroy, from North Pascack Road in Spring Valley, New York." Hinkel said that sounded about right. Then he put out his hand, introduced himself as David Hinkel and led us inside.

We entered to find a beautiful girl sitting at the table, John giving her a tattoo. He looked up and said, "What the heck are you doing here?" When he found out that I was in town for a game, the next night, he gathered up 20 of his biker buddies and the Hellions had our most boisterous road cheering section ever. All game they screamed things like "Kick ass, Mulroy!" I think that was the only time my brother ever saw me play, and he did it in style.

CHAPTER SIXTY

TOO MUCH FOR HER TO ENDURE

Three years later, I would be called to visit Houston again. From the outside, it seemed my brother had found peace. Although he had parted ways with Glenda, the biological mother of his first child, John Jr., JT had married a wonderful lady named Jackie Bell. Jackie had a daughter about the same age as little John and they were happy playmates. My mom had occasional contact with my brother and her sense was that John and his family were doing well.

Apparently, Jackie's mother didn't see it that way. She did not approve of Jackie's biker lifestyle. She got a court order that declared Jackie an unfit mother, which gave her custody of Jackie's little girl. Well, losing her daughter was too much for Jackie to bear. A few days later, while JT and little John watched TV in the next room, Jackie would take her own life by gunshot. This would be the first time, but not the only time, my little nephew John would see a helicopter land on his front lawn to take a body out of the house.

When my mother got the news, she called and said we had to visit John and his son. We both flew to Houston International where we rented a car. As we pulled up to John's house, Little John was riding a Big Wheel in the street. Harley-Davidsons and pickup trucks filled the driveway and the front lawn. Mom and I were the only two people with no denim or leather. We were what my brother and his friends called "normal people." John walked out of the garage and gave Mom a huge hug as they cried together. I could tell that Mom, little John, and I were the only people not high on something.

The next day John showed me the bikes and hotrods that he kept in the garage. When we came to the last car, he opened the trunk and it was full of guns. There were pistols, rifles, and shotguns, and even a box of hand grenades. I asked him what he was doing with all this. He said, "In my tattoo business, I do a lot of bartering. When people don't have cash, they pay for tattoos with valuables. Guns, drugs, and sometimes even a little sex." He smiled and laughed.

Soon, we were getting in the rental car to head to Jackie's funeral. I'd bet that was the first time that little John sat in the back seat of a vehicle. When my mom strapped him in, he didn't know what a seat belt was. My brother insisted on riding his Harley-Davidson and told me to stay close behind. It was quite the caravan: 30-plus motorcycles, hot rods and pickup trucks, and us in our economy-size rent-a-car. It was like being in a biker parade. We didn't need a police escort; we had all the security we needed.

Other than the bikes and hot rods in the parking lot, this funeral parlor looked like any other. Inside, however, none of the other rooms were being used. My guess is they didn't want to mix the clientele. It was a closed casket ceremony, but John said she was in leather and denim because she was one of them. Her mother was not allowed to attend. John blamed her mother and Jackie's family for her death.

There was no priest, no person in charge of sending her off. John spoke, then a few of his friends shared some words. It was sad, but they spoke from their hearts. It seemed like everyone was high on something. There was no sign of the funeral parlor staff. They were likely hiding in their offices. When the ceremony was over, they put Jackie in a hearse. The caravan followed the hearse to her resting place. The next day mom and I flew home, but my poor mom could not stop thinking about little John. He was now her biggest worry.

CHAPTER SIXTY-ONE

"YOU SEE, THE DEVIL'S NOT READY FOR ME YET."

In the summer of 1985, I had just finished the season with my Louisville Thunder indoor team. Keith Tozer, our player-coach, and I were in charge of the club's summer camp programs. We were running a camp in Lexington and the staff was staying in a hotel downtown. Most weeks during the summer I would work the club's camps on Mondays and Fridays. Mid-week, my contract allowed me to fly around the country doing juggling demonstrations and speaking engagements. I would make more money doing a 90-minute demonstration than most coaches earned for working camp all week. Often, I would do two different camp demos in one day.

As I returned to Lexington that Thursday evening, I joined the guys in the hotel bar. Keith wore a serious look and told me we needed to talk. He hung his arm on my shoulder and walked me to a quiet spot in the lounge. He said, "Brother, sit down, I have something to tell you. I just got a message from your mom. Your brother has been shot." With little emotion, I asked, "Is he dead?" Keith was surprised by my reaction. He blurted out, "I'm serious. Your brother's been shot!" Had Keith been with me when I went to Jackie's funeral in Houston, I'm sure he would have understood why I wasn't even a little surprised.

I asked again if my brother was dead. Keith answered, "No, he's in a hospital and just came out of a coma, and your mom wants you to call her now." I hustled to my room and called my mom. She was very shaken, and I think she was most concerned about little John. She said, "John needs us, and I don't have the emotional strength to go through that again. Can you please go to Houston? Pray for little John."

The next morning, I left for Houston. There were no direct flights so I did not arrive until almost midnight. My mom had not spoken with anyone, and we did not know where little John was or who was caring for him. No one knew that I was coming. I decided to stop by the Black Dragon first. As I reached the hood at 1 a.m. on a Friday night in summer, there were thousands of people roaming the street.

I stopped at a light, and two hookers came up and asked if I needed company. When I rolled up in front of the Black Dragon, I saw two young kids racing in supermarket carts along the sidewalk. Both wore blue jeans and sleeveless denim jackets. One kid had long blond hair, and I knew it was little John. He had just turned five years old. I thought to myself, *Thank God my mom did not make the trip.*

As I walked up to little John, I was thrilled to see he recognized me. He ran up and jumped into my arms, and then he and his friend brought me into the Black Dragon. A lady was giving a guy a tattoo on his shoulder in the back of the parlor. It was Karen, my brother's newest *"Old Lady"*. I had heard about her but this was the first time we had met. Little John introduced her as his mom. Karen was good people. She said with John laid up, she had to tattoo to pay the bills.

The next morning, we went to see my brother in the hospital. As we left the elevator on John's floor, I could hear him screaming from across the way. "Give me some more fucking morphine! I need more fucking morphine!" We followed the yelling to his room. Inside, we found John and Hinkle, his best friend, the guy I met on my first visit. He was always a loyal friend in John's time of need. My brother gave me a smile and I gave him a gentle hug. After our greeting, he said, "Hey, you're normal; they'll listen to you. Go tell the doctor I need more fucking morphine." I found his doctor, introduced myself, and asked for an update. The doctor pulled John's file from a cabinet. He took out an X-ray and held it up to the light. Then he said my brother had been shot in the chest. The bullet had somehow passed between his heart and his spine and exited out his back. The doctor added that the odds of a bullet fitting between the heart and spine are incredibly small. "Your brother is a very, very lucky man," he said.

At that moment, my brother screamed, "Where's my fucking morphine?" The doctor said, "We have been giving your brother the normal dose of morphine, but he seems to have a high tolerance to our drugs." He smiled, I smiled back, and I headed back to John's room. When I told JT what the doctor said about the bullet, he smiled and said, "You see, the devil's not ready for me yet."

I went to a pay phone, called my mom, and told her that both Johns were in good care. Later that day, I had learned that my brother had given little John a few small tattoos: one on the base of his right thumb and two in the same spot on his left hand, just little dots, like freckles. This way, if little John ever got kidnapped by a biker gang, my brother would be able to identify him.

We stayed with John all day. That night his friends started to pile in. I'm sure the hospital loved this group. His room was standing room only, as loud as any biker bar. Soon John stopped complaining about the morphine; his friends were helping him self-medicate. Little John and I were probably the only people not high. At one point, I realized I didn't know how John got shot. So, I leaned in and asked him. John started to tell the story and the room got quiet. He said, "I was letting Rick and his old lady stay over at my house. We were all a little high. We had been shooting heroin and he started arguing over something bizarre. One thing led to another, and with guns all over the house, bullets started to fly. The next thing I knew, I was being put into a helicopter on my front lawn and I woke up here."

I asked what happened to this Ricky guy. John said, "I'm not sure what happened to Ricky; no one has seen him around." First there was a light giggle and then the room broke into laughter. I felt I had missed the punchline of a good joke. Well, a few weeks later, Ricky was found in a cornfield outside of town, his head blown off. It happened while my brother was still in the hospital, so it wasn't him, but I think most people in the room knew who it was.

The next day I flew home. My mom convinced my brother that until he was on his feet, it would be best for little John to move to Monterey, MA, where he could live with Grandma and start kindergarten. I believe that move saved little John's life.

John Mulroy Jr. in front of the Black Dragon Tattoo Studio

JT hanging out at the Black Dragon Tattoo Studio

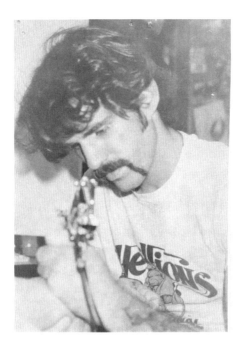

JT working his tattoo magic

**JT & His Boys at The Black Dragon
Tattoo Studio, Houston TX**

CHAPTER SIXTY-TWO

JT'S NEW LOW: A 13-HOUR STANDOFF WITH A HOUSTON SWAT TEAM

On September 7, 1987, the front-page headline of the Houston Chronicle read: **Police arrest gunman after 13-hour standoff**. Here is the story:

"A tattoo parlor owner armed with a shotgun kept Houston SWAT officers at bay for 13 hours in Montrose Sunday before he came outside and was arrested without incident. John Thomas Mulroy, 31, address undetermined, was arrested about 8:30 p.m., police spokesman Dan Turner said. Mulroy is charged with attempted capital murder of a police officer. Bond was denied. About 7:30 a.m., police received a call about a disturbance with a knife at the Black Dragon Tattoo Studio, 1202 Westheimer. Turner said Mulroy fired two shots at arriving officers, who returned fire, then took cover and called for assistance. Turner said there was another brief flurry of gunfire, and then another man ran from the parlor. He told police that Mulroy was intoxicated and extremely upset, Turner said.

The SWAT team was called, and police sealed off several blocks of the lower Westheimer area. SWAT negotiators tried to talk to Mulroy, but he destroyed his phone. A robot was used to deliver another phone to the front of the business, and police re-established contact. Turner said police had many conflicting stories about the type and number of weapons in the building and considered the standoff a 'high-risk situation.' After hours of negotiations, Mulroy finally stepped outside. Turner said police had not determined why Mulroy fired on the officers or why he was upset. He said there were rumors Mulroy was angry because a friend had been arrested recently."

My brother's reckless lifestyle had finally boiled over. He landed in a maximum-security state prison, the Beto Unit in Anderson County, Texas. John served three ungodly years. The Beto Unit was known as a "prison for gladiators," where inmates fought because they liked to or they had to. Worse, if you were in for attempted capital murder of a police officer, you were a marked man. In those days, the police and the prisons had no mercy.

Being a freehand tattoo artist did earn John some benefits. Back then most people associated tattoos with sailors, soldiers, biker clubs, social deviants, and criminals. There were plenty of those kinds of people behind bars, so tattoos were a hot commodity. John also learned to draw kinky porn, a popular commodity that, along with the tattoos, gave John a stream of income and a fighting chance to survive.

CHAPTER SIXTY-THREE

JT REVEALS THE BETRAYAL

While John was serving time, he would occasionally call Mom so he could talk to little John. One day when John called, Mom could tell he was not doing well. She asked him what was bothering him. In a broken voice, John asked, "Do you remember Father Kearns?"

After a pause, Mom said, "Of course I remember him."

John got right to it. "Well, when I was an altar boy, he was molesting me. He did horrible things and he made me do horrible things. I never told anybody before. I didn't think anyone would believe me. When I was younger, I actually thought it might have been my fault. Mom, you're the first person I ever told this to, and it's the first time I ever said it out loud."

They both began to weep uncontrollably. They got the one-minute warning and soon the call was disconnected. Mom cried hysterically, thinking of each little sign that she might have seen. My mother was a devout Catholic. In fact, she never divorced my father because she wanted to be able to receive communion, one of the seven sacraments. With her upbringing, she figured the ideal male role model for her sons was a priest from the local parish.

Once she regained control, she called me. I could tell right away something was off, and for the next two hours, we cried together. She kept saying she should have known. It's always easier in hindsight. There may have been clues. For example, one night at a catechism class, John nearly duked it out with Father Reynolds, who was Father Kearns' superior and part of the authority that John despised. John never wanted to go to church; he did not want to continue being an altar boy. His reckless ways—the drugs, the risk-taking, and the disrespect for authority—were part of his cry for help. In our household, the highest authority was the church. I believe all forms of authority, the government and police, in some way represented to John the church's authority, and he rebelled against it all. To this day, my mother blames herself. In some small way, her raising little John was like having a second chance.

When we got off the phone, I wondered how I was not able to sense the burden my brother was carrying. I also knew that had I not found soccer, I would have been dead or in jail. My love for the game kept me away from becoming an altar boy. Soccer was like a spiritual force that steered me away from trouble and onto a life path of happiness and fulfillment. I also took stock in how lucky I was to have so many caring people in my life. That started with my wonderful mother, Agnes, who had handled the highs and the lows all by herself with strength and resilience. My coaches were my mentors; they were always there for me. Many people do not realize the influence a coach can have on a young person's life. Let me tell you from personal experience, it can be lifesaving.

Unfortunately, my brother had Father Kearns and Father Reynolds. True, Reynolds did not take part in the molestation, but he covered it up and that made him equally culpable.

JT's way of saying that he loved me

How JT signed his letters from jail to his son.
"To John Love Dad"

CHAPTER SIXTY-FOUR

"FINALLY, YOUR BROTHER IS AT PEACE."

John Thomas "JT" Mulroy died on February 17th, 1992. Shortly after his release from prison, John was found hanged in a closet in his apartment in Houston, with a rope around his neck and a needle in his arm. Was it a suicide, or was it an act of sexual asphyxiation gone wrong? We will never know. What I do know is that my brother lived a deeply complicated life. As they were about to shut his coffin, I remember my mother looking at him and then at me and saying, "Finally, your brother is at peace." Yes, for the first time in many years, he was at peace. He left behind a wonderful wife, Karen, and two sons, Little John and James.

This portrait was drawn on a white handkerchief with a black ink pen by JT as a gift to his son little John while JT was serving time in a maximum-security state prison in Texas.

CHAPTER SIXTY-FIVE

LIVING THE DREAM

My first season as a pro was coming to an end, with only two road games left. One would be against the New York Cosmos on Tuesday night, August 10th, at Yankee Stadium. At this point I had earned regular time on the field. As we boarded the plane for New York City, I realized this would be the first time I would play professionally in my hometown, and the first time I would spend a night in a Manhattan hotel. *How cool was that? I thought that only rich people stayed in hotels in Manhattan.* Even more important, I was going to face my idol, the King, Pelé. We arrived on the Monday before the game, and since Yankee Stadium was not available for us to train that day, Coach Myers took us for a light jog and a kick-around in Central Park.

As I put my head on the pillow that night, I knew I would struggle to sleep. I'm not sure how to describe this feeling, but it was some form of positive energy. I eventually nodded off and the next day we were stepping off the bus at Yankee Stadium. When I was growing up, we had once lived with my grandmother on Valentine

Avenue and 187th Street, off the Grand Concourse in the Bronx, just a few subway stops away. This neighborhood was familiar turf.

Coach Rottenbucher had organized a pregame exhibition between my old team, Clarkstown Sports Club, and another youth club. He was waiting to greet me as I got off the bus and we fell into a hearty hug. My teammates and I made our way to the locker room, the nicest one I had ever seen. I don't know why I was surprised, since this was the house that Babe Ruth built.

The day before, from the hotel phone I had tried to reach my Pomona Junior High School guidance counselor, the guy who years ago had told me to quit dreaming, that I would never be a professional soccer player. Although we never talked, I left a message at the school asking if he needed a ticket. Not sure if he ever got the message. For all I knew, he was in the stadium. Regardless, I was glad I made that call because I had to get it off my chest.

We never knew the starting eleven until right before the kick-off, except for maybe the goalkeeper. As Coach began to write the lineup on the board and got to the midfielders, I saw him write "M-U-L," and adrenaline raced through me. I didn't even hear the last few names of the lineup. Heading out to warm up, I felt like I was gliding on a cloud. When we reached the pitch, the stadium was filling up and the crowd was full of life. It was everything I dreamed it would be and more.

We were told to clear the field to make way for pre-game ceremonies. We huddled on the sideline in front of the dugout. Coach Myers gave us a few last inspiring words. He said, "Stick to the plan—whenever Pelé gets the ball, make sure we double-team him." That sounded good to me, as we would not saddle any one person with marking him. They directed us to the field to line up for the national anthem and team introductions.

There I stood with my hand over my heart, singing the national anthem. I was getting ready to play on the same field that had been home to Joe DiMaggio, Babe Ruth, and Mickey Mantle. As the anthem came to an end and I wiped away tears, the PA announcer began to introduce the players. *In goal for Miami, number 18, Van Taylor. Defender, number 9, Jim Holton.* Finally, I heard, *In midfield, number 14, Tommy Mulroy.* It seemed like the entire stadium got up and shouted for me. The roar was so loud they wrote about it in the papers the next day. Aside from when they introduced Pelé, no other player got a warmer welcome.

Two huge signs hung from the rafters. One read, "Mulroy, chuck a moon," which was the rave back in the day. Now, I never did that in public, but after a high school game, our goalkeeper Mau stuck his bare butt out the window of our team bus at some nuns at Albertus Magnus High School. Yes, Mau got suspended. So, that message on the banner may not have been the best choice of words, but my friends' hearts were in the right place. Whenever I see that banner in the background of the game photos, I laugh, even 50 years later.

This was a pivotal game for the Cosmos. They needed a win to secure a good seed in the playoffs. It was the first full year that Pelé had been on the team. They had added some other big-money stars like Italian striker Giorgio Chinaglia. The Cosmos needed this game. We, on the other hand, were out of the playoffs, and some of our key players on loan had already returned to England. As we stood in our positions waiting for the referee's opening whistle, I could hear my friends chanting, "Mulroy, Mulroy." *Wow, this is surreal.* The ref blew his whistle and off we went. Soon the Cosmos had moved the ball down the flank into our defensive third. The ball was played inside to Chinaglia, who fired toward the near post but was robbed by our young keeper, Van Taylor. Alas, Pelé was there to blast in the rebound.

We had played only two minutes and twelve seconds, and we were behind. The crowd of 18,103 stood cheering. I was jogging back for the kickoff when I saw Coach Myers waving at me. I sprinted over while the referees tried to break up the Cosmos' celebration. Coach told me there was a change of plans, that we were giving Pelé too much room. "I want you to mark him out of the game, Tommy. I want you to follow him wherever he goes. If he goes to the bathroom, you go with him. He is yours."

It happened so quickly I didn't have time for nerves. Looking back, the order Coach gave me was monumental, one of the best things that ever happened to me. I had to look at the game and my mission differently. As one newspaper wrote the next day about me marking my idol: "Mulroy and Pelé were face-to-face, back-to-back, side-to-side, underneath and on top of each other throughout the game. Mulroy and Pelé did a respectable version of me and my shadow."

The Cosmos' lead did not last long. We played the ball out wide from the kickoff, where our wing sent a cross into the box. An unmarked Nico Bodonczy rose up and scored on a header that took the air out of the crowd. I thought this game was going to be a barnburner; after three minutes each team had scored. A few minutes later, Chinaglia and our keeper Van Taylor met in a brutal collision, and Chinaglia was taken off the field. He returned a few minutes later with three stitches in his right shin. Unlike today, back then you did not have to wear shin guards.

This man-to-man marking was new for me. When I was in college, I was the guy being marked. Now here I was, running when Pelé ran, stopping when he stopped. At all times I had one eye on him and one on the ball. A few times I took the ball from him, which made me realize he was human. Okay, superhuman, but still human. I admit that here and there I held his shirt and grabbed his shorts. I even took him down once or twice, but only with the ball. I could tell he respected that I was playing the ball and not kicking him. Players all over the world had gone out of their way to get a piece of him, ball or no ball, but not me. That is not who I am.

Every time I got the ball, the stands went berserk. My family and friends from Rockland and Ulster Community College, as well as my German American League teammates, were all cheering for me. My mom was there with my Uncle Frank and the entire Fuchs family. Every time I touched the ball, whether toe-poking it away from Pelé or dribbling up the field, the fans were yelling for me the entire 90 minutes. It was amazing.

The Cosmos started to chip away and 28 minutes in, Chinaglia smashed in a great ball from Tony Field. Mike Dillion extended the lead when he converted a through-ball from 12 yards. After each goal, on my way back to midfield, I was thinking, *I am so glad that Pelé did not score that one.* I was beginning to think that I could contain him.

At the 37-minute mark, a Cosmo played the ball from midfield to the left flank, where Brian Rowan sent a left-footed cross that overshot our box. The ball was retrieved by his fellow Scotsman Charlie Mitchell, who chipped it high. The ball started to come down between the penalty spot and the keeper's box, about ten yards off the back post. It was a perfect serve, with a touch of backspin and not too hot. It was also going to drop in the most dangerous spot, which was anywhere near Pelé.

When Charlie hit the chip, I was running toward the goal alongside Pelé, one eye on him, one eye on the ball. As the ball started to curl away from the goal, Pelé began to backpedal, his head moving from side to side. He was using his peripheral vision to see what was around him, so he would know what to do next. He always had one eye on the ball.

The box was crowded. Four of my teammates and I stood within playing distance of where that cross would land. In addition to Pelé, three other Cosmos jockeyed near the ball. I was staying goal side of Pelé, and as he started to backpedal, I thought, *that ball is so high, it's coming down like a floater*. On a ball with that little pace, it is hard to generate a dangerous header on goal. I figured if Pelé was going to head it, I could give him a little space. And then it happened. Pelé was not going to head the ball. He had turned his back to goal, positioning himself to perform one of the most difficult and spectacular athletic feats in all of sport—the "bicycle" kick, or overhead kick.

By the time I realized this, it was too late. Up Pelé went, his back to goal, his body parallel to the grass, his eyes never leaving the ball. He swung his left leg up and then whipped his right boot into the ball. He was only 5'8", but when his boot met that ball, that boot was at least six-and-a-half feet off the ground, upside-down. On a bicycle kick you must strike the ball above the center to keep it below the bar. Keep in mind that this kick is amid a forest of players. His shot whizzed past my jumping teammates and me, sailed past our diving keeper, and stung the net in the corner. The crowd broke into screams and cheers. I had never heard anything like it. Time seemed to freeze. Normally when the other team scores, everyone is upset.

Not after this one: we were all in awe. It was like having front-row seats to a magic show. That would prove to be a historic moment, not just for Pelé, but for our sport here in the United States.

After the game, Pelé would say it was one of the best goals he had ever scored, which was no small feat, this being his 1,254th goal. His goal was so spectacular and so unusual the American media referred to it as an upside-down somersault. This was another example of how little the U.S. sports media knew about the world's game. This goal epitomized why Pelé had decided to unretire and bring the beautiful game to our country. He wanted to promote the wonder of soccer and import to the U.S. the passion felt by billions around the world.

Pelé's goal that night on August 10, 1976, was so historic that five years later in 1981, Paramount Pictures released a soccer film called *Victory*. Starring Sylvester Stallone, Michael Caine, Max von Sydow, and Pelé, the film follows Allied prisoners of war who are held in a German prison camp during World War II. In it, the prisoners play an exhibition match of football against a German team whose captain was Cosmos star, Werner Roth. Pelé wins that game with a spectacular bicycle kick against the German soldiers. That goal, portrayed in the first mainstream soccer movie ever released in the U.S., was a reenactment of the goal Pelé had scored that night in Yankee Stadium. The audience for that bicycle kick ballooned from the 18,000 people who saw it live to millions of people seeing it in slow motion on the big screen. In some small way, I felt a part of it.

Back to the game at Yankee Stadium. A few minutes after Pelé's goal, we were awarded a penalty kick. My roommate Roman Rusol stuck a bullet into the corner, beyond the reach of Shep Messing, the Cosmos' goalkeeper and my lifelong friend. The first half ended with the Cosmos up, 4–2.

As we made our way to the tunnel leading to the locker room, I was greeted by spirited fans. As the second half started, it was back to the one-on-one dance with the King. My dream-come-true was also a lesson in how soccer is played at the highest level. In every game he played, Pelé was marked tightly, usually by multiple players. This is why he was even better off the ball than he was on the ball. He did things that I had never seen anyone else do. He would make me think he wasn't paying attention, and then, bang, he was gone. He would act like he was tying his shoe, or talking to a fan or teammate, and suddenly he was gone again. With his speed and technical ability, all he needed was a half-step to strike fear in his foes.

There were times that night when Pelé used other players as a pick, a common tactic in basketball. He would run me into other Cosmos players, and sometimes he would lead me to the blindside of my teammates, who would unknowingly help Pelé free himself. Soccer is a game of inches played on a huge field. I never saw another player in any sport change speed and direction more often or with more success than the King. That is how this man, despite being double or triple-teamed, scored over 1,200 goals.

Halfway through the second half, the Cosmos had a corner kick in the part of the field closest to the fans. Pelé did not normally take corner kicks; he was the guy on the end of the kick. As the Cosmos set up for the kick, I was all eyes. Pelé started his run into the penalty area but then darted out toward his teammate, who was about to take the kick. I thought they were going to take a short corner and give Pelé the ball. I was close enough to grab him, but chose to shadow him instead. I was using all seven of my senses to try to offset his superhuman nature.

Most people think there are only five senses. But if you are covering Pelé, you need more than touch, hearing, sight, taste, and smell. There are actually two more senses: vestibular, the sense of balance and movement, used, for example, to ride a bike or dribble a soccer ball. And proprioception, the conscious awareness of the body and limbs. This sense helps you know where a body part is without looking at it. The truth is I used only six of my seven senses, each one but taste. As Uruguay's Luis Suarez will tell you, there is no upside to using taste on a soccer field.

The fans were excited to get a close-up look at the King as he ran toward his teammate about to take the corner. I was fixated on the King, and then bang, he bolted off. After three quick steps, he came to an abrupt stop. I was running backward and nearly lost my balance. He had made the run because he knew I was following his every move. It was like a game of Follow the Leader. I realized that he had done that little jig only to have me follow him, and the fans knew it too. Pelé looked at me, smiled like only he can, and waved his index finger as if to say, I GOT YOU.

The crowd laughed and cheered. A few seconds later, Pelé shot off again, three quick steps. I backpedaled like my life depended on it. Pelé had become the puppeteer, and I was his puppet. He stopped and the fans erupted again; Pelé had made them laugh at my expense. I believe that he did not do this with mean intent; I think he was trying to throw me off my game. I considered it an honor to be covering him. Looking back now, I liken this episode to Daniel LaRusso being mentored by the wise master Mr. Miyagi in the movie *The Karate Kid*.

A few minutes later, the referee stopped the game for an injury. As the team trainer went out to tend to the downed player, Pelé walked over to the sideline, me right behind. Some fans were yelling, "Mulroy, Tommy Mulroy." Pelé had asked for water. I was thinking, *If he runs into the bathroom, am I really going to go with him?* For sure. He was not getting away from me, no matter where he went. As I stood a few feet away, a man jumped off the Cosmos' bench, filled a cup with water, and walked it to Pelé.

I had one eye on Pelé and the other on the field, where play had not resumed. I was on high alert, thinking he was going to take off as soon as I took my eye off him. Pelé drank the water, handed the cup back, and said in his Brazilian accent, "Please, another cup." The man filled the cup and handed it to Pelé. He turned to me and said, "You look thirsty, you like water?" Then he handed me the cup. This was a "wow" moment in my life. With a big smile and a "Thank you very much," I enjoyed the best cup of water I ever drank.

After the game resumed, Pelé wasn't doing much, but Chinaglia was. He scored in the 73rd minute, and then again in the 79th minute. Frustration set in, especially for our older English players. They began to tackle harder than usual, and the English can tackle hard. One of my teammates yelled at me to kick Pelé. As we fell farther behind, he was screaming, "Kick that fucking N****r." I knew Pelé could hear him. How sick was that? I thought if my mother Agnes had heard my teammate, she would have come onto the field and dragged him off.

Yankee Stadium was hallowed ground, but the dirt infield of the baseball diamond was a poor surface for soccer. Occasionally the ball would fly out of bounds to the other side of the infield and it took a while to retrieve it. I remember Coach Myers telling me after the game that Pelé made more money waiting for the ball boys to retrieve the ball than I made in a month. At the time, Pelé was the highest-paid athlete on the planet. He had a $7 million, two-and-a-half-year contract. They estimated he was going to play in about 85 games, some of them exhibitions overseas. Do the math and that is $82,352.94 per game, or about $915 per minute, or $15.25 per second.

Late in the match, Chinaglia scored two more goals. At that point, most of my teammates couldn't wait for the final whistle, but I was living the dream. I had a front-row seat for the best goal in history. My idol was teaching me all manners of soccer nuances, and he even served me a refreshment. Huge banners bearing "Mulroy" hung from the rafters and fans were screaming my name. I wanted the game to last all night. Then something happened that was almost as sublime as the game itself.

Seconds before the final whistle, the ball got played out of bounds at midfield, near the player benches and locker room. Pelé turned to me with a smile. He grabbed his shirt with both hands and said, "You like my shirt?" My jaw dropped, no words coming out. I think Pelé read my body language, as we had built a bit of a bond during the match, helping each other off the ground when the occasion called for it. The King whipped off his shirt, handed it to me, and ran through the dugout toward the locker room. The ball got thrown in and a few seconds later, the referee blew the final whistle.

Fans rushed the field like they always did when Pelé played, which is why he would sneak off before the final whistle. I rolled up the King's treasure and hid it under my shirt. I hurried toward the locker room and away from the thousands of fans, most looking for Pelé, some others screaming my name. Soon I was surrounded by my cousin Frank Fuchs, Erhardt Kapp, and many of my former youth club teammates. They escorted me to the entrance of the tunnel without letting anyone rob me of one of soccer's most cherished jewels. I stepped into the tunnel, where newspaper and TV reporters jockeyed for a quote from Pelé or Chinaglia.

As I made my way through the media chaos, a man stepped up to me, a pad in one hand and a pen in the other. He said, "Tommy Mulroy, I'm Bill Varner with the Journal News. Do you have a minute?" I was a rookie and still excited about giving interviews. In that moment, I would have given one to my junior high school paper. The Journal News, my hometown paper, had covered me when I played in high school. The next day, I would frame Varner's story and hang it on my wall, where it has been ever since.

I finished the interview and went to the locker room, where my teammates were surrounded by reporters, VIPs, and sponsors. As I started to undress, I still had Pelé's jersey in my hand, and no way would I put it down. Who could I trust to protect it? My mother was outside with my family, waiting for me. But if I gave it to her, would I be putting her life at risk? Wearing only a towel, I approached Coach Myers, who was sitting in front of a locker answering questions in front of a few microphones. I said, "Coach, can you please look after Pelé's shirt for me?"

Coach smiled and said, "Tommy, I will guard it with my life. But hurry up because there is a chance someone will kill me for it." I handed it to Coach and took my fastest shower ever.

By the time I got dressed, most reporters had left and I thought the hoopla was over. But when I walked out to the bus-boarding area, a large crowd milled about. As I came into view, they went crazy. Just when I thought the dream was over, the place was lighting up like the fourth of July. People ran to me screaming and asking for autographs. I saw my mom, Agnes, my Uncle Frank, Aunt Nancy, and my cousins standing to the side, glowing with pride. I recognized many friends from my school days, teammates and opponents alike. It was amazing. As one newspaper reporter wrote, "When Mulroy stepped out of the players gate to the stadium after the game, he was greeted by screams of 'Tommy, Tommy, Tommy,' from a large crowd of fans who pressed around him and held out pieces of paper and even soccer balls for him to autograph. 'Who is that guy?' asked a guard at the gate. As Mulroy made his way slowly through the crowd, his dreams were still very much in progress."

Even today, that photo from our game opens doors and gives me instant credibility. When people see it, they say, "You played against Pelé!"

I joke back, "No, Pelé played against me." Then I tell them the story of that wonderful day as if it was yesterday.

Living The Dream

Look closely "Mulroy Chuck a Moon."

CHAPTER SIXTY-SIX

THE FINAL REFLECTION

That night, I reflected on my journey. Eight years earlier, I had never seen a soccer ball. No one in my family had played soccer or knew much about it. Now Pelé had given me his match jersey. After most of his games, players and fans had begged him for his shirt. On this day, he offered it to me. Sure, I was marking him, but that alone did not earn me the honor, or so I believe in my heart.

I believe that Pelé was the most important force in elevating soccer from an ethnic cult to a mainstream sport in the U.S. He helped millions of Americans understand, appreciate, and embrace the beautiful game. In some way, when Pelé gave me his jersey, I think he was handing me a torch. There was a message in that jersey, a call to continue on with his quest, to promote soccer as if I were his disciple. People ask if I traded my jersey with Pelé. I tell them he did not want mine. I still have both our jerseys hanging together on the wall with the other shirts I wore during my professional career.

This was one of the best days of my life, outdone only when my beautiful wife Paola gave birth to our daughter, Sabrina. I know this day would never have happened without the support of my wonderful mother, Agnes Mulroy, my family, as well as all of my club, high school and Cinema 45 teammates, all of whom contributed to who I am. I was so lucky to have wonderful coaches and mentors, the guys who guided me from age 12 right through to the pros. They are John Sautner, Frank Rottenbucher, Fred Bloom, Rich Meszaros, Gary Schoonmaker, George Vizvary, and Greg Myers, who gave me the task to mark Pelé that night. I am who I am because of all of you. Thank you for being such an important part of my life. Love always, "Soccer Tom."

POSTSCRIPT

On and off the field, "Soccer Tom" Mulroy has devoted his life to soccer. Here are a few highlights.

Playing Career

Tom became a professional soccer player at age 19 when he signed with the Miami Toros of the North American Soccer League (NASL). He competed at the pro level for over a decade, playing for 13 different teams in 250+ games, scoring over 50 goals and winning both outdoor and indoor championships. In 1986, Tom was among the first American players to represent the USA in a world all-star game. This match was held in Lima, Peru, to honor the retiring Nene Cubillas, Peru's best player ever and a FIFA Top 100 player.

Soccer Executive/Entrepreneur

In 1986, Tom became founder and president of Soccer Marketing and Promotions and Se Habla Futbol. He soon emerged as an accomplished entrepreneur, creating new ways to promote the game across the country. From 1992 to 2007, he conceived, owned, and ran Copa Latina, the largest multiethnic soccer tournament in the USA. At a Copa Latina final, Tom married his sweetheart, Paola, in front of 5,000 fans. He also launched a new kind of event that paired music with soccer. Tom promoted a Brazil-Mexico game featuring a concert by Carlos Santana, and a Germany-Argentina match with a performance by the Gypsy Kings. In 2012, Tom became president of the NASL's Fort Lauderdale Strikers. He led the club to the NASL finals and markedly increased the team's fan base.

Tom has made many contributions to multiple FIFA World Cup tournaments. After his playing career, he was named official spokesperson for the 1994 FIFA World Cup, then held for the first time in the USA. He performed at the World Cup draw held at Madison Square Garden in New York City in front of a live audience and a television audience in 164 countries. He was a member of the South Florida Soccer Bid Committee for the 1994 World Cup, the 1996 Olympic soccer games held in the Orange Bowl, and the 2026 World Cup Committee. Tom has attended nine consecutive World Cup final matches, beginning in Mexico in 1986 and running through Russia in 2018.

Spokesman and Entertainer

A natural showman, Tom once held the world record for juggling a soccer ball with 12,295 taps, keeping the ball airborne for over two hours. He performed this feat atop the Empire State Building as a promotion for one of his professional teams. He also performed during halftime at a Harlem Globetrotters basketball game. As the soccer spokesman for the "Just Say No to Drugs" campaign, Tom appeared on *Late Night with David Letterman*, ESPN's *Just for Kids*, and Nickelodeon. He also served on national TV as a color commentator for College Soccer Weekly.

Tom resides in Miami with Paola and his daughters, Sabrina and Militza. John Mulroy, Jr. is happily married with a young son of his own. He followed in his Uncle Tom's footsteps and is a full-time youth soccer coach. James Mulroy has gone on to become an accomplished, professional guitarist. He lives close to his mother Karen, who is also a tattoo artist. Tom and his company continue to work with youth clubs, leagues, federations, and sponsors to nurture and promote soccer in the USA

Thank you all for reading this book.
I hope you enjoyed reading it as much as I enjoyed writing it.
You can view more about me and my soccer world
at the following places:

To Contact "Soccer Tom" Mulroy
Website: http://soccertom.com/
Email is: tom@copalatina.com

World Cup 2026—Here We Come!

ACKNOWLEDGEMENTS

We all know the saying, "It takes a village to raise a child." In my case, it took a soccer community of loving family and friends to make me who I am. My journey to publish *90 Minutes with the King* has been no different. The encouragement, direction, and hard work put in by my clan is what made this book possible. There will be some public-school teachers rolling over in their graves when they find out Tommy Mulroy wrote a book.

Let me begin by thanking my mother, Agnes. She inspired and encouraged me at every level of my life right up until her last few days as I read her the manuscript. My devoted friend William Derella guided me from the beginning and provided creative ideas at every step of the way. Soccer journalist Bill Summers skillfully edited the book and gave me sound advice on the publishing process. Thanks to my good friend Shep Messing, the American soccer legend who wrote the Foreword from his heart.

Next, I thank my editorial committee, which was made up of some of my most valued friends and family members. It starts with my roommate and best friend Rick Derella, who helped me remember the wonderful journey. My junior high coach, Rich Meszaros, worked in the publishing industry for many years and brought his experience and insight to the project. Art Turpel, a successful business executive and soccer fanatic, helped me run Soccer Marketing and Promotions and stage its most spectacular soccer events. Ben Markus, who worked for me at the Fort Lauderdale Strikers, brought his business insights and proofreading to the team. My little cousin Dan Fuchs, a school teacher, helped with fact-checking that could only be done by a member of the Cinema 45 crew.

My village also include friends like Tom Byer. This Ulster soccer brother and author of *Soccer Starts at Home* shared many useful publishing tips. I also received valuable advice from Mike Gorszczaryk, a member of the MLS Charlotte FC academy coaching staff. Mike started his coaching career at my Weston Select youth club and, at age 26, has written two soccer books. Thanks to Josh William, a book industry friend who recommend Bookbaby, and to Christiana Ellis, who walked me through the logistics of publishing. I am so grateful to Ryan Zighelboim for his artistic talent in the design of our wonderful 90 MINUTES WITH THE KING book cover.

Most important of all, I thank my family, friends, and my entire soccer community. You have supported me throughout my adventure and shared in the amazing evolution of soccer here in the United States. Finally, I recognize soccer, the sport I love and the game that saved my life.

TESTIMONIALS

"What a wonderful read. *90 Minutes With The King* is not only an entertaining soccer story, but an inspirational life's journey that exemplifies how soccer's core values can shape a person's life. Soccer Toms self-motivation, dedication and determination is a textbook example for inspiring young men and women who truly are committed to reaching their dreams on and off the field." —**Anson Dorrance**

Head Coach first Women's World Cup (1991) & 21 Time NCAA Division I Tournament Champion with UNC.

"Tom Mulroy deceived me, he made me think I was about to read a great soccer story but it's so much more - it's a great American success story…From his rough and tumble beginnings to his soaring soccer success and his intense caring for kids of all skills and sizes this is truly a must-read story for anyone looking for inspiration. Great Job Tom!" —**Brian Kilmeade**

Co-host of Fox & Friends

"Tom, while anyone who grew up with the beautiful game in the 1970's-1980's can attest to your considerable soccer skills, little did we know of your outstanding writing abilities.

Your book *90 minutes with the King* was a fantastic read. As a player who grew up in New York during those wonderful days of club soccer, your book brought back such vivid memories. Through your words, I could almost smell the confines of the Met Oval, I could hear the sound of my metal cleats of my adidas boots while walking to and from the Met Oval.

I was fascinated to learn of your journey in life, so rich and full of greatness. We all knew you to be the Pied Piper of soccer! Whatever it took to promote the game, you were there, and your book has taken us with you.

Richly written and stunningly accurate *90 Minutes With The King* will enrich every reader." —**Hank Steinbrecher (The Preacher)**

Secretary General/CEO US Soccer

"Pele is a soccer legend, arguably the greatest player of all time. Tommy Mulroy is also a soccer legend, whose passion for the game is unmatched. In *90 Minutes With The King*, through Mulroy's storytelling, you will get a rare behind the scenes glimpse of Pele and will also see why everyone who meets Mulroy falls in love with The Beautiful Game." —**Michelle Kaufman,**

Miami Herald soccer writer, who has covered 6 World Cups and Messi's arrival at Inter Miami

"I fully enjoyed this memoir about the perseverance of a young Tom Mulroy who uses his success in soccer to build his self-confidence at a time when educators had little knowledge of how to truly help a kid who could barely read and struggled in school. His journey could have gone wrong at many turns, but soccer kept him on the right path. This is a great read for those looking for a model of how to overcome adversity." —**Kevin Gailey,**

Chair of the Board Learning Disability Association of America

"Tom Mulroy's book is a compelling story of the power of soccer, and his complex life story. It clearly defines the ability to make a career out of one's passion, and the importance of athletes making good decisions. Tom, who has helped American Soccer's popularity during its early years clearly tells the story how times have changed for the better.

It is a must read for those who lived during his journey and a powerful read for the young people that are now involved in soccer." —**Al Miller**

Member of the National Soccer Hall of Fame / Former Collegiate and Professional Team Coach

"Regardless of the sport, every player has a dream…the bigger the dream, the more unrealistic and most often an ending of disillusion and disappointment.

In *90 Minutes With The King How Soccer Saved My Life*", Author Tommy Mulroy, known throughout the US as "Soccer Tom" shares his hopes, dreams and accomplishments along with his sorrows and pain growing up as a neophyte soccer junkie in the soccer starved 1960s and '70s.

Mulroy's story is extremely personal and heartfelt while at the same time serving as a historical reflection on the state of the world's game in America.

It will pique the memories of seasoned soccer observers, inspire those whose dreams are now more realistic than ever and reinforce the importance of a hero in every young person's life.

While soccer legend Pele may have been Tom's hero, readers will soon find a hero worthy of their own admiration; a true survivor and in many ways a King in his own right!

Thank you, Tom, for sharing your story!" —**Dr. Joe Machnik**

National Soccer Hall of Fame Inductee / Soccer Rules Analyst, Fox Sports TV

"Tom has inspired thousands with his skill, showmanship and as an ambassador of the Beautiful Game. His story is a journey of determination, swagger and love of the sport that changed his life. For everyone that he entertained, supported, and inspired- this book will show you what it took to achieve so much."
—**Mike Moylan**
Owner of Soccer.com and COO at Sports Endeavors Inc

"I was so impressed with your book. This has to be read by parents, soccer coaches and soccer players who want to improve their game. There was also so much history about soccer starting with Clarkstown, the ethnic leagues, the ethnic players that you played with and against to prepare you for the professional game. During your career you had very devoted and knowledgeable coaches. You proved that by being positive, working hard and never giving up helped you to become a great professional. As a former player and coach for over 60 years I highly recommend your book to youngsters who want to play the beautiful game. Your book is not just about soccer, but it is also about life and how to make good decisions. Loved your book "Soccer Tom". —**Arnie Ramirez**
Director of Pele Soccer Camps & 40 Years Collegiate Soccer Coach

"When I was growing up playing soccer many of my friends idolized Pele, Franz Beckenbauer, Johann Cruyff, George Best and more. My idol was Tom Mulroy! Tom had perhaps the biggest influence on me wanting to play soccer more but even more on wanting to be a coach. I was lucky enough to consider Tom as a big brother. He made all of his friends feel the same way. I learned more about life than I did about soccer hanging around with Tom. He taught me the importance of friendship, kindness and sharing. Tom never let his younger friends pay for anything. I mean anything. He was a Leader to all, even if that meant paying the lunch or dinner bill for the entire group. He was, and still remains, a role model to all of his friends and family. On the field he was a fierce warrior, but off the pitch he was the most kind, gentle human being I have ever had the privilege of being friends with! Tom's book is an amazing story about an outstanding person. Tom has proved that even faced with such adversity, you can make it in America. His contribution to Soccer in America cannot be overstated. Tom Mulroy is Soccer Royalty who invented the term, "Soccer Clinician!" I copied as much as I could from Tom and applied it to my own Soccer Clinician career. For that, I owe Tom a great debt of appreciation!" —**Tom Byer**
"Author of SOCCER STARTS AT HOME / adidas Golden Boot Winner"

"This is truly an inspirational story. "Soccer Tom" Mulroy's book *90 Minutes With The King* is a wonderful read. It's motivating and a reality check for inspiring young players dreaming to make the professional ranks."—**Jerry Yeagley**
Coach Indiana University / National Soccer Hall of Fame Inductee

"Everyone who loves soccer, who loves sport, or just wants to see how hard work and focus can bring success, should read *90 Minutes With The King* Well done!"

—Skip Gilbert

CEO US Youth Soccer

"*90 Minutes With The King* is so much more than a story of a kid and his dream of playing professional soccer. It is a story of survival in which Soccer Tom overcame challenges with traditional schooling through soccer which fed his passion and sharpened the skills that he did have. Formal education in the '70s truly did not accommodate students with learning disabilities. Tom's perseverance and determination helped guide him throughout his life. These skills were developed through his experience with soccer. Schools have for years focused on the results of tests, which has killed students' development of passion to explore and learn. If Tom were to take a standardized test today, I am sure he would not score well on it, however, he is one of the smartest people I know. His people skills are second to none, he can run a multi-faceted business, and he can relate to a young developing soccer player as well as a Fortune 500 executive.

Tom's story is so inspirational. It should be marketed to schools to show students with learning disabilities that anything is possible, you just have to find your PASSION. Teachers should be focusing on what makes kids jump out of their seats and go after things that inspire them. Once they learn how to learn, the world will be their oyster." **—Dan Fuchs**

38 Years in Education

"Tom I am pleased to be part of your unsurpassed dedication to the beautiful game." **—George Vizvary**

NJCAA Soccer Coaches National Hall of Fame. Mentor to "Soccer Tom"

"This is my favorite kind of book. Must-read for any soccer enthusiast who wishes they could do what they love has to read this. I have many words to describe this book- funny, entertaining and authentic. Follow along with "Soccer Tom", his journey from youth, college to the professional game. As a pioneer and trailblazer, you will share his passion and dedication in promoting and advancing the game of soccer in the United States. Tom's enthusiasm is contagious, and he is a true ambassador for the game of soccer. I highly recommend!" **—Van Taylor**

Professional Goalkeeper 30 + Years collegiate coach

ABOUT THE AUTHOR

"Soccer Tom" Mulroy became a professional soccer player at age 19, seven years after he first touched a ball. He played professionally for more than a decade, scoring over 50 goals.

After his playing career, Tom was named the official spokesman for the 1994 World Cup, the world's largest sporting event. In 2012, Tom became the president of the Fort Lauderdale Strikers, leading the club to the NASL championship game.

For nearly 40 years he has run his own global sports marketing agency specializing in soccer promotions and events. His clients have included Coca-Cola, McDonald's, Snickers, Budweiser along with FIFA, CONCACAF and CONMEBOL soccer federations.